IMAGES
of America

LYON TOWNSHIP

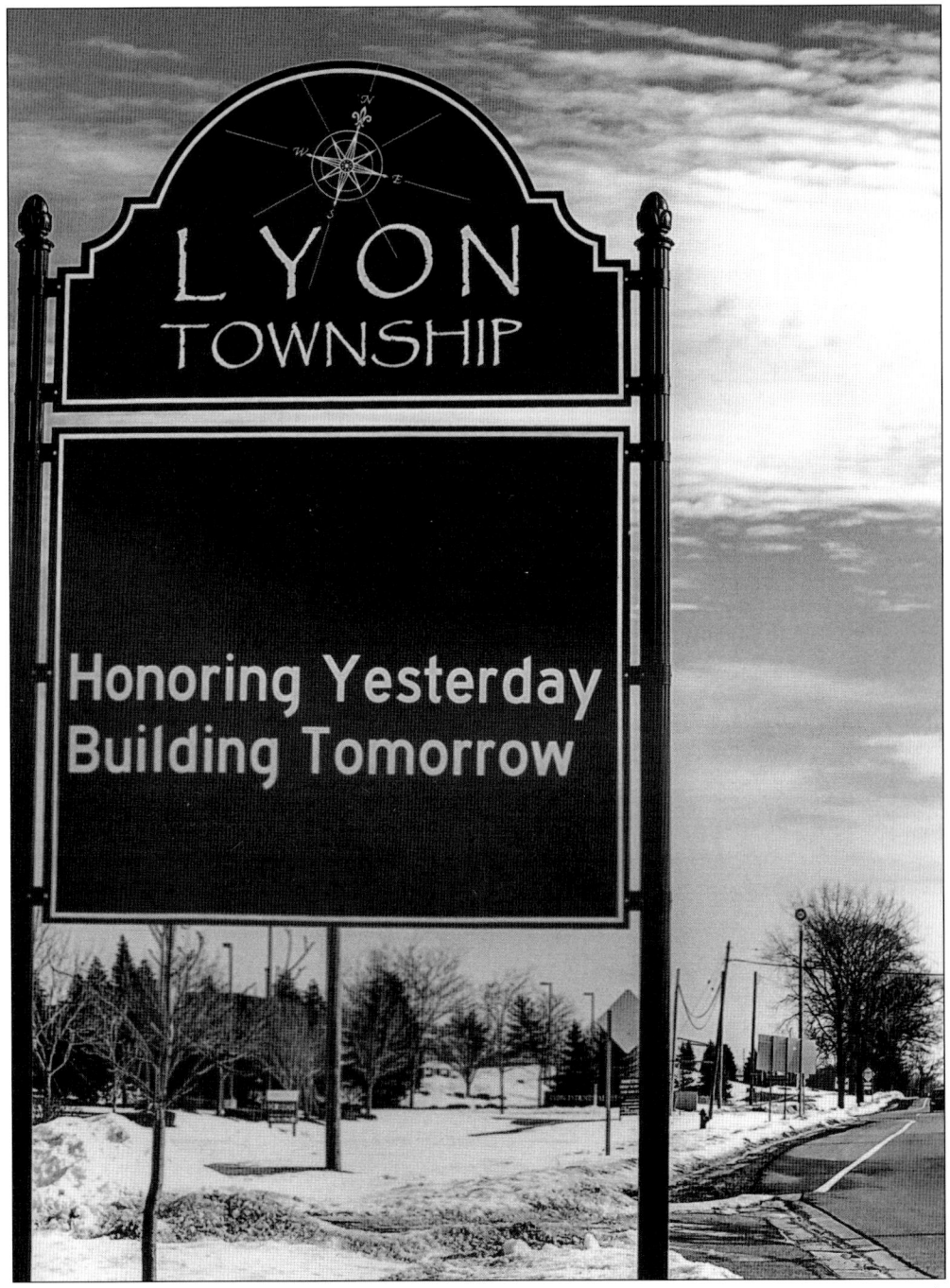

"Honoring yesterday, building tomorrow," the township's motto, captures the community's growth from the early 19th century to the new millennium. (Courtesy of Jane and Jack Purslow.)

ON THE COVER: The South Lyon Community School District is one of the highest rated in the state. These New Hudson School second graders in 1955 are the youthful pioneers who helped lead the township's ride to excellence. (Courtesy of Sdunek files.)

IMAGES of America
LYON TOWNSHIP

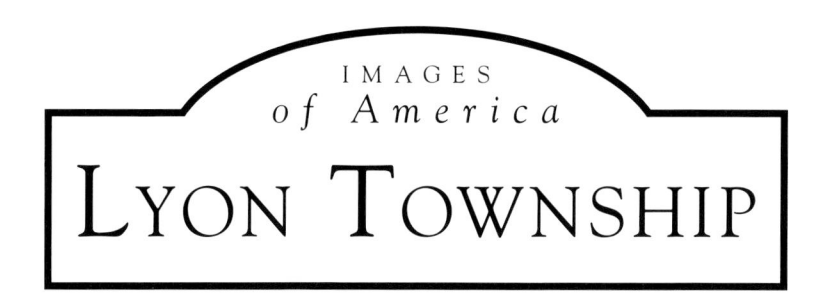

John Bell and Diane Andreassi
Foreword by Hugh D. Crawford

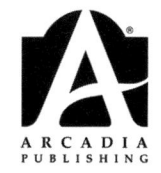

ARCADIA
PUBLISHING

Copyright © 2014 by John Bell and Diane Andreassi
ISBN 978-1-4671-1245-1

Published by Arcadia Publishing
Charleston, South Carolina

Printed in the United States of America

Library of Congress Control Number: 2014945508

For all general information, please contact Arcadia Publishing:
Telephone 843-853-2070
Fax 843-853-0044
E-mail sales@arcadiapublishing.com
For customer service and orders:
Toll-Free 1-888-313-2665

Visit us on the Internet at www.arcadiapublishing.com

This book is dedicated to the Charter Township of Lyon Board of Trustees and the Downtown Development Authority members who had the vision to preserve history for current and future generations.

Contents

Foreword		6
Acknowledgments		7
Introduction		8
1.	Early Residents	9
2.	Social	19
3.	Old New Hudson	31
4.	Agriculture	43
5.	Schools	67
6.	Cemeteries	87
7.	Interstate 96 Expressway	91
8.	Today	95
9.	Community Services	109
10.	Future	125

Foreword

Lyon Township is a thriving community with a rich history and promising future. John Bell and Diane Andreassi's book gives glimpses into the township's deep-rooted history in our state, taking readers back 200 years and giving us a historical perspective of the people and events that occurred. The book continues the depiction of Lyon Township's history right up to the present day. As vice-chair of the Downtown Development Authority and a reporter at *South Lyon Herald* (Hometownlife.com), Bell and Andreassi are the perfect people to tell this story. John Bell and Diane Andreassi have the community connection and knowledge to tell the story of this great area's past and give us a glimpse of its future.

Lyon Township is ideal for residential, commercial, and industrial growth in the coming years. In supporting manufacturing, retail, and corporate development, Lyon Township has become a great community to live, work, and play. It was recently named the fastest-growing township in Oakland County. Lyon Township is a wonderful community, and it has been my honor to serve as the township's state representative since 2008.

—State Representative Hugh D. Crawford
38th District

Acknowledgments

We give our greatest gratitude to Jane and Jack Purslow, whose photographic contributions made this book possible. Jane also contributed to the construction of the book.

We also want to thank Ann Polan for her keen editing eye and providing a tremendous amount of material for the book.

Other thanks go to Cathy Cattone, a genealogist with the Lyon Township Public Library; Holly Teasdle, library director; and all other library staff who helped. Other contributors were the John and Mary Canfield family; H.C. Arms; Bruce and Carolyn Sdunek; Roy Cash; Phil Elkow; Clinton and Bonnie Cook; Ruby Templeton; Pat Haas; Josephine Scheffer; Lyn Rhodes; April Talaga; the Erwin family; Doug Canfield; Giffels-Webster Engineering, Jason Mayer; McKenna Associates, Chris Doozan; Civil Engineering Solution, Leslie Zwanda; Irene Raney; James Peters; Bob and Dolores Seccombe; Clair Haack; Elaine Cash; Sue and Jerry Knapp; Richard Fairfield; the Fletcher family; Margaret Heidt; Bill and Jackie Carey; Mark Spencer; fire chief Ken Van Sparrentak; fire marshal Don Collick; and Oakland County sheriff deputy Mark Snider.

We would also like to thank our family members for their patience, including John Bell's wife, Jackie; Jane Purslow's husband, Jack; and Diane Andreassi's husband, Domenic.

Introduction

After French explorer Antoine Cadillac landed in Grosse Isle in 1701, it took 130 years before Bela Chase and his family forged northwest to become one of Lyon Township's first settlers.

Native Americans lived in the area before Chase arrived. The natives traded their baskets with settlers for wheat, beans, and bread. New settlers learned many local roads and lakes were named for Native Americans. Pontiac Trail, for instance, was named for famed Chief Pontiac.

Around 1830, new area settlers petitioned the state legislature to separate the six square miles from Novi. They wanted to name their property Fruitland, but state legislators decided to recognize Lucius Lyon, a territorial delegate, senator, and surveyor.

One of the first town meetings was held on April 7, 1834, with Thomas Salmon as moderator and William G. Smith as clerk, according to Gertrude Sibley Clapp in the "Oakland County Pioneer Papers." Some of the positions they filled included highway commissioner and director of the poor.

Around 1832, a small hamlet in Lyon called New Hudson was formed. A plank road from Detroit to Grand Rapids crossed the township through New Hudson. Stagecoaches ran, and two tollgates required payment for passage of animals. By 1834, log schoolhouses were built.

Meanwhile, a small community named Kensington was founded in the northwest corner of Lyon Township. A lumber mill was erected for the homes and businesses that were expected. The Kensington Bank Company soon followed in 1833. Kensington wildcat banknotes, however, were deemed worthless, and the community failed when the banks fell.

In the early 1890s, New Hudson was a thriving community with businesses that served travelers to Detroit and northern communities.

When Interstate 96 was under construction in the 1950s, travelers remained on Grand River Avenue. But when the expressway was completed, the motorists left the township roads in favor of the fast-moving highway.

In later years, however, the I-96 expressway heralded in new businesses lured by the proximity and visibility to the many drivers. By 2013, Lyon Township was named the fastest-growing community in Oakland County, as developers built homes and businesses at a rapid pace to meet the growing interest of people who wanted to leave big cities and experience the flavor of a rural atmosphere. Capturing this dichotomy in its history, Lyon Township's motto is "Honoring yesterday, building tomorrow."

One

EARLY RESIDENTS

Throughout Lyon, there are still reminders of the bygone days of early settlers. One of the biggest vestiges of the past is the New Hudson Inn, which has gone by different names and has been used for various purposes, ranging from a dance hall to a tavern and a gentlemen's place for relaxation. It was opened for business about 1831 and is still operating. It is often referred to as one of Oakland County's oldest buildings.

Some of the early residents include the Purdy, Bidwell, Thayer, Hopkins, Renwick, Taylor, Covey, Canfield, Cash, Goldy, Spellar, Blackwood, Waldron, Sprague, Fawcett, Peters, Jones, and Musoff families. Some descendants of these early residents still live in the township in 2014.

In 1831, the Purdy family left Seneca County, New York, to establish a homestead. John Thayer and Eliphlet Sprague, also from New York, settled in the northwest corner of town. Russell Alvord and Daniel Richards followed. It has been said that Richards erected the first log cabin around 1834, and the post office was opened around the same time with Dr. John Curtis serving as postmaster.

Starting in 1830, Eliphlet Sprague operated one of the first farms. Jonas Hood was the first carpenter, and Garrett Houghtalling was the first blacksmith. It is also believed the road bridge over the Huron River at Kensington was the first in the township.

In 1834, Curtis and John A. Hand opened the first general merchandise store, and the opening of a blacksmith business, owned by John Elder, came next. In the 1830s, land purchased from the government sold for $1.25 an acre.

Around 1836, New Hudson's first log school was erected, and Thomas Bogart was the first teacher. As more and more children came, the schoolroom became cramped, and a frame building was erected next door. A brick building on three acres followed the wood-frame school, and it served the community until April 13, 1921, when it burned. Classes were held at Maccabee Hall and other locations. A new school building was constructed the following fall.

By 1877, New Hudson had two general stores, the New Hudson Inn, a post office, and a wagon shop, as well as a blacksmith shop, two harness shops, and two churches.

Near the end of the 19th century, E.J. Rice was a beloved teacher, and he owned the elevator where farmers marketed their produce. He also owned a general store where farmers' wives traded eggs and butter for groceries.

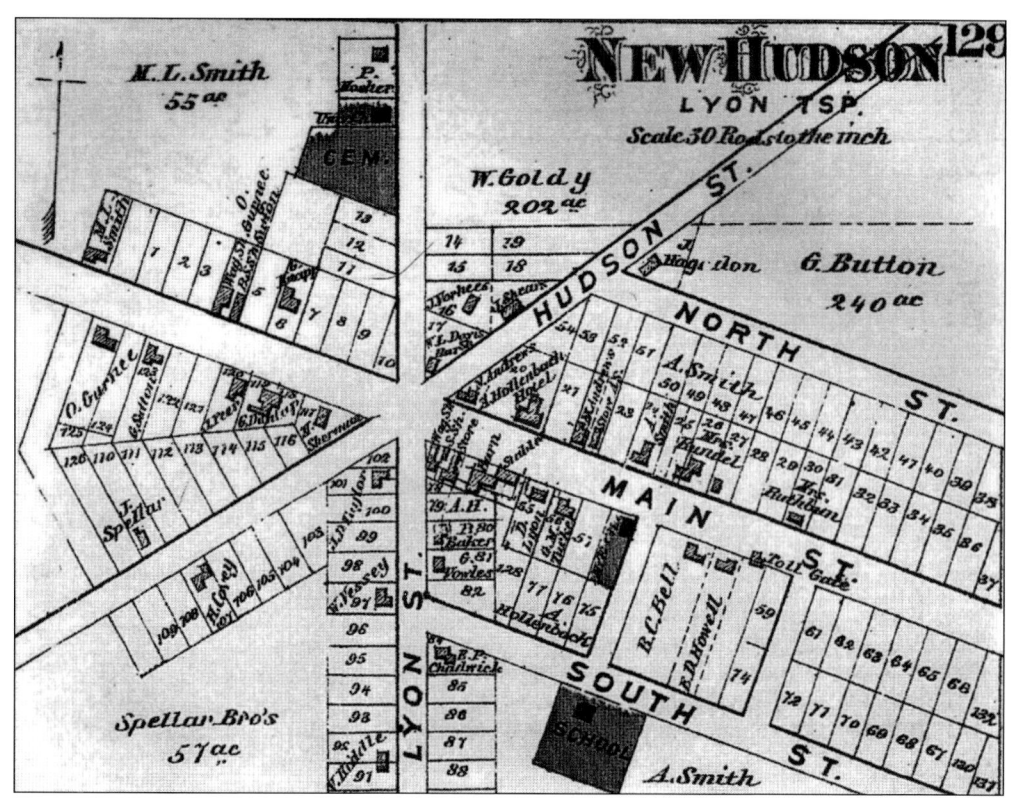

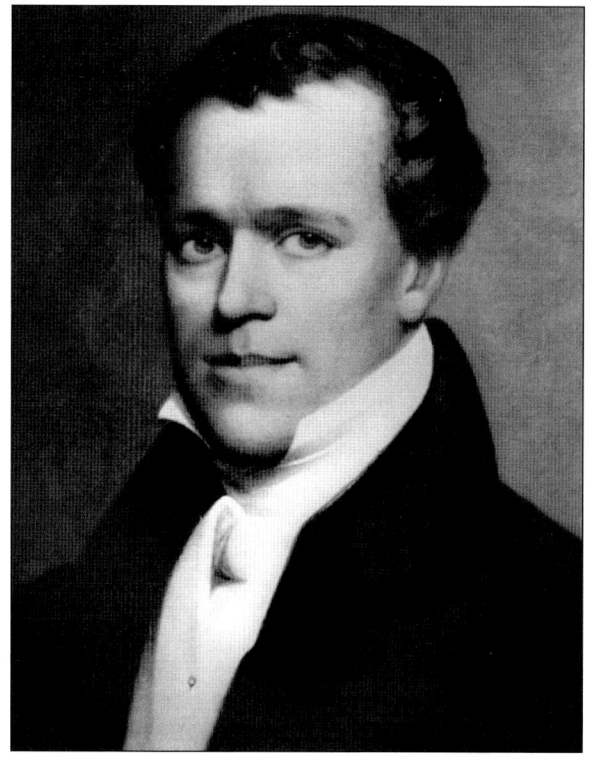

This plat of New Hudson in 1872 shows the early development of the community that included a school, a cemetery, church, and social gathering places. Many of the streets shown have changed names. Main Street is now Grand River Avenue, Hudson Street is Pontiac Trail Road, Lyon Street is Milford Road, and South Street is Rice Street. (Courtesy of Lyon Township.)

Lyon Township was named for Lucius Lyon after state legislators declined to use the name Fruitland, as suggested by residents. Lucius Lyon was a territorial delegate and surveyor. He was born in 1800 and died in 1851. Although not a resident of the township, he was a prominent state senator. (Courtesy of Oakland County.)

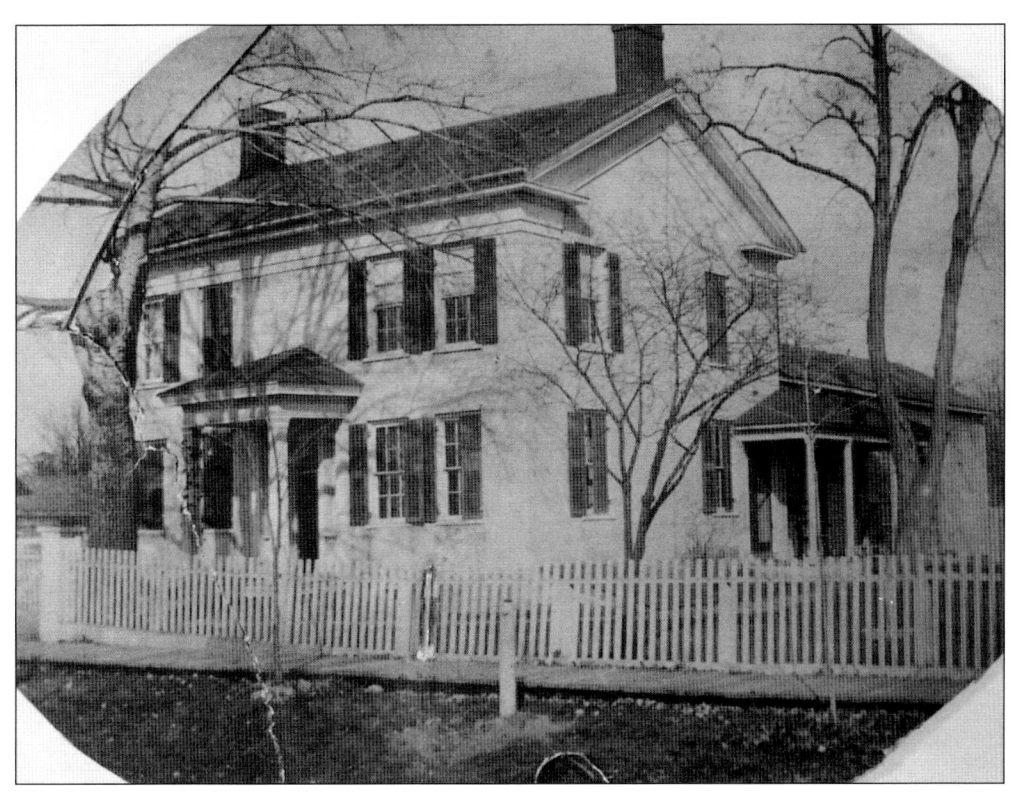

This home was built around 1895 and was owned by Frank and Nettie Renwick. The property on Grand River Avenue was L shaped and had about seven acres of farmland at the rear and to the east. In 1929, Jesse and Lee Pearce modernized the structure by adding plumbing, a coal-fired steam boiler for the new central heating system, and running water pumped from the basement cistern to each faucet. The building is currently home to the Bon-a-Rose Catering Company. (Courtesy of Lyon Township.)

From left to right, Jesse, Robert, Max, and Della Pearce are seen in front of their home on Grand River Avenue in New Hudson. Local folklore has it that a ghost in the form of a young boy had been regularly seen in the upstairs of the home. (Courtesy of the Lyon Township Library.)

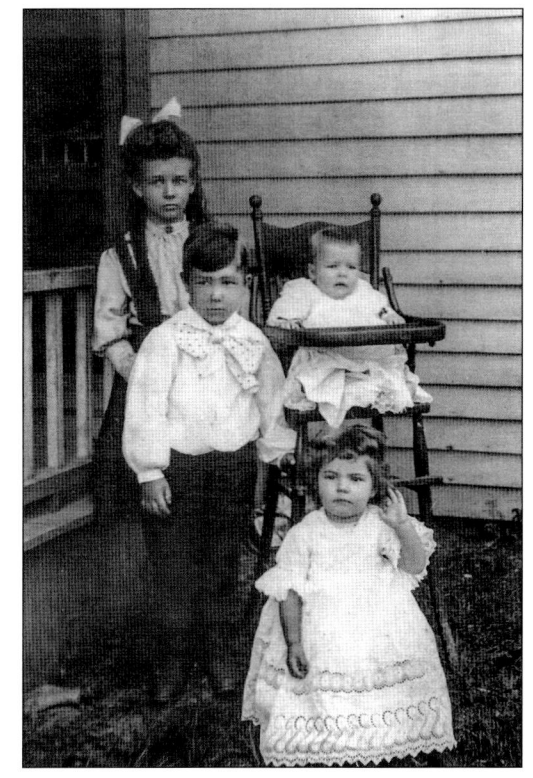

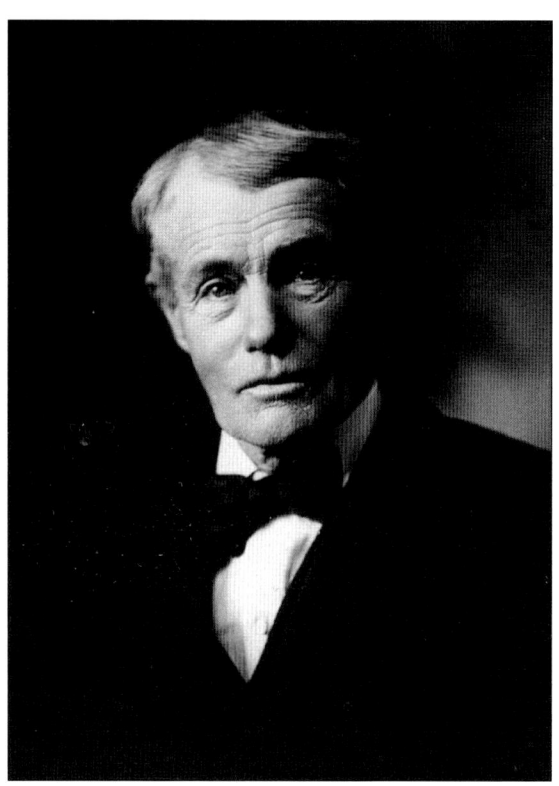

This image of Lew Rose was found in the Lyon Township Library among photographs of early residents. It is believed Rose family members lived on a 40-acre farm on the corner of Eleven Mile and Martindale Roads, which is currently the Hornbrook subdivision. Cemetery records show that Lew Rose died in 1928 and is buried in the Rose Bullard Cemetery. (Courtesy of the Lyon Township Library.)

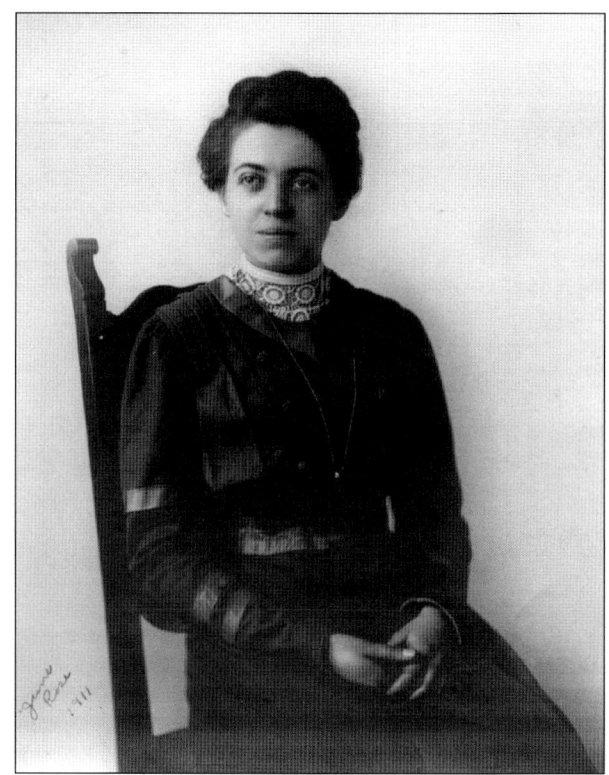

This 1911 photograph of June Rose, Lew Rose's wife, was donated to the Lyon Township Library genealogy department. (Courtesy of the Lyon Township Library.)

Silas and Louise Rose sit for a photograph around 1890. Cemetery records show Silas died at age 76 in 1893. (Courtesy of the Lyon Township Library.)

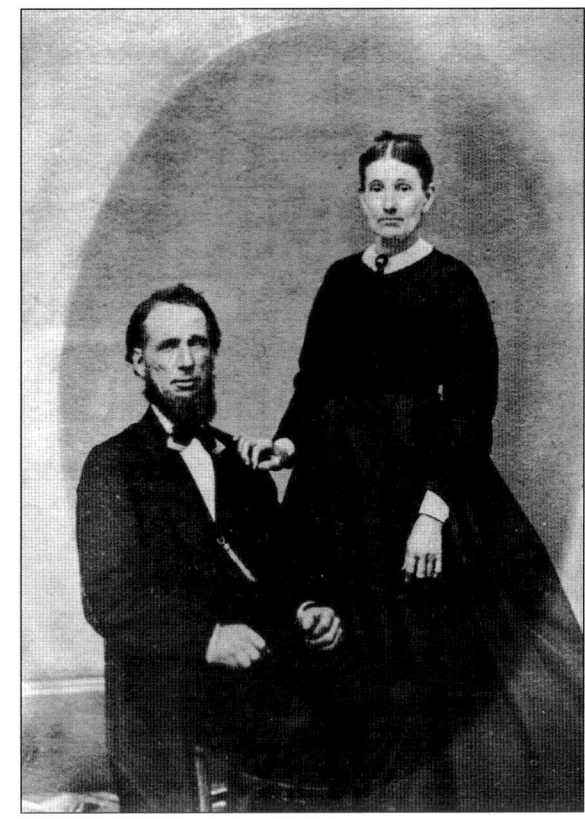

From left to right, Bertha Hamilton Mackey, a Miss McIntosh, a Miss Terwillager, and Elsie Harding Canfield are dressed for an outing in the late 1800s. (Courtesy of the Lyon Township Library.)

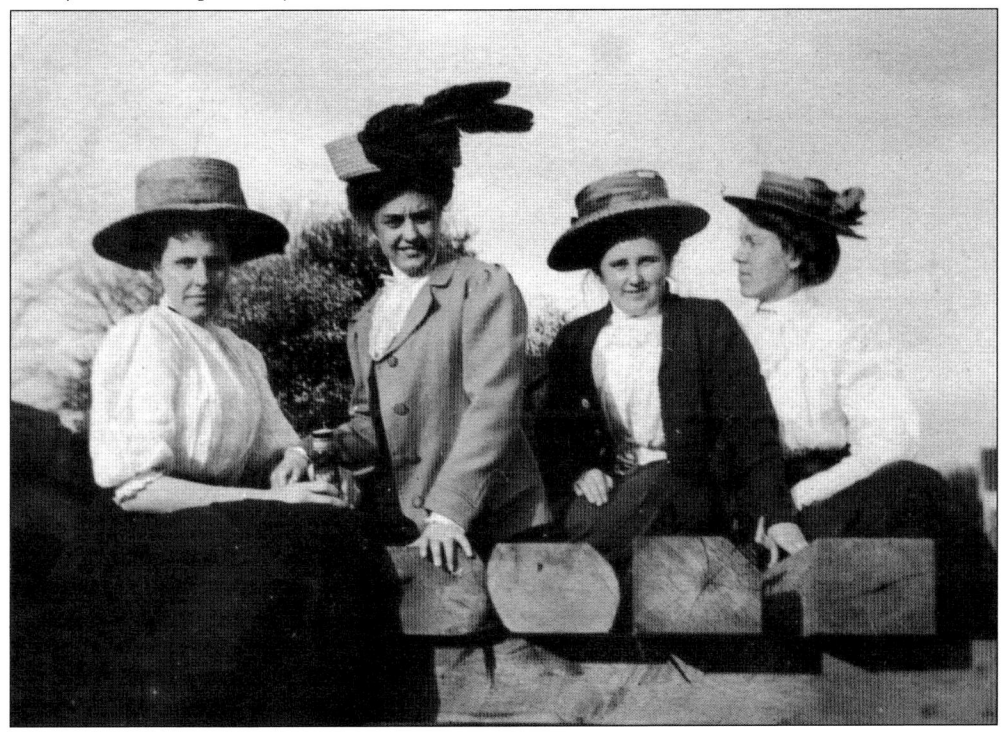

13

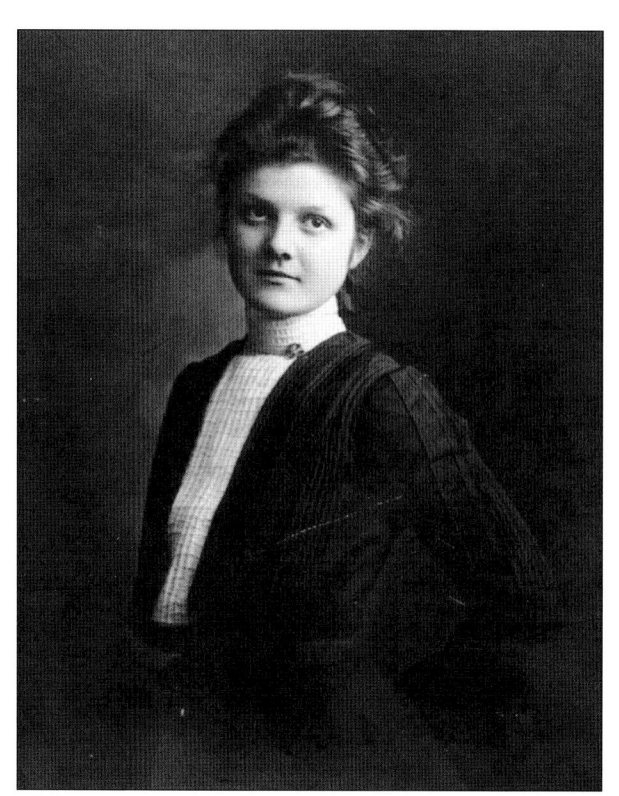

Jesse Renwick Pearce Kingsley with her husband, Bill, operated one of the many restaurants in New Hudson. (Courtesy of the Lyon Township Library.)

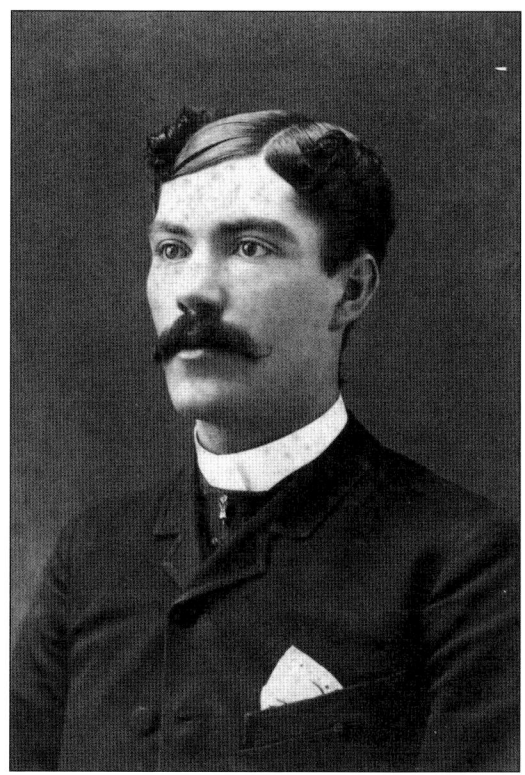

Will Dowling sports a one-of-a-kind haircut. (Courtesy of the Lyon Township Library.)

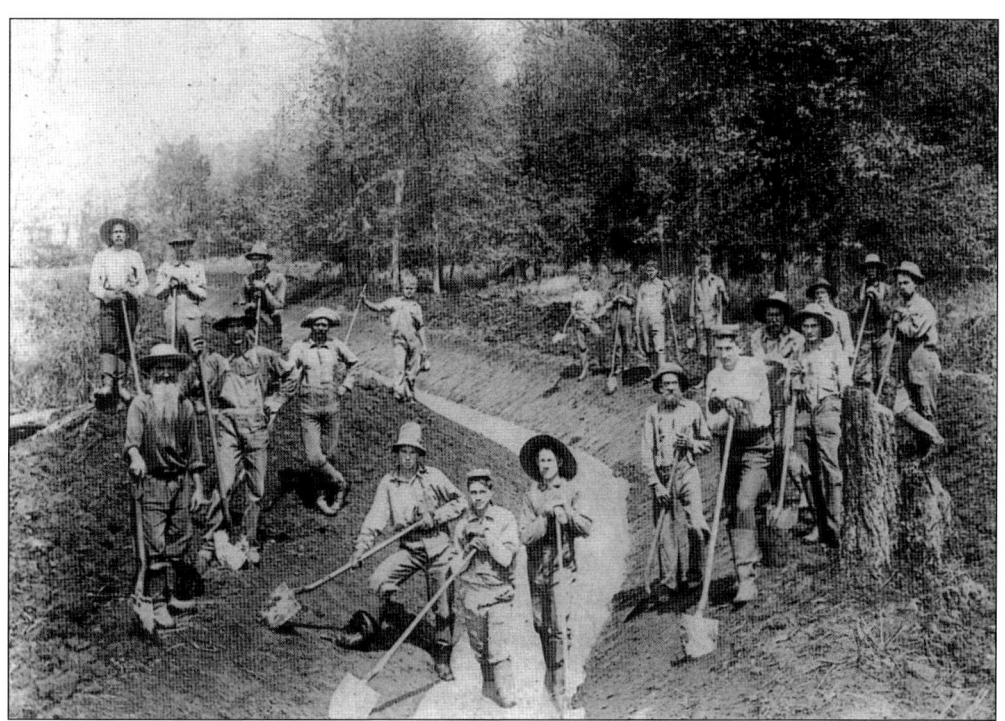

Men dig a drainage ditch by hand on South Hill and Eleven Mile Roads to relieve swamps in the area. Note there are no backhoes, bulldozers, or other modern-day equipment—just shovels and men. The man in the center of the ditch is Claude Underhill. This photograph was taken around 1900. (Courtesy of the Lyon Township Library.)

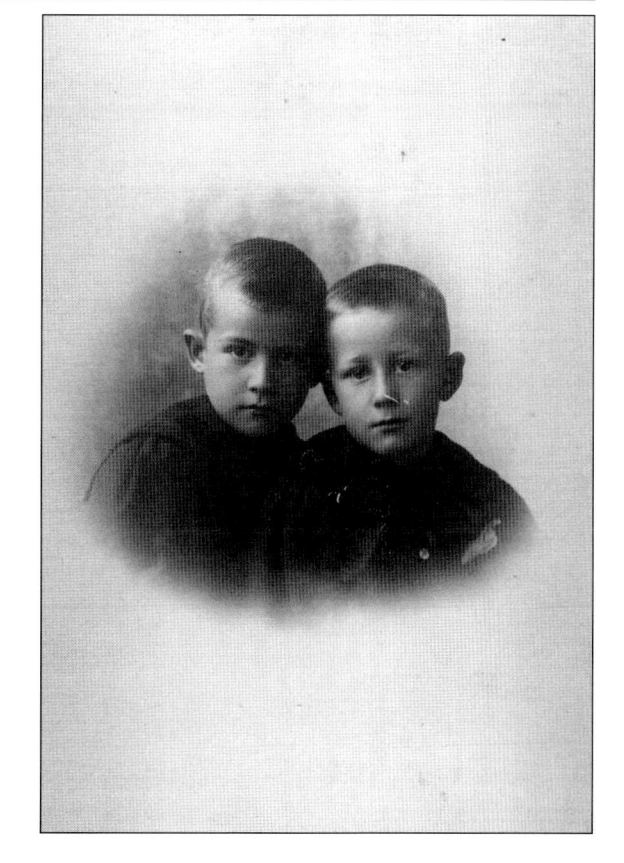

Dewey and John Shear, brothers of Bruce Shear and Dulah Shear Cole, are shown here. The family was associated with the Kingsley restaurant in New Hudson. (Courtesy of Lyon Township.)

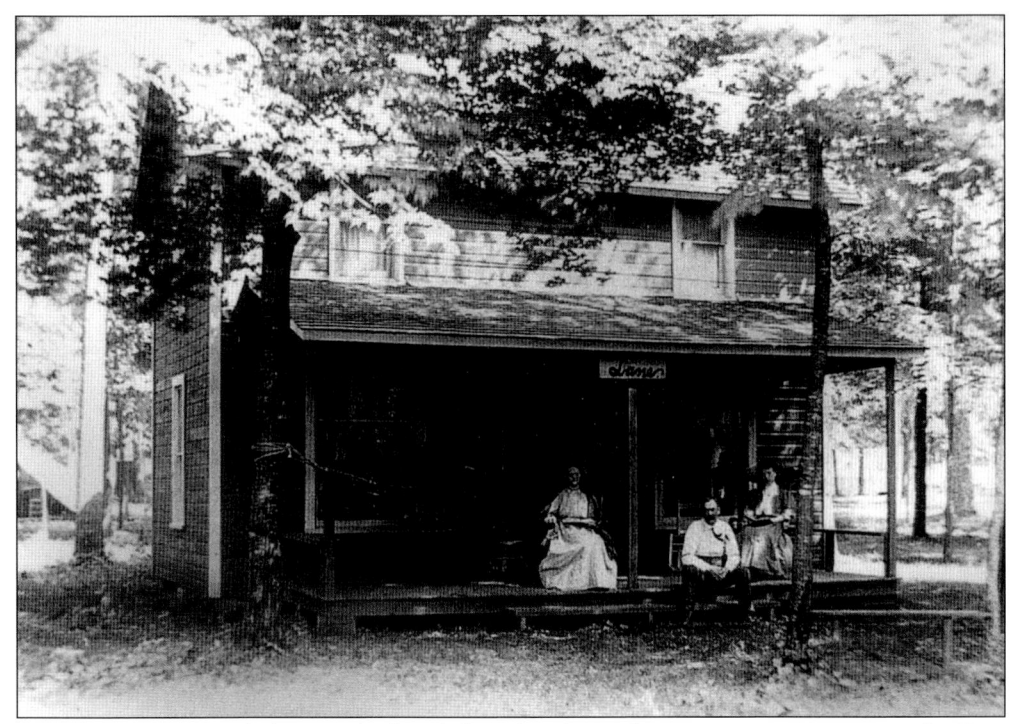

This is the Lane family home, which is believed to be in the Kensington community by Kent Lake. Idamae Canfield Lane and Oscar Lane are shown on the porch. Idamae was born in 1866. (Courtesy of Darrell Lane.)

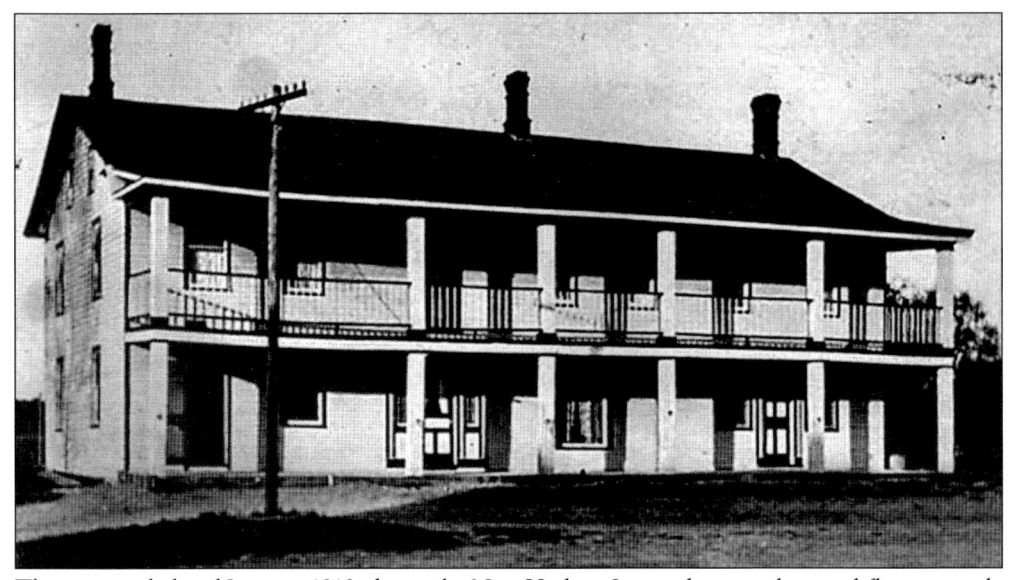

This postcard, dated January 1910, shows the New Hudson Inn with a grand second-floor veranda for the guests of the hotel. It was a stagecoach stop and a meeting place for locals. (Courtesy of Lyon Township.)

Donald and Gabrilla Zunek Donley pose with their daughter Cara in the late 1800s. (Courtesy of the Lyon Township Library.)

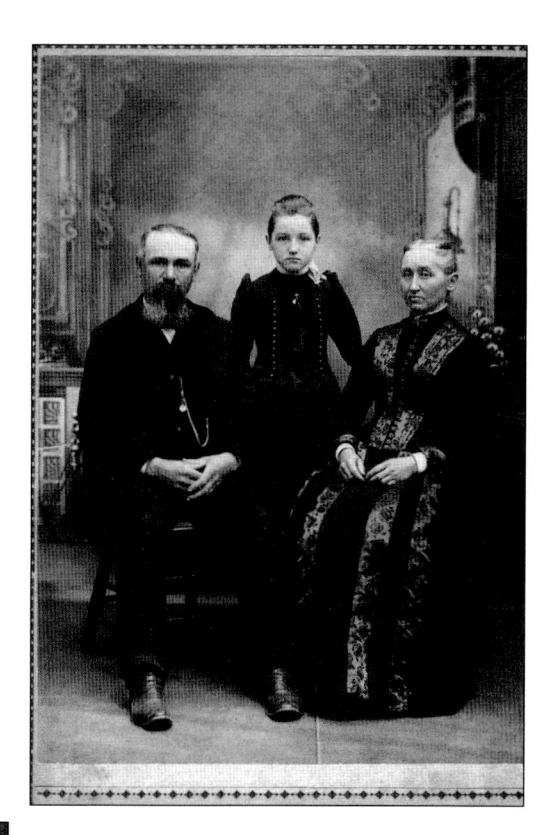

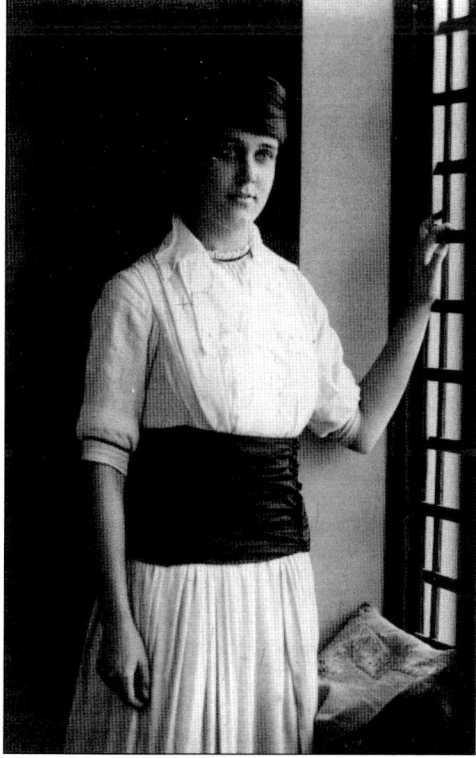

Leota Baker was the daughter of New Hudson resident Lewis Baker. Lewis was born in 1857 and died in 1924. He was part owner of the Commercial House Hotel in South Lyon in the 1800s. Leota was in the New Hudson graduating class of 1914. (Courtesy of the Lyon Township Library.)

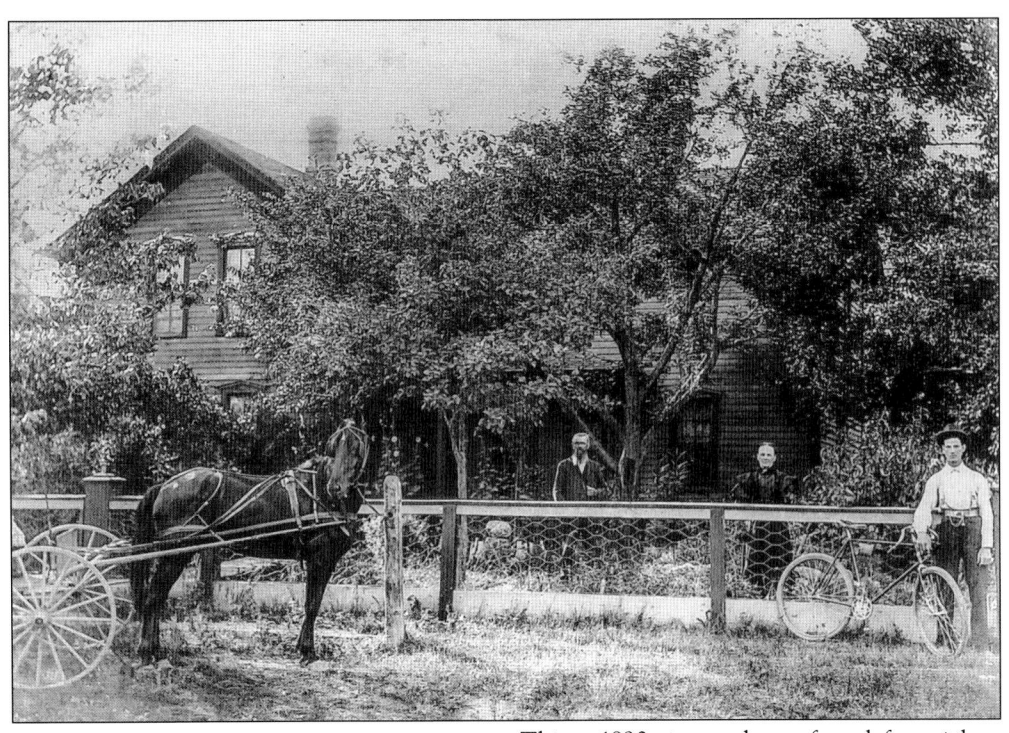

This c. 1890 picture shows, from left to right, John and Mary Spellar with Burt Goldy in front of the Spellar home on Pontiac Trail Road. The house is located next to what was to become Lyon Township Hall, library, and fire station. (Courtesy of the Canfield family.)

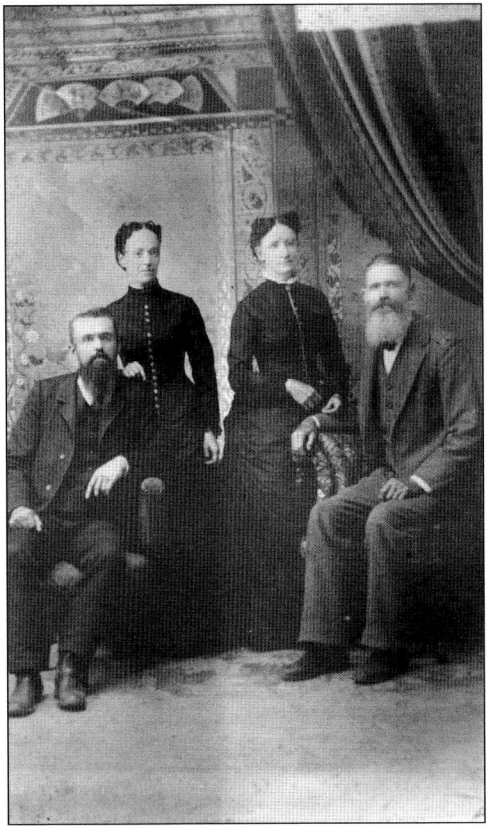

John and Mary Spellar (on the left) are pictured with Rebecca and Mark Spellar around 1870. (Courtesy of the Lyon Township Library.)

Two

SOCIAL

Constructing what is now known as the New Hudson Inn in 1831 was one of the first things the early settlers did, and it turned out to be good for the local merchants. The tavern was a stagecoach stop for travelers who were inevitably hungry and thirsty on their journeys. The New Hudson Inn is believed to be the oldest building still standing in Oakland County. At this publication, the restaurant was still in business as a tavern.

The tavern reached its peak of popularity in the early 1840s when it was purchased by Herman Smith who added a ballroom with a spring floor that became the delight of area dancers. It was also known as the Temperance House and was the entertainment hub for people who lived miles away in all directions.

In 1843, Herman Smith built a church in New Hudson that was alternately used on Sundays by the Presbyterians and Methodists.

The Universalist Church was built in the mid-1800s next to the New Hudson Cemetery on Milford Road. The church building was jacked up and moved by sled to Grand River Avenue in 1905. It later became known as Maccabee Hall.

As the years passed, other popular meeting places were Ruth's Cottage Inn and the Jack-O-Lantern Sandwich shop, which was painted bright orange. The Jack-O-Lantern was a popular spot for schoolchildren to gather after classes, socialize, and eat the restaurant's famous pie, according to Ruby Templeton, a longtime New Hudson resident.

The quality of life in Lyon Township today is also measured by the abundance of golf courses, including Lyon Oaks, Kensington Metro Park, Coyote, Pebble Creek, Tanglewood, and Cattails.

Also, James F. Atchison Memorial Park has become the setting for annual festivals that have attracted families near and far.

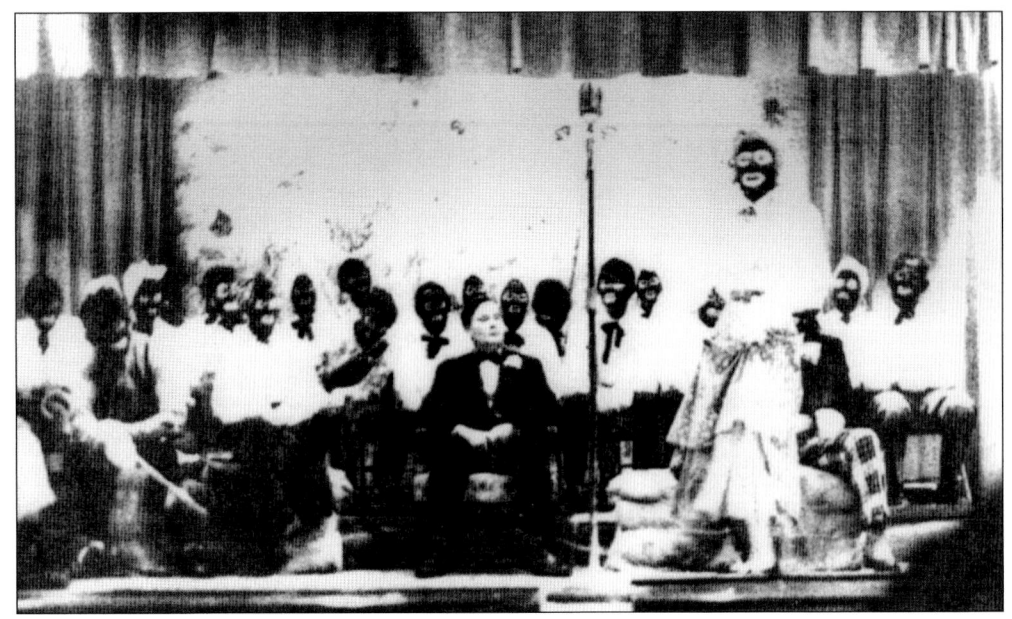

Area residents revealed their talents during a minstrel performance around 1950 at Maccabee Hall. This type of entertainment consisted of comic skits, variety acts, dancing, and music. The minstrel genre continued until the 1960s in high schools and local theaters. Lyon resident and postmaster Harold Haas was the master of ceremony who introduced the various acts. Charles Sdunek, shown in the back row, was a prominent New Hudson resident. Maccabee Hall was torn down in the mid-1980s. (Courtesy of Ruby Templeton.)

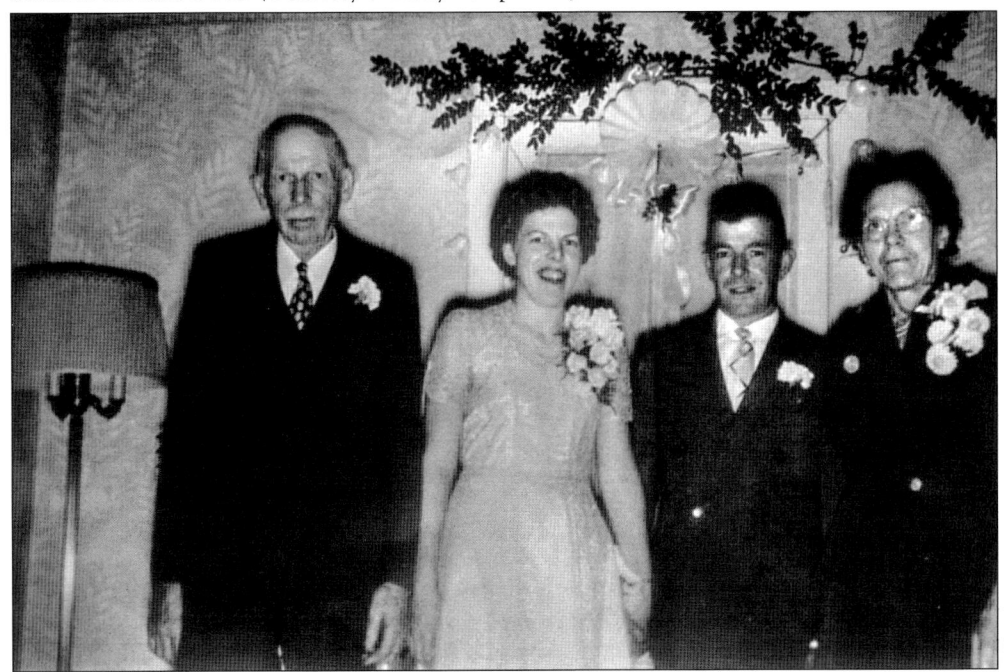

Mary E. Canfield was married to Lawrence Marvin. The couple is flanked by her grandparents, William and Elsie Canfield. Mary's brother John was a well-known farmer who later formed a seed company that sold hybrid varieties through the Midwest. (Courtesy of the Canfield family.)

Ralph Bidwell, 39 years old, is pictured in his baseball uniform in 1937. He played on a local baseball team in New Hudson. (Courtesy of Ann Polan.)

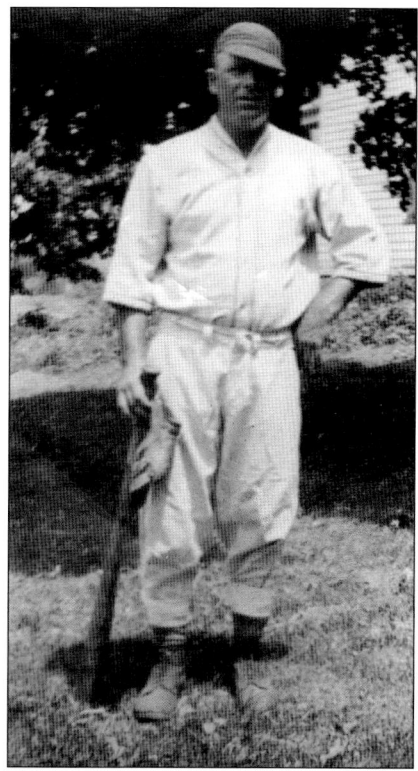

Here, Knights of the Templar New Hudson baseball players take a team picture c. 1910. (Courtesy of the Lyon Township Library.)

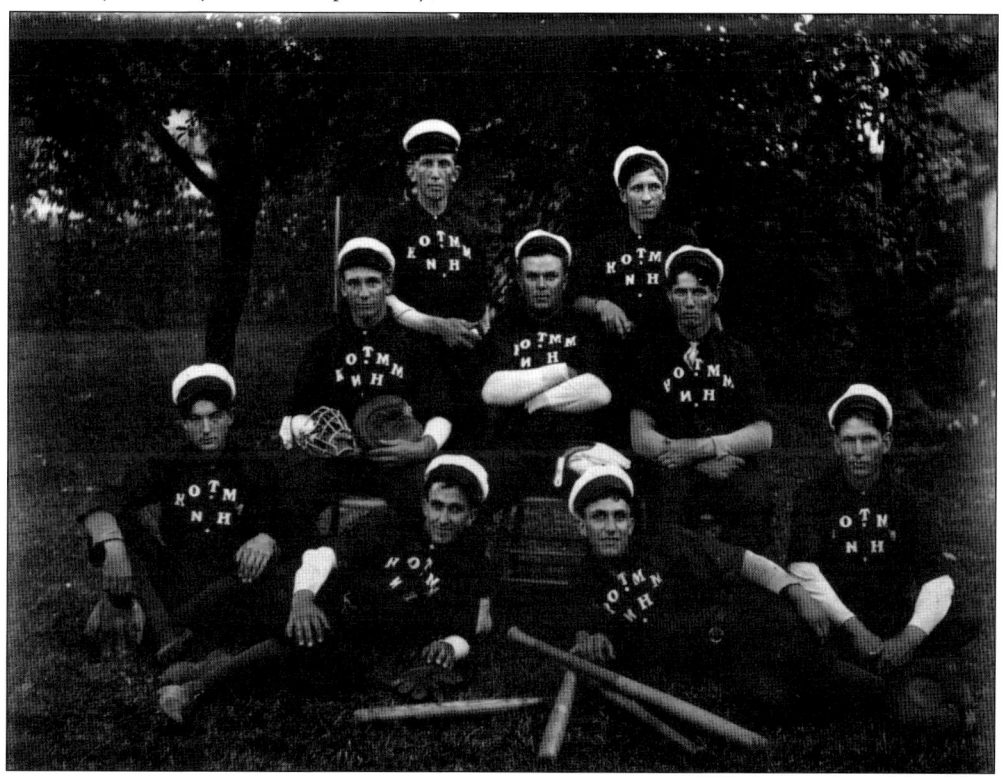

21

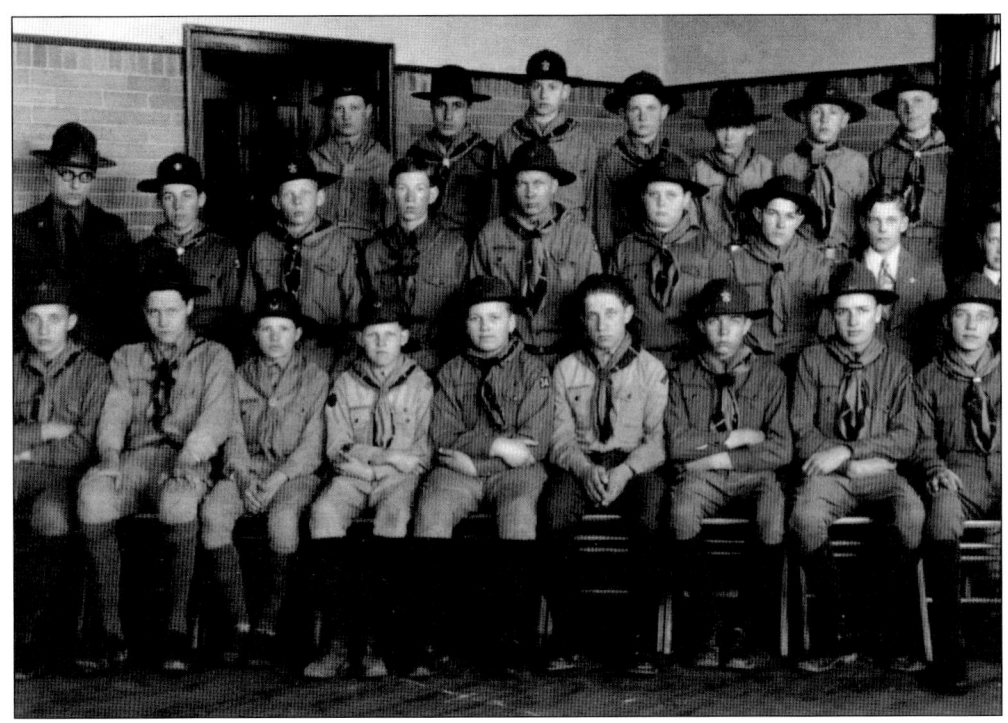

A Boy Scout troop meets in the New Hudson School in the 1930s. (Courtesy of the Canfield family.)

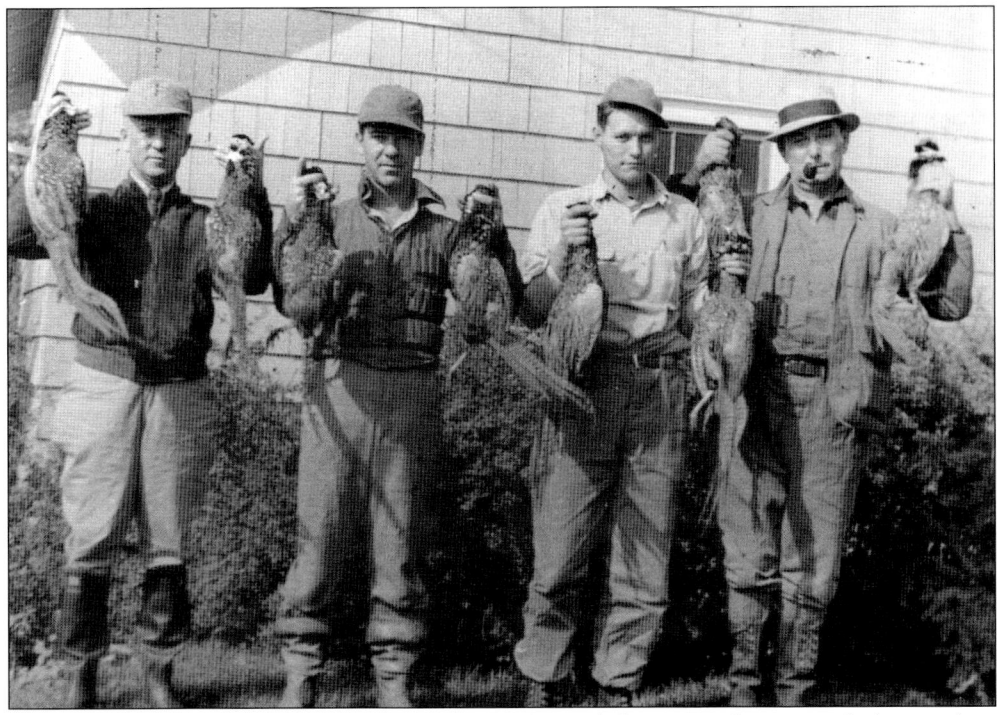

From left to right, Perry Miles, Floyd Nast, Bill McKinley, and Elmo McKinley pose with their trophies after the 1941 opening day for pheasant hunting. (Courtesy of the Lyon Township Library.)

In 1947, fifteen-year-old Duane Bidwell leaves his Johns Road home to check his trap lines. Trapping animals, such as muskrat and mink, was a productive way for young people of the time to make an income. He earned between $2.50 and $4 a pelt for muskrats, and mink pelts went for $25 to $32.50 each. (Courtesy of Ann Polan.)

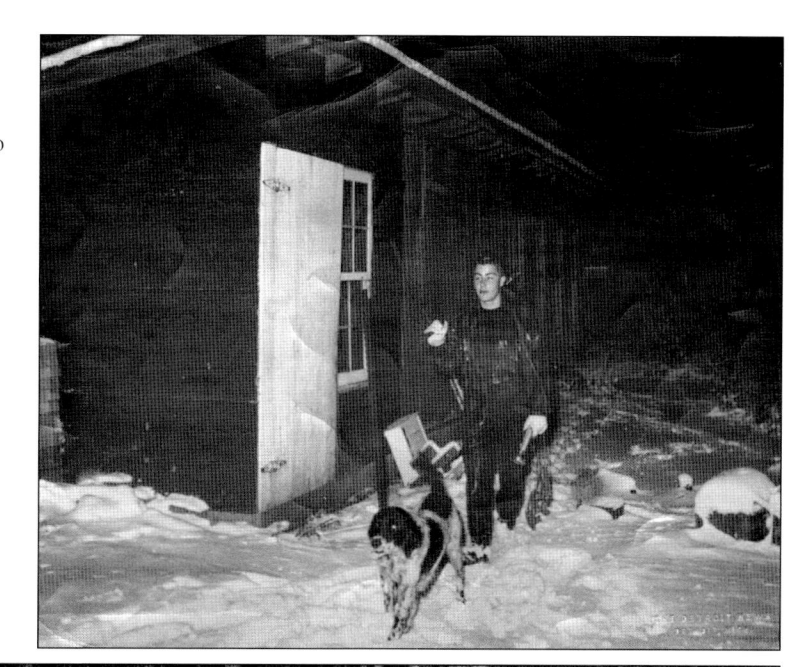

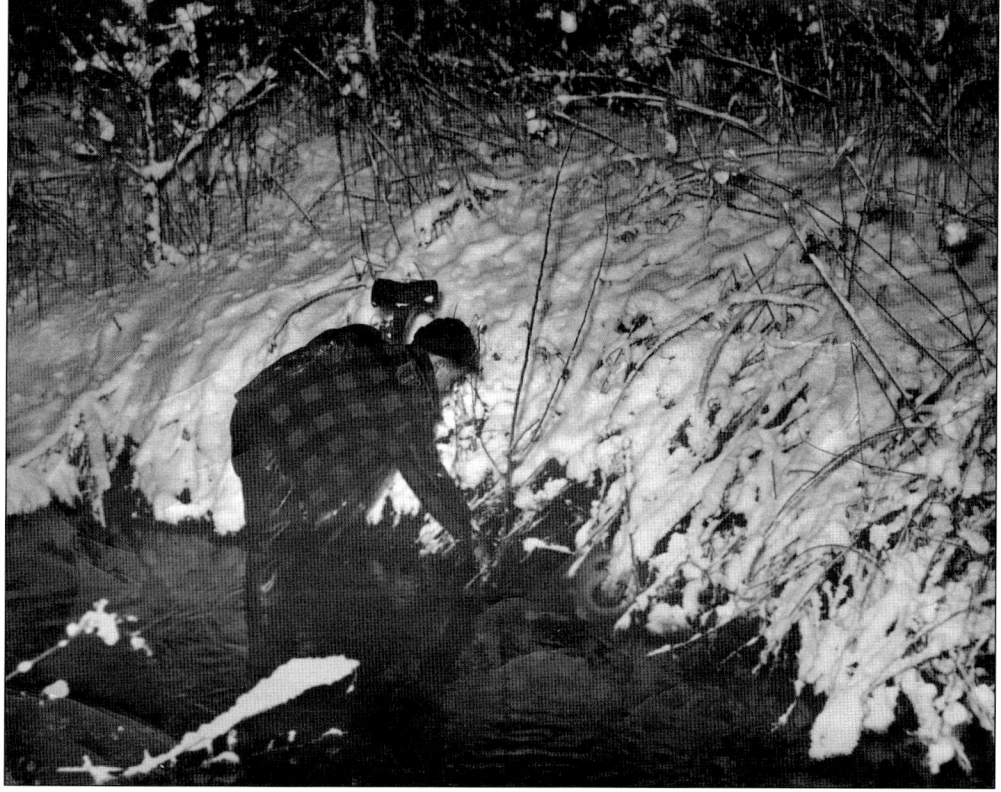

This is another c. 1947 photograph of Duane Bidwell as he runs his trap lines along a drainage ditch in Lyon Township. He learned to trap from his father, Ralph Bidwell Sr., who trapped the same marsh creek 20 years earlier. His father also taught him to fashion pelt-drying boards. (Courtesy of Ann Polan.)

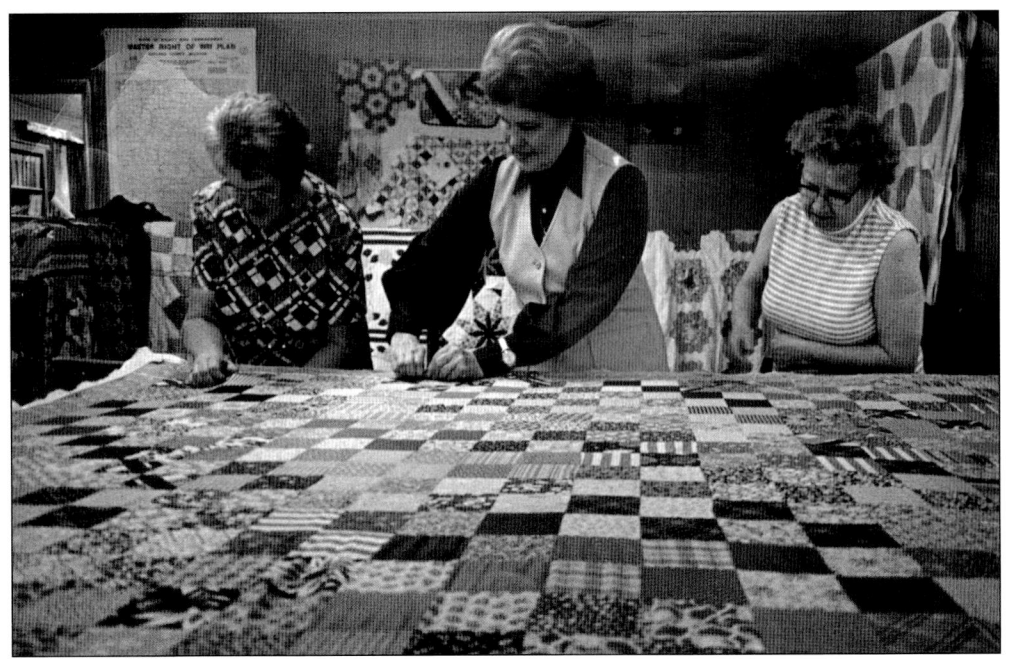

From left to right, Geraldine Knapp, Ruby Templeton, and Mary Canfield tie a quilt top at the community center, which is located in the Lyon Township Library on Milford Road. (Courtesy of the Canfield family.)

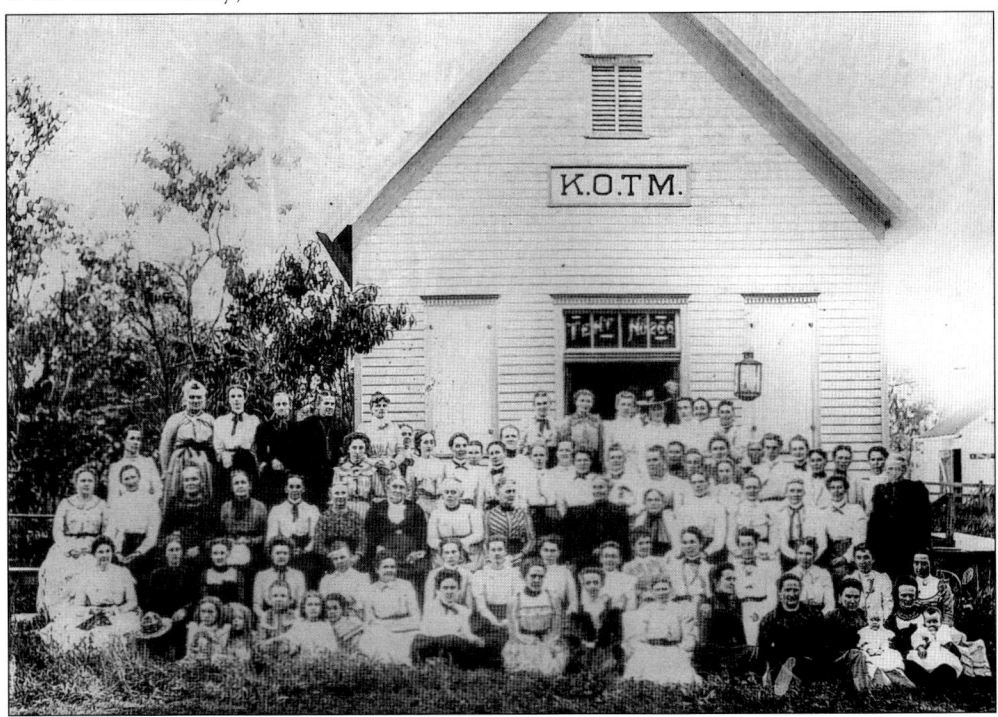

This gathering of the Women's Auxiliary of the Knights of the Templar Maccabees, Tent No. 266, was a social event for women of the time. The building was also used as a polling precinct for elections. (Courtesy of the Lyon Township Library.)

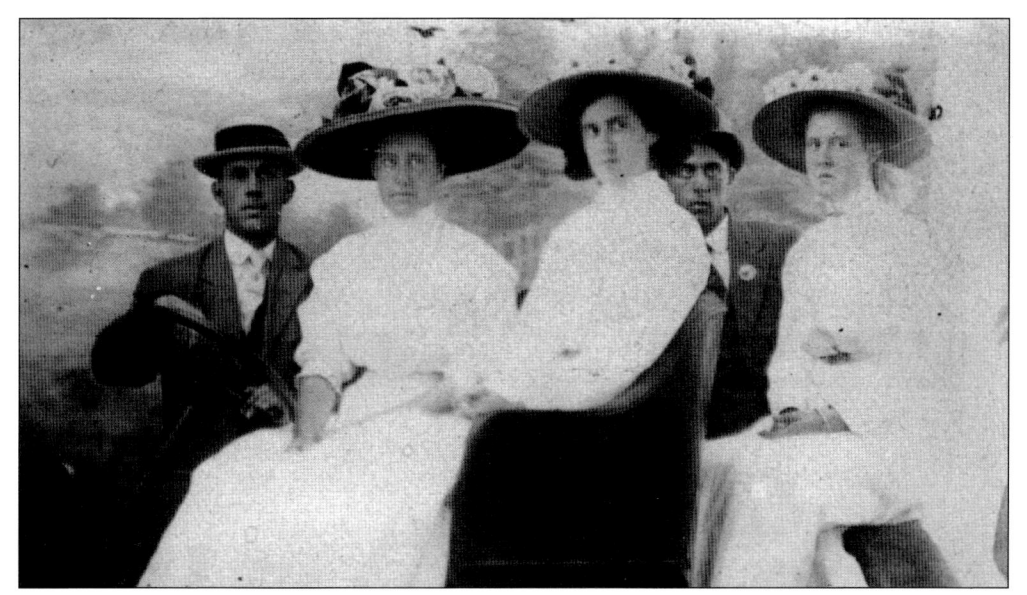

This open car in 1914 was common during that time period. Pictured are (first row) John Chamberlain, Sadie Hopkins, and Beryl Hopkins; (second row) Clair and Blanche Hopkins. (Courtesy of Ann Polan.)

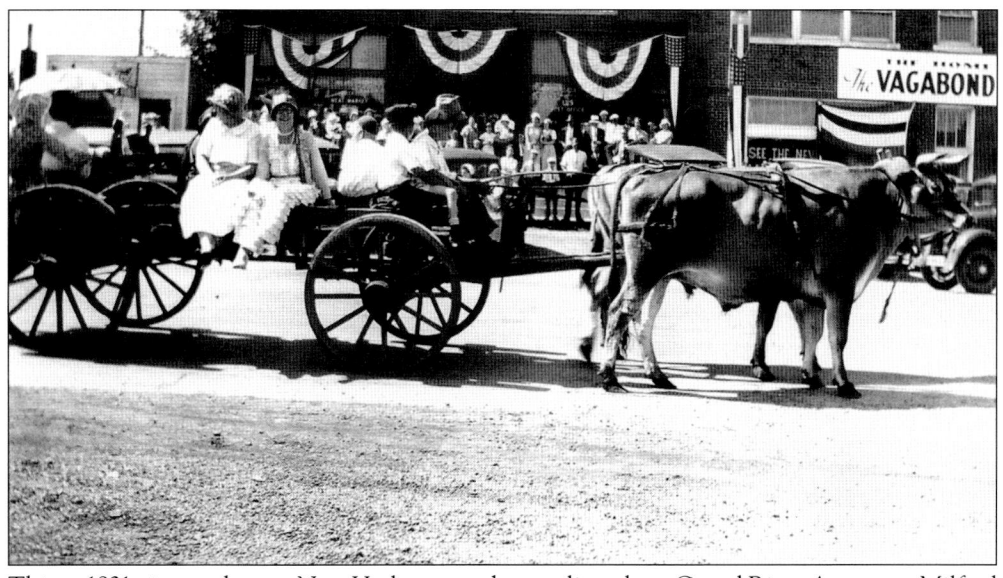

This c. 1931 picture shows a New Hudson parade traveling along Grand River Avenue at Milford Road. The sign in the background shows a sales office for the Vagabond Coach Manufacturing Company. The company produced one of the first over-the-road recreational trailers and was the Airstream of its time. (Courtesy of Lyon Township.)

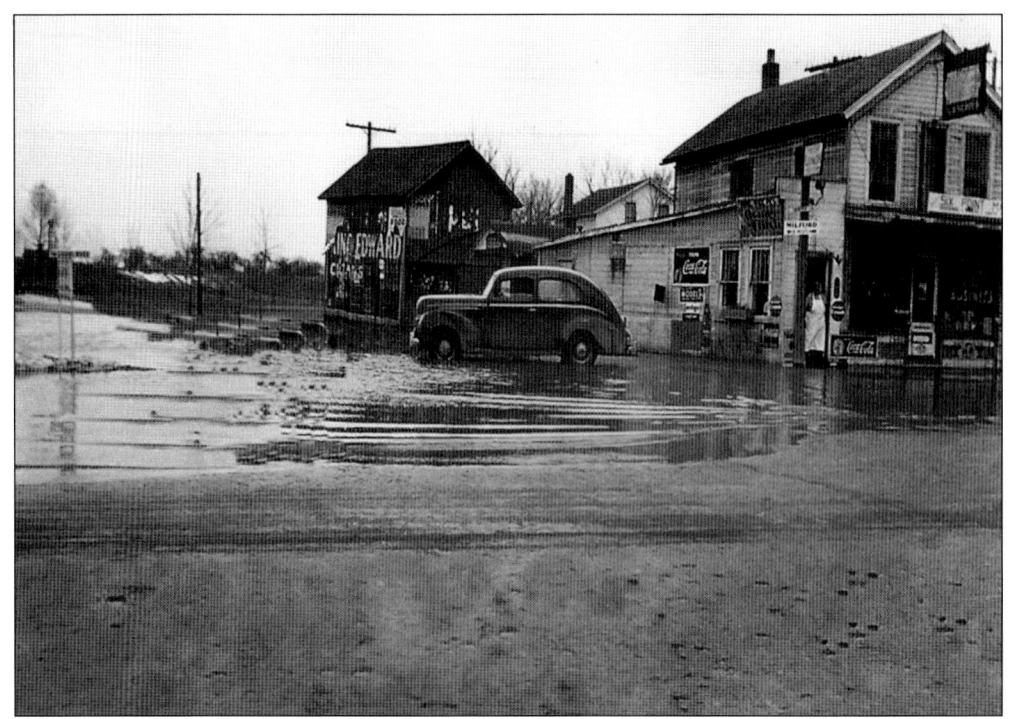

A spring thaw at the intersection of Grand River Avenue, Milford Road, and Pontiac Trail Road resulted in a flooded roadway. The building on the right was a grocery store. It was first opened as a drugstore and post office by Dr. Tucker. The balcony was removed, and the small structure on the side was added for storage. Later, a sandwich shop opened there, around 1947. (Courtesy of the South Lyon Herald.)

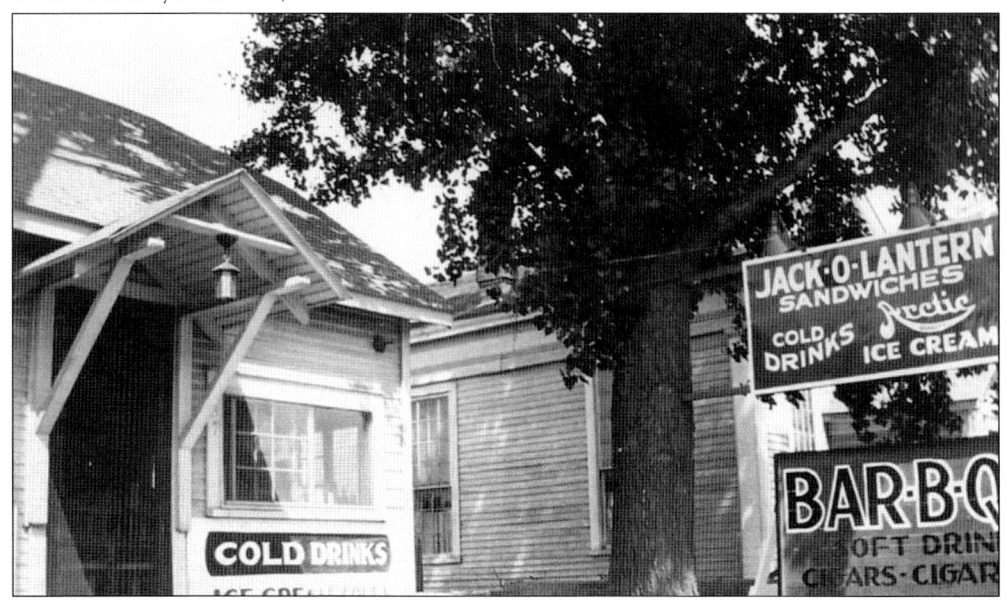

The Jack-O-Lantern Sandwich shop, around 1938, was located on Grand River Avenue between Maccabee Hall and Washburn gas station. The building was painted a bright orange. (Courtesy of Ruby Templeton.)

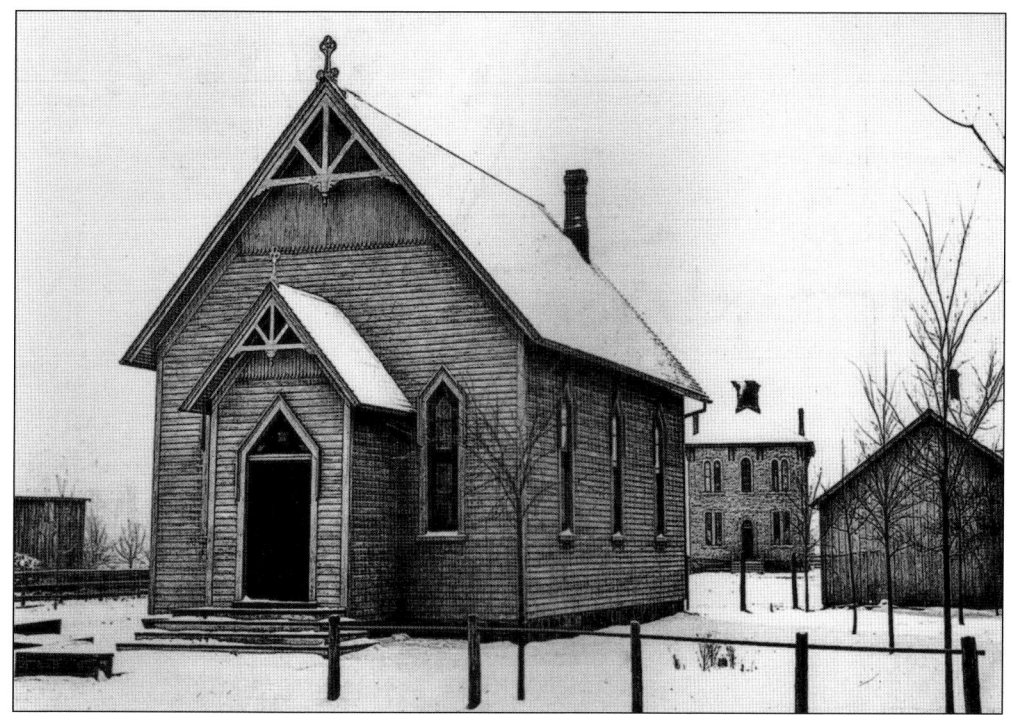

In 1837, eight people organized a congregation of the Methodist Episcopal church in New Hudson. In 1884, this building was constructed on Grand River Avenue. When the road was widened in 1930, the church building was set back from the road and turned 90 degrees, facing on what is Wells Street today. The building served as the congregation's meeting place until 1969, when a new church was constructed directly across the street. (Courtesy Lyon Township files.)

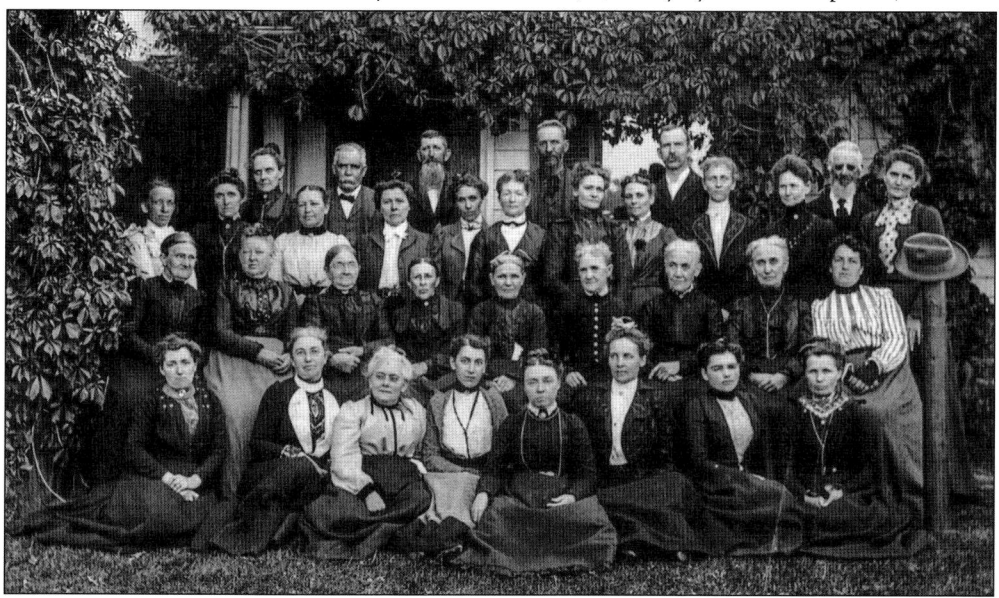

The Ladies Aid Society of the New Hudson Methodist Church is pictured at Norman Spencer's house across from the church on Grand River Avenue. (Courtesy of the South Lyon Area Historical Society.)

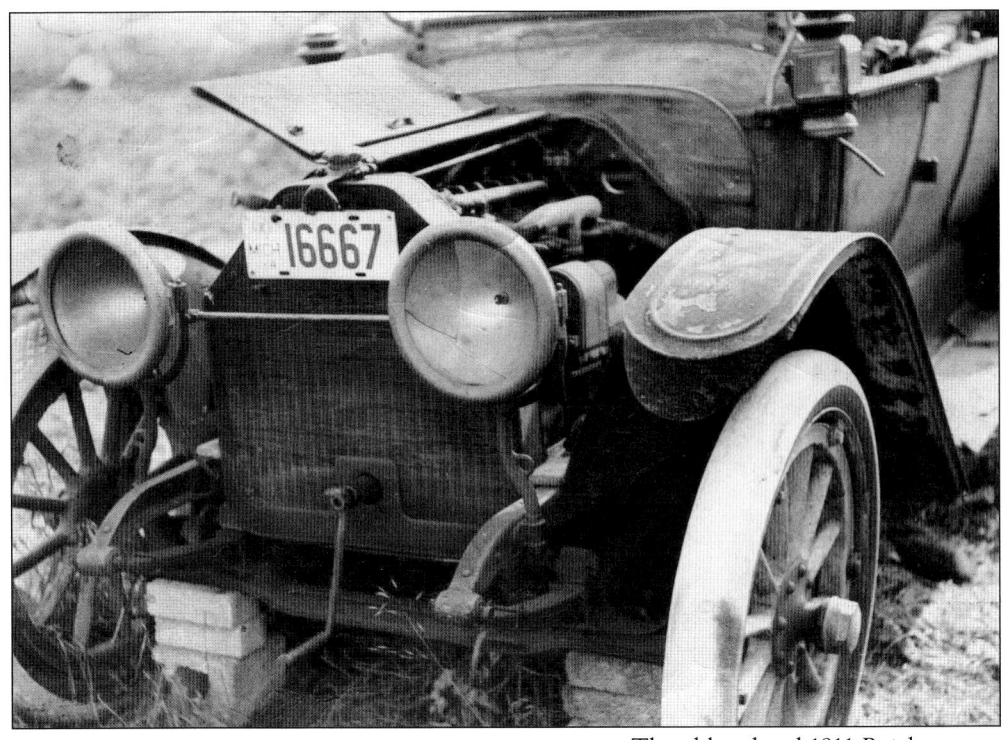

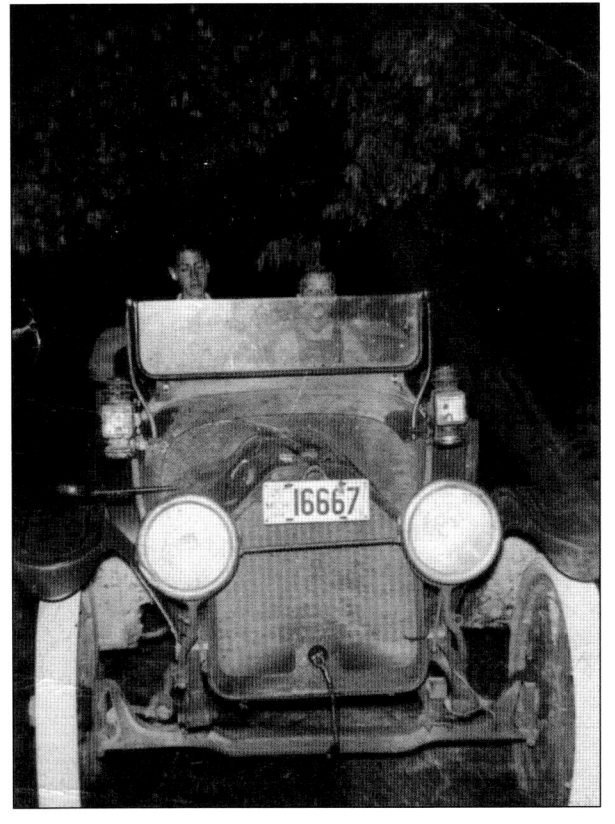

This dilapidated 1911 Buick was on blocks at the Bidwell home on Johns Road. The car originally belonged to Adelbert Hopkins. (Courtesy of Ann Polan.)

Lawrence and Calvin Bidwell sit in this 1911 Buick that once belonged to their grandfather Adelbert Hopkins. The car was never restored to operating condition. (Courtesy of Ann Polan.)

Residents met at the post office to conduct business and share stories of the day. The post office has been located in multiple buildings throughout New Hudson. In 1967, a new building was constructed at Grand River Avenue and Shefpo Street where it is currently located. Contrary to popular belief, the post office is not owned by the US government. It is privately owned. An early postmaster was Harold Haas. (Courtesy of the Lyon Township Library.)

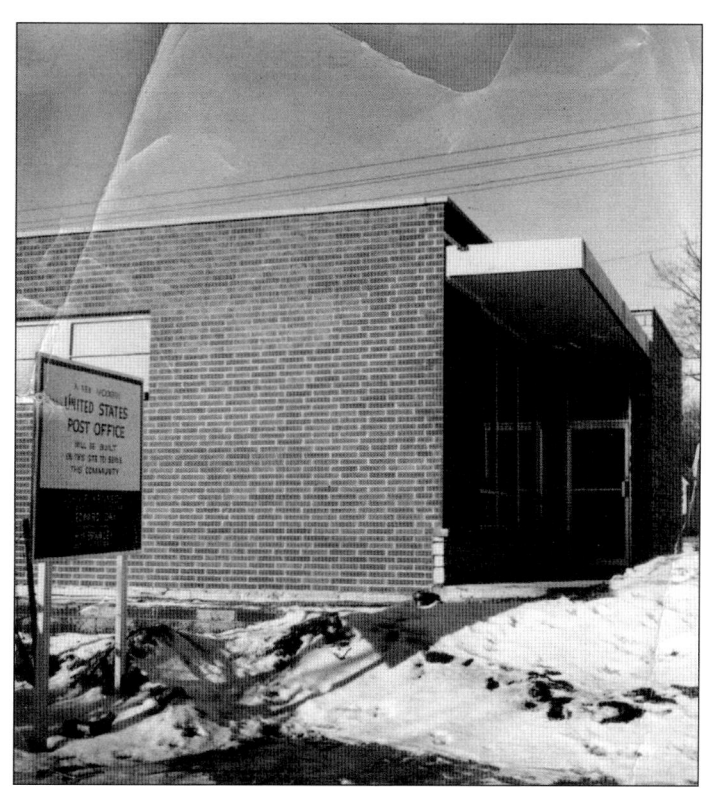

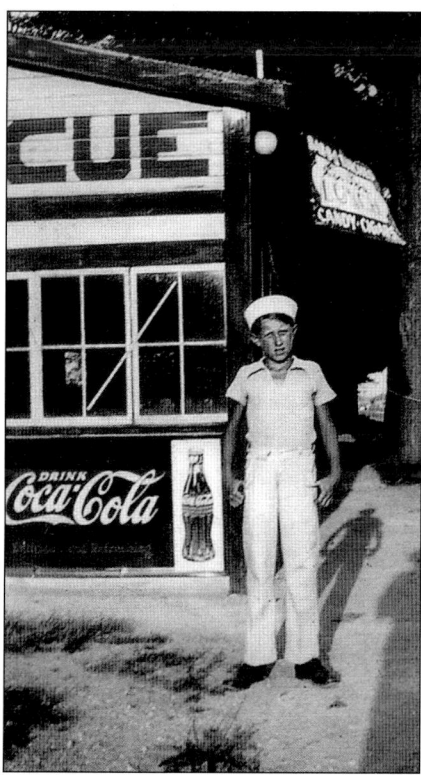

Arthur Templeton stands in front of New Hudson's barbecue restaurant around 1930. (Courtesy of Ruby Templeton.)

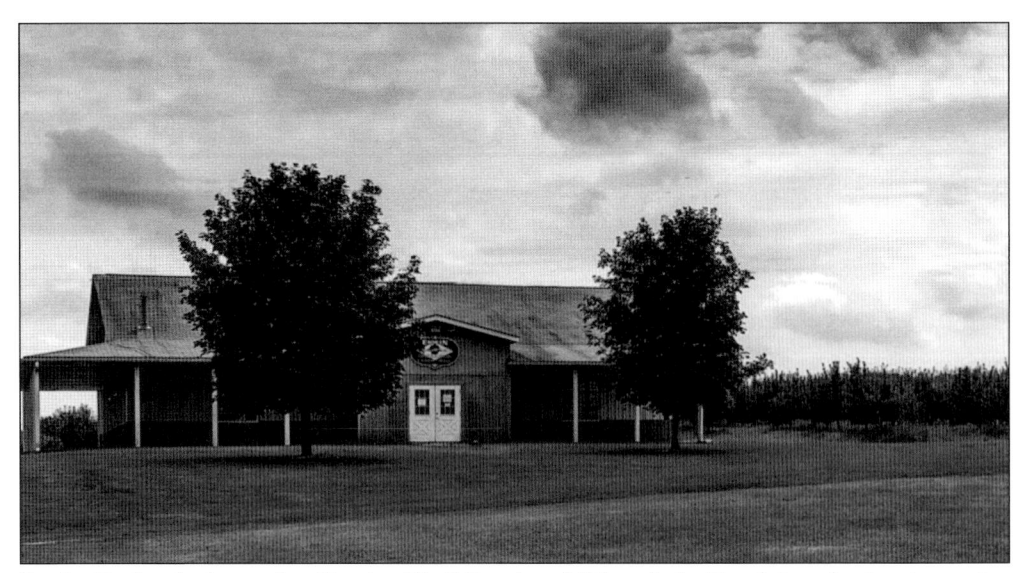

Erwin Orchards, located at Pontiac Trail Road and Silver Lake Road, is a destination point for regional visitors. It offers a cider mill, doughnuts, and U-pick fruits and vegetables. Tractor wagons take customers out to the field to pick produce. The popular enterprise was established during the 1950s. Recent activities include a haunted house at Halloween. (Courtesy of Jane and Jack Purslow.)

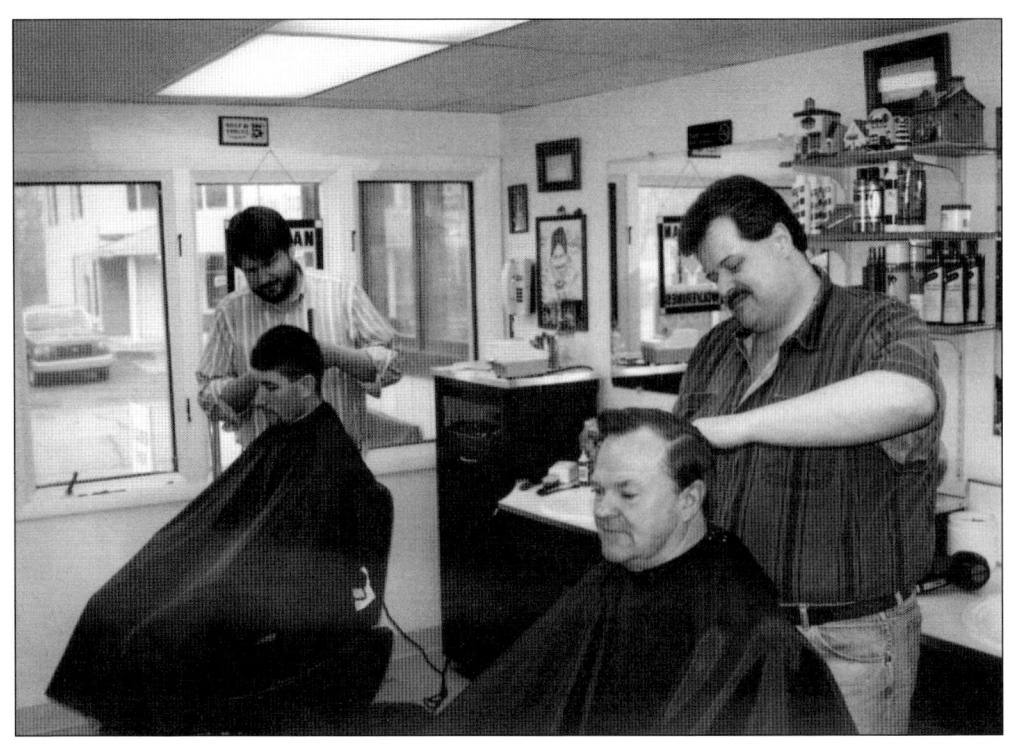

More stories have been told at the local barbershop than anywhere else in town. Tim (in the foreground) and Dennis Miner, owners of Miner's Barbershop on Grand River Avenue, tend to customers. The shop was previously Lumby's Barbershop. (Courtesy of Lyon Township.)

Three
OLD NEW HUDSON

The New Hudson Inn was the most notable business in the hamlet. The Grand River Avenue business opened in 1831 as the Old Tavern and reached its peak of popularity in the early 1840s.

In 1834, Curtis and John A. Hand opened the first store. A blacksmith business soon followed. Billy Sidell made boots to order. Dr. Tucker's drugstore was located at Milford Road and Pontiac Trail Road; the building also housed the post office for a time and served as the residence for Dr. Tucker's family. In later years, Lena Bailey operated a small restaurant attached to the building.

Burt's Buggy and Machine Shop on Grand River Avenue operated around 1880 as a blacksmith and machine company. Judd Burt and his son Fred repaired farm equipment and later built buggies. In 1931, Judd's grandson Fred started the Vagabond Coach Manufacturing Company and built one of the first recreational trailers. The Rice Building, located on Grand River Avenue east of Milford Road, was opened around 1880 and operated as a general merchandise store. The structure caught fire and burned, and only its first floor was rebuilt.

The Cheese Factory was owned by a Mr. Towar and was opened in 1911 on Rice Street next to where Dolsen Elementary School is today.

Knapp's Mobil gas station, west of the New Hudson Inn, was in operation in the 1920s. It was a full-service station where the attendant checked oil, cleaned windshields, and filled tires. The Knapp station was joined by Washburn full-service gas station, which was a thriving business in the 1930s. It was on the east side of the New Hudson Inn.

The Jack-O-Lantern Sandwich shop was another popular enterprise in the 1930s. The eatery, painted a bright pumpkin orange, was on Grand River Avenue between the Maccabee Hall and the Washburn gas station.

Other businesses in New Hudson in the 1940s included the New Hudson Lumberyard, Vagabond Coach Manufacturing Company, New Hudson Tool and Manufacturing Co., Ruth's Cottage Inn, the New Hudson Welding Shop, a Detroit Edison service center, and the Dairy Bar, which was operated by Arthur Travis and the Shear families.

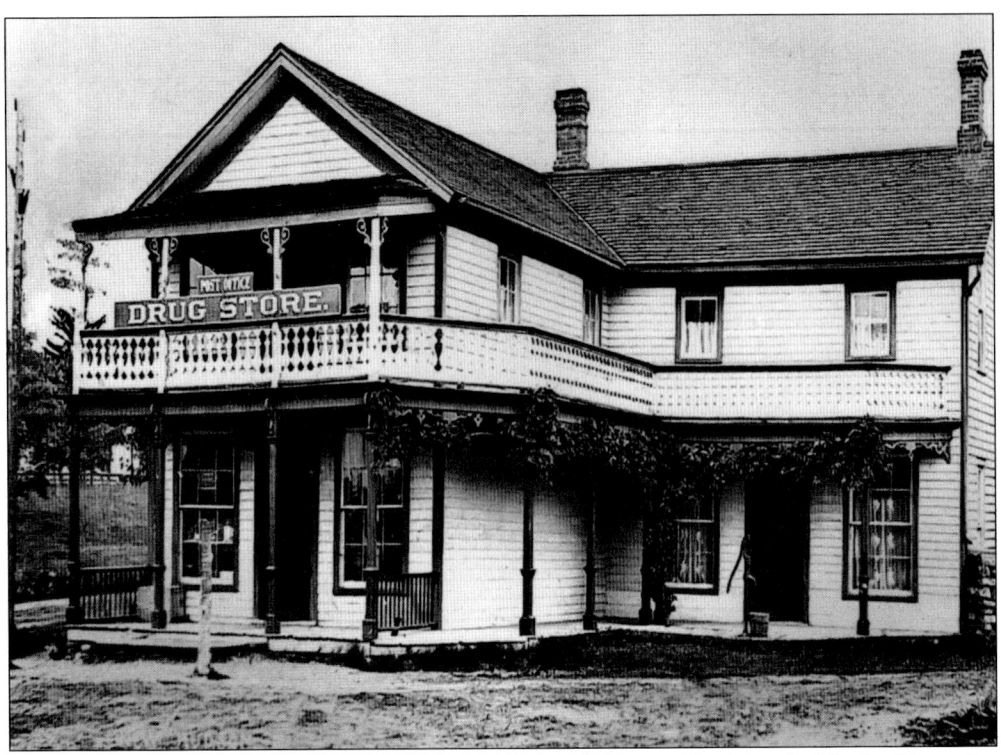

Dr. Tucker's Drugstore was located between Milford and Pontiac Trail Roads. The building also housed the post office and served as the residence for Dr. Tucker and his family. (Courtesy of Lyon Township.)

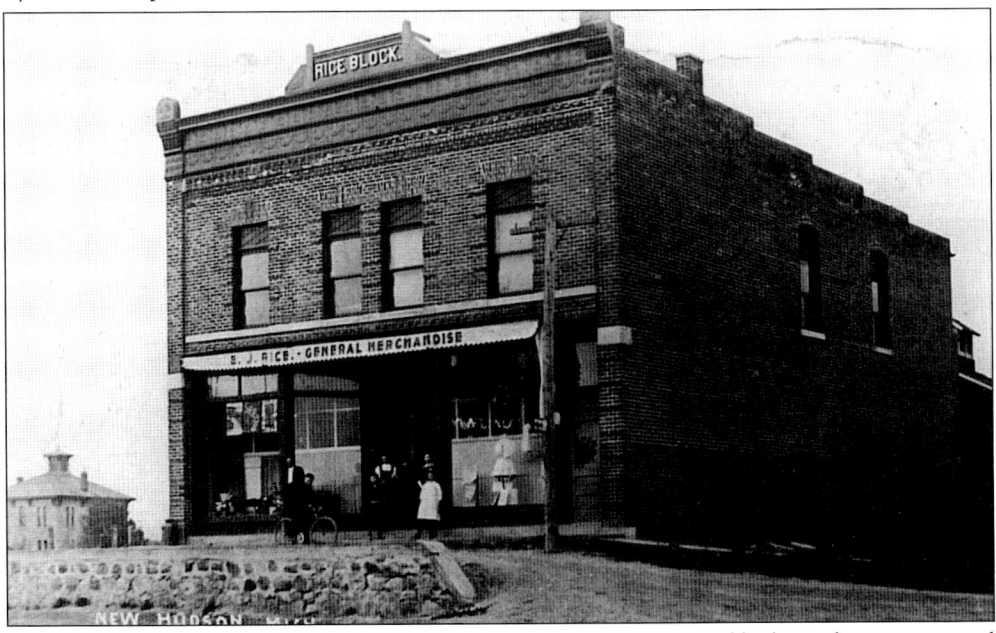

The Rice Building prior to 1921, on Grand River Avenue east of Milford Road, was a general merchandise store. Pictured in the background and to the left was the New Hudson School. (Courtesy of Lyon Township.)

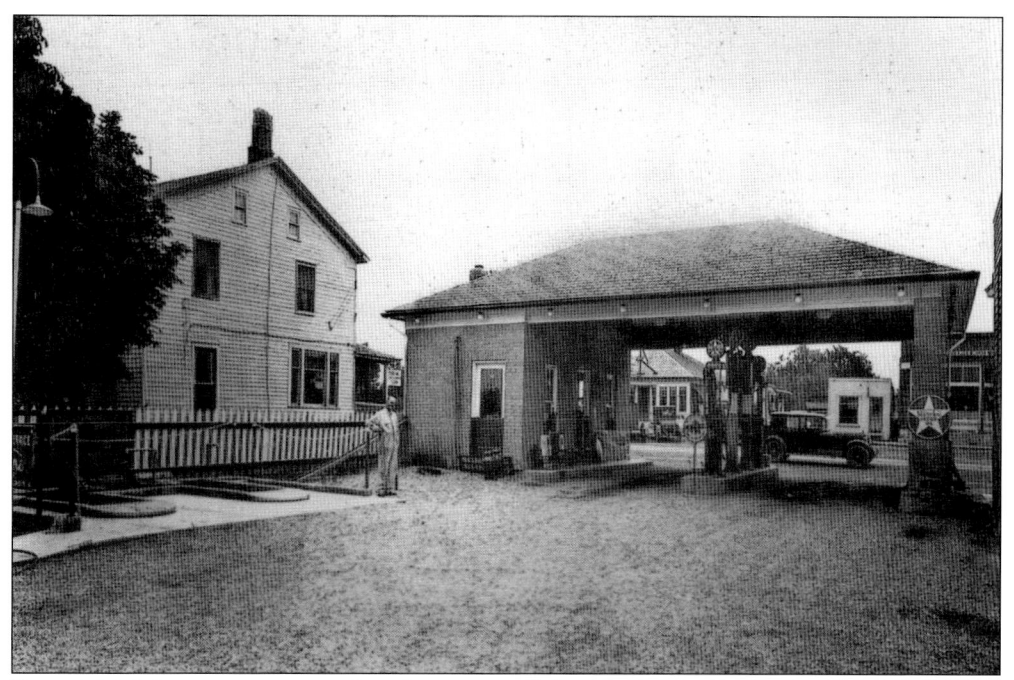

Knapp's Mobil gas station, around 1925, was west of the New Hudson Inn. This was a full-service gas station. Open pits for oil changes and underbody work were also available. (Courtesy of the Knapp family.)

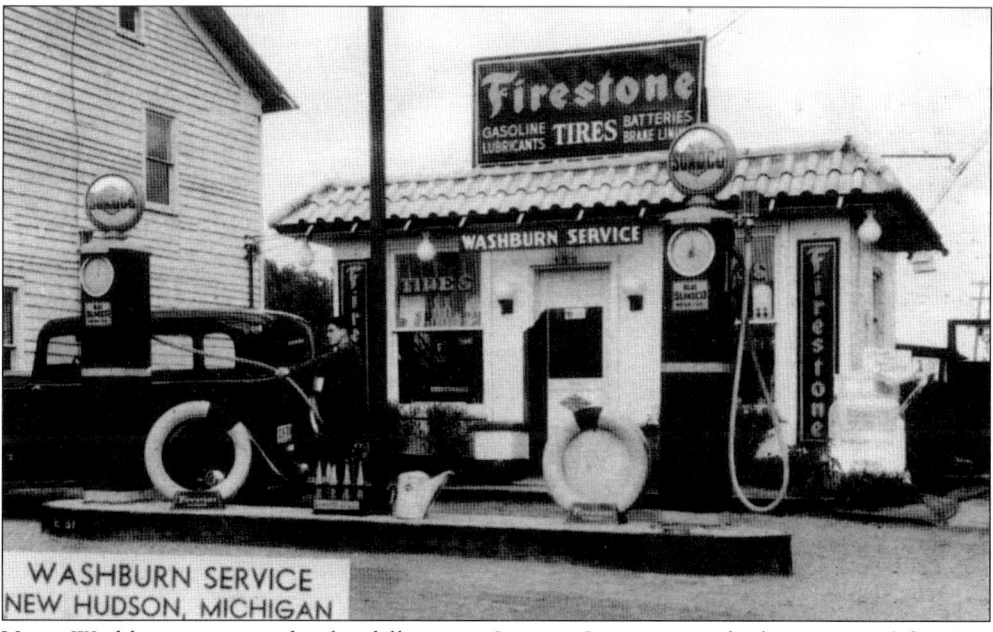

Vince Washburn is pictured at his full service Sunoco Gas station, which was east of the New Hudson Inn. At the time, car tires were wrapped, and motor oil was dispensed in glass bottles with tapered funnels for the cap. Underbody service was conducted in cement-lined pits. (Courtesy of Lyon Township.)

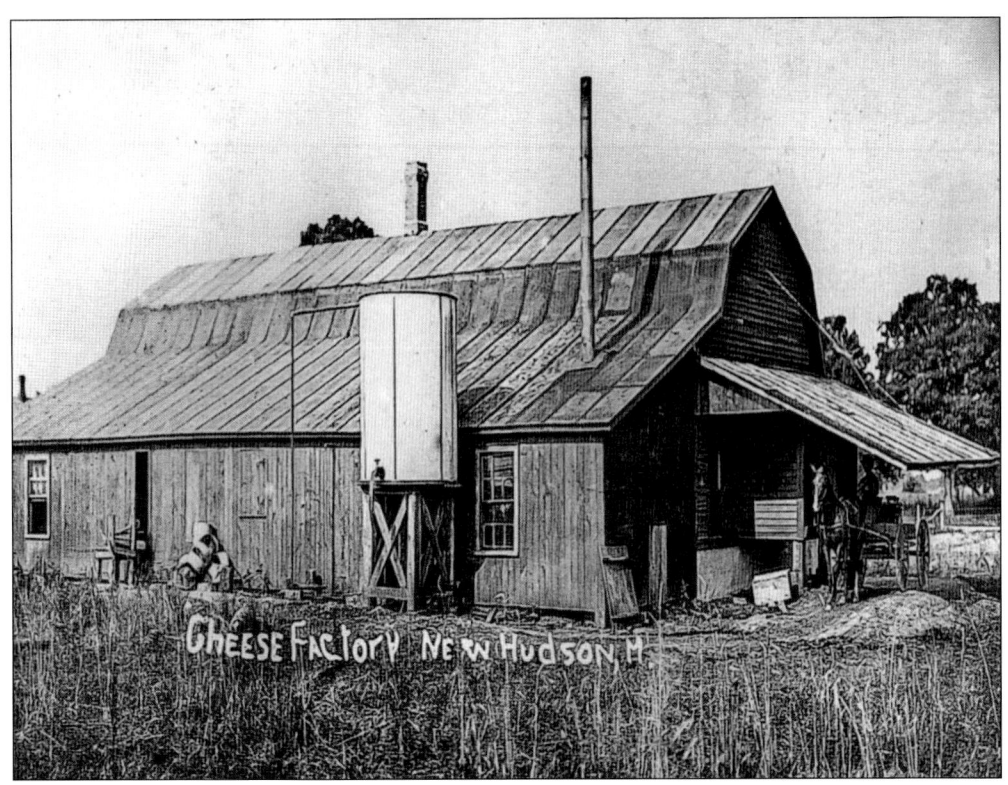

The New Hudson Cheese Factory was located adjacent to Dolsen Elementary School on Rice Street around 1900. The owner, a Mr. Towar, had a home on Grand River Avenue. He moved his house to Milford Road near the school to make it more convenient to keep an eye on his business. The building was later used as a bus maintenance garage. (Courtesy of the Lyon Township Library.)

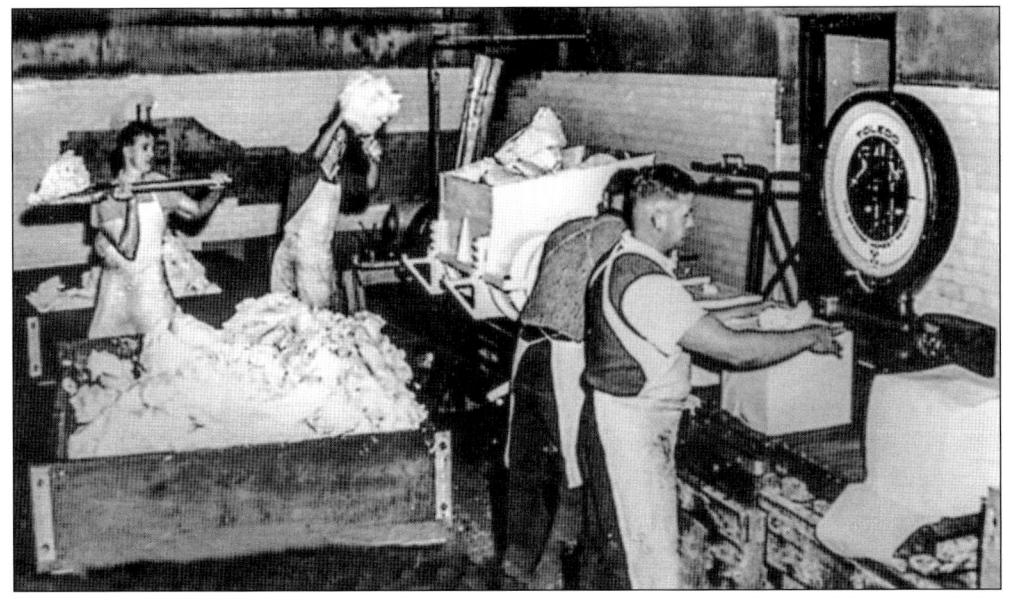

Workers at the New Hudson Cheese Factory are seen completing a day's task. (Courtesy of the Canfield family.)

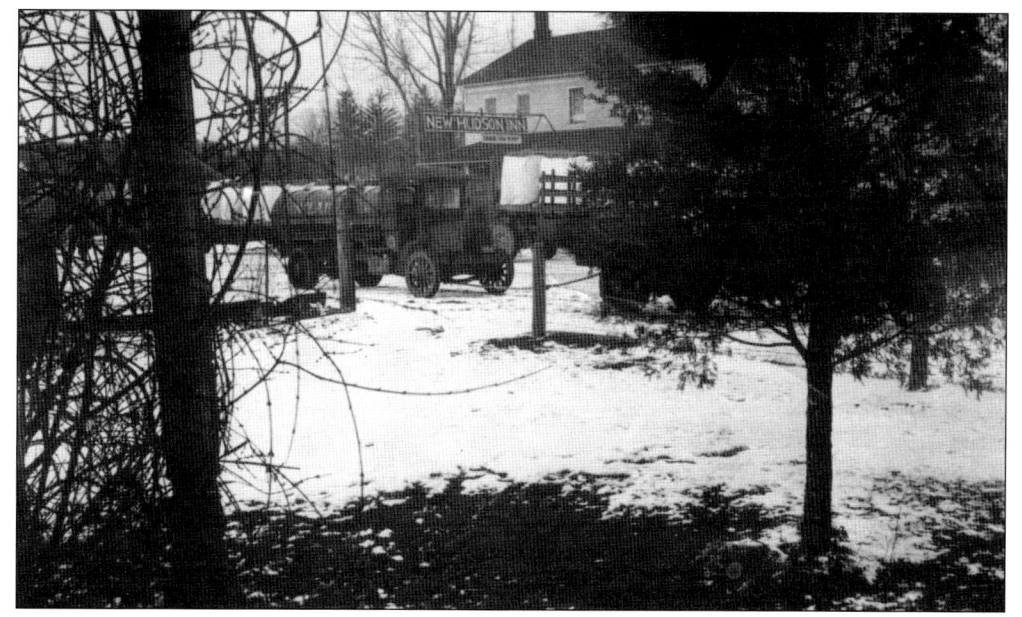

This c. 1915 picture of the New Hudson Inn shows the area before Grand River Avenue was fully developed. (Courtesy of the Lyon Township Library.)

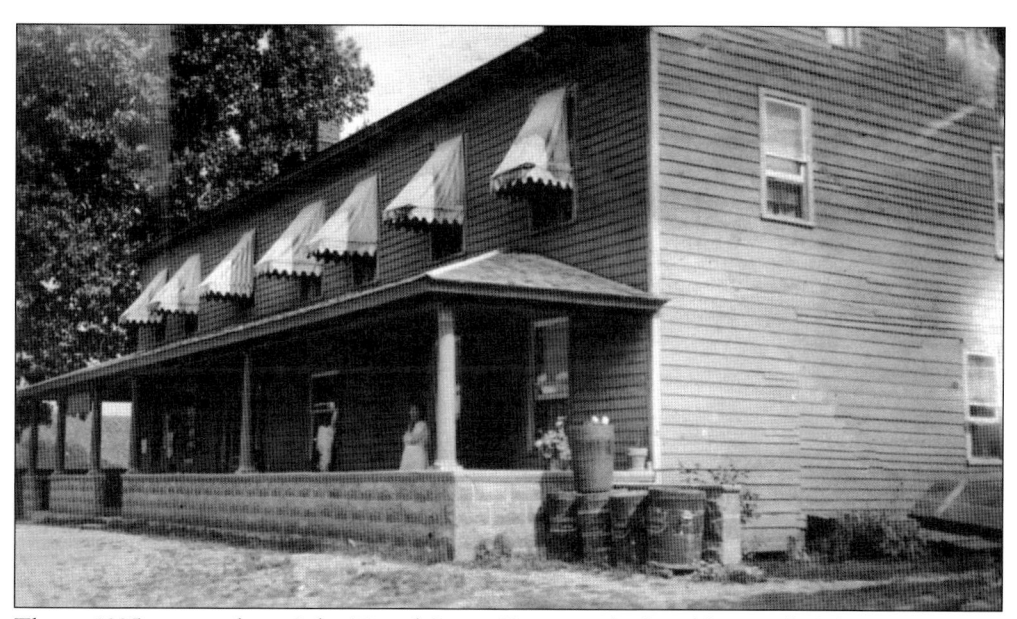

This c. 1925 picture shows John T. and Carrie Kitson at the hotel later called the New Hudson Inn. They acquired the property in 1916. (Courtesy of the Lyon Township Library)

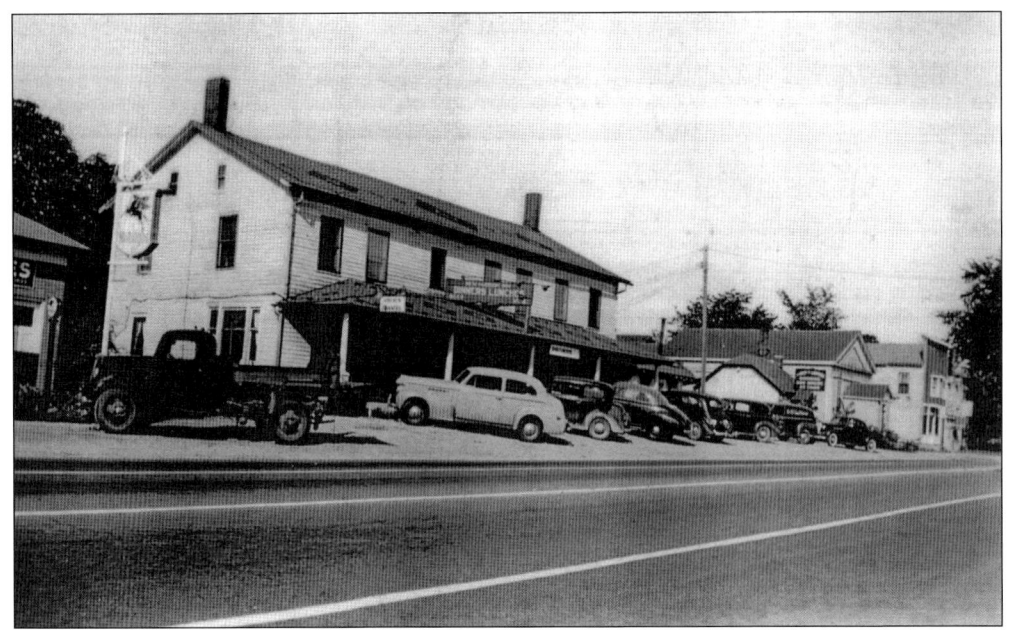

This is a c. 1946 panoramic view of the north side of Grand River Avenue looking east. The structures are the New Hudson Inn, Junior Knapp's Mobil gas station, Vince Washburn's gas station, Jack-O-Lantern Sandwich shop, Maccabee Hall, a two-story apartment building, and Ruth's Cottage Inn restaurant. (Courtesy of Lyon Township.)

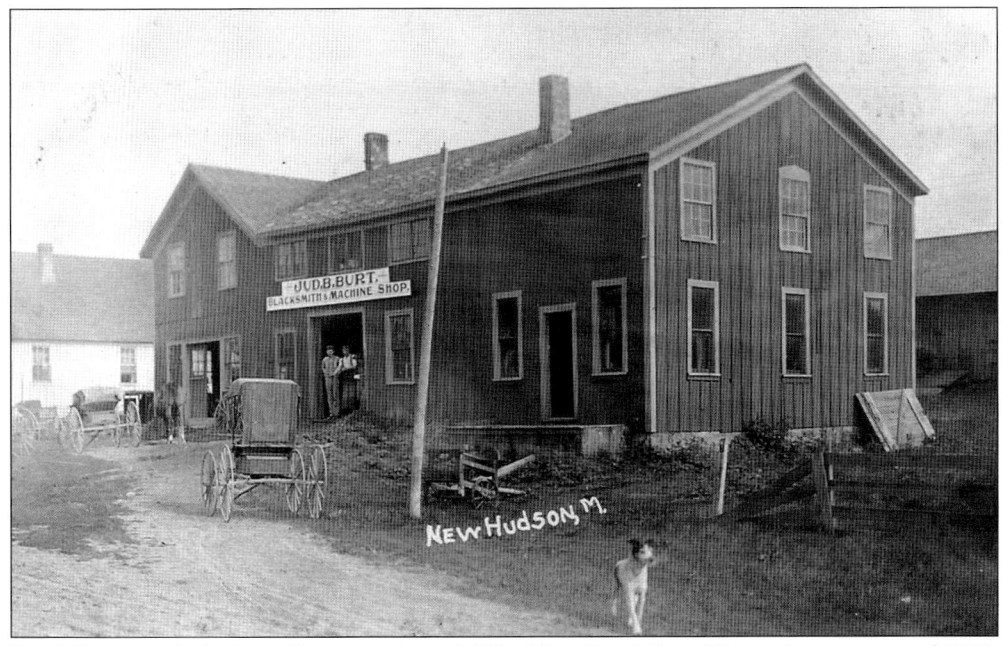

Burt's Buggy and Machine Shop stood near Milford Road and Grand River Avenue around 1880. It was a blacksmith and machinery company where Judd Burt and his son Fred repaired farm implements. (Courtesy of the Lyon Township Library.)

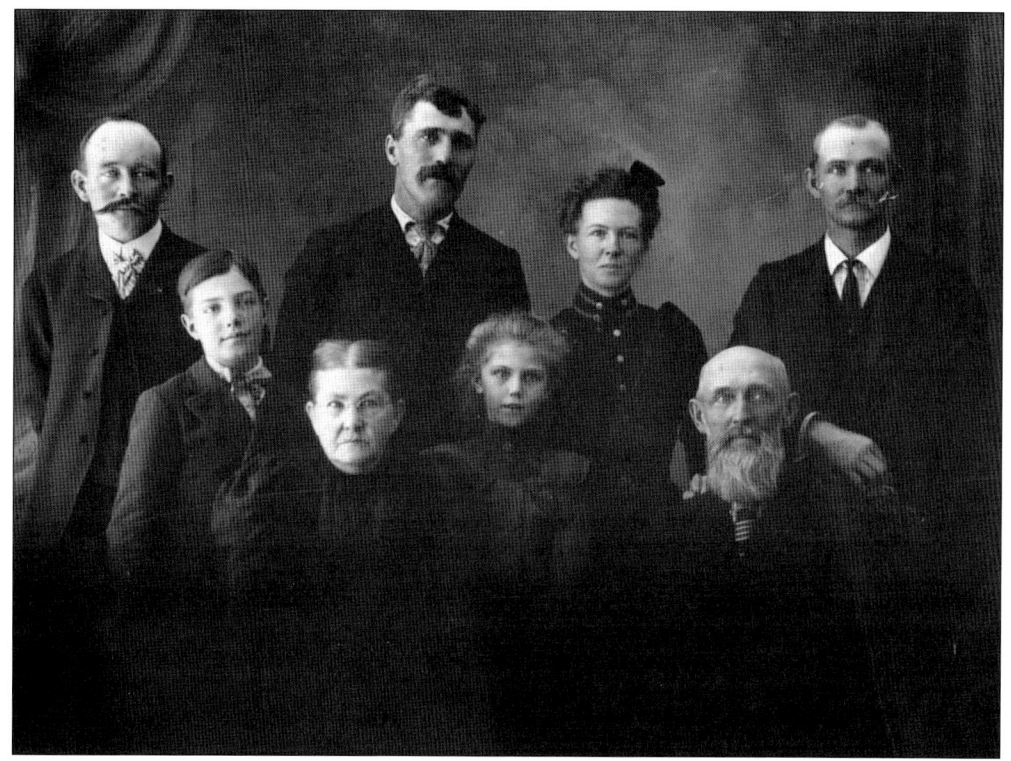

The Knapp family members were prominent early residents who owned land on Pontiac Trail Road. The acreage ultimately became the Gerald Knapp Airport. (Courtesy of the Lyon Township Library.)

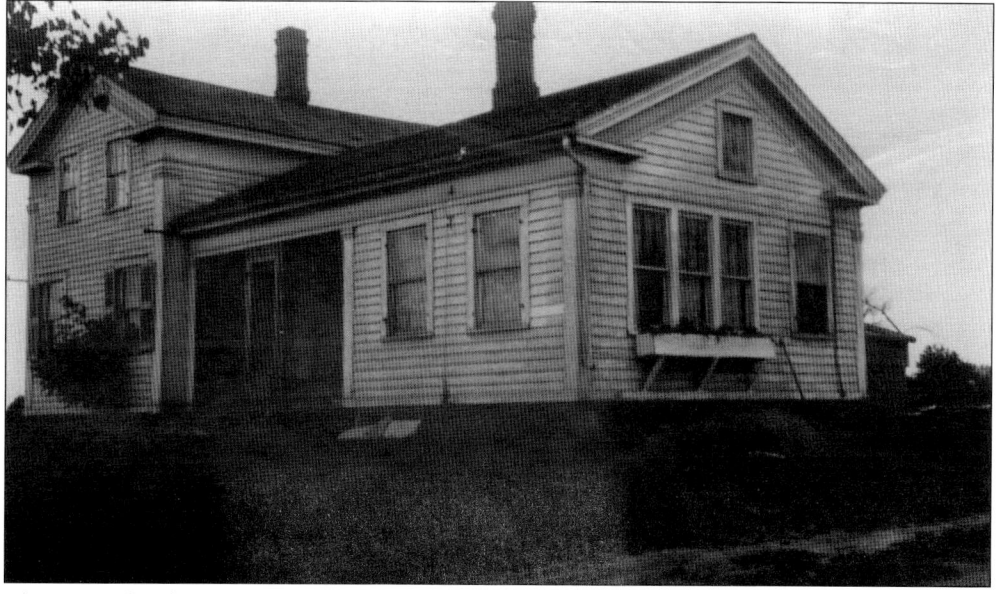

The Knapp family residence still stands on Pontiac Trail Road across from what is now the Oakland County Southwest Airport. (Courtesy of the Lyon Township Library.)

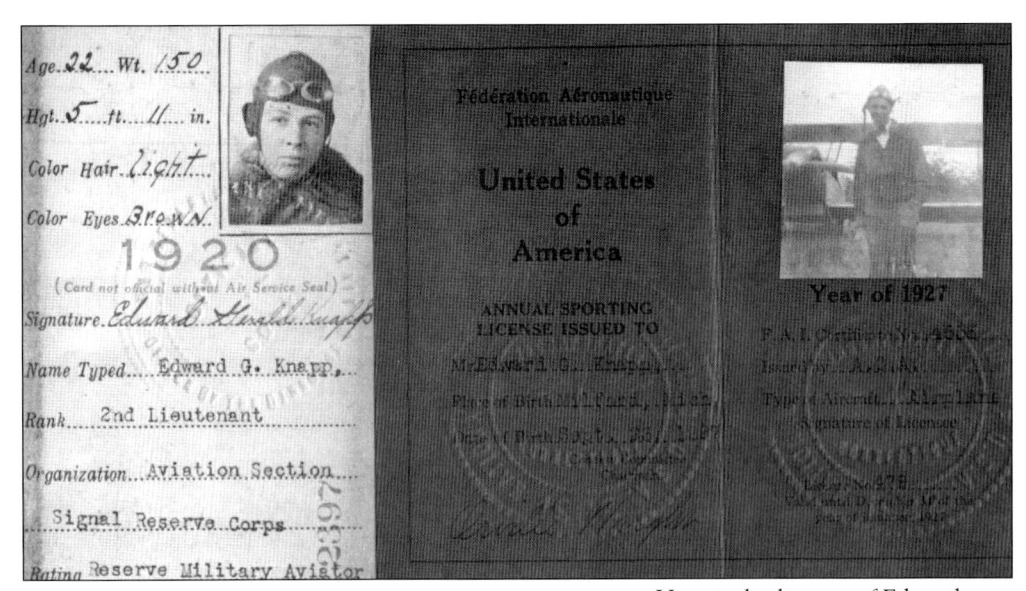

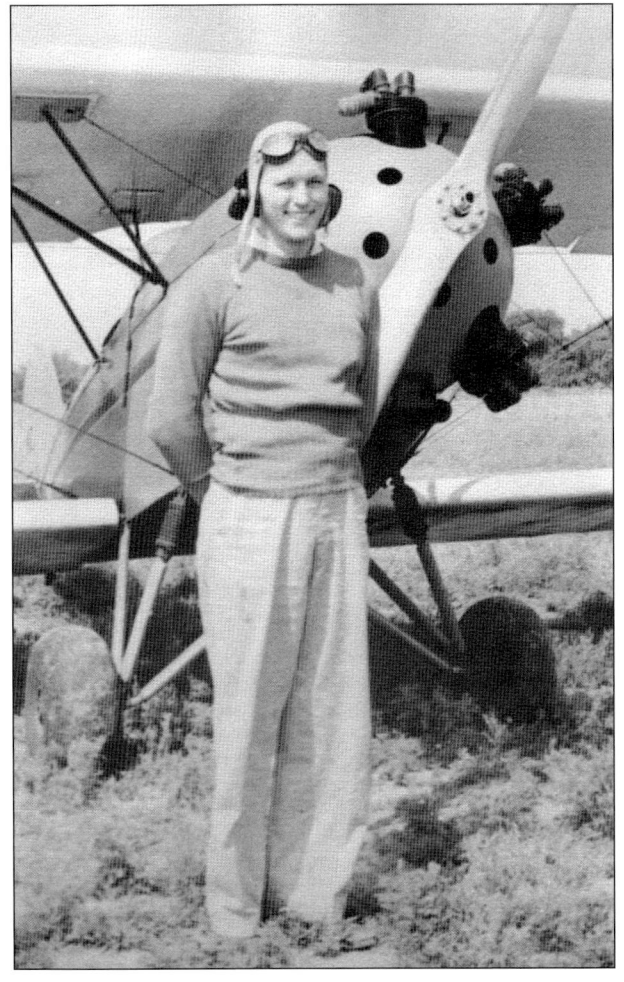

Here is the license of Edward Gerald Knapp, a second lieutenant in the Aviation Section of the Signal Reserve Corps. He was killed in an airplane crash in Texas. His uncle Harvey Knapp opened an airport in 1947 on land that had been used as a family farm. During the airport's dedication ceremony, a parachute demonstrator miscalculated his flight and landed in a pigpen on Cash Street, according to Roy Cash, a longtime New Hudson resident. (Courtesy of Jerry Knapp.)

Bill McKinley was the operator of the airport and worked at Vagabond Coach Manufacturing Company in the late 1930s. The Knapp Airport was also known as New Hudson Airport and is currently referred to as Oakland/Southwest Airport. An airport beacon often shined in bedrooms of local residents, explained nearby resident Roy Cash. (Courtesy of the Lyon Township Library)

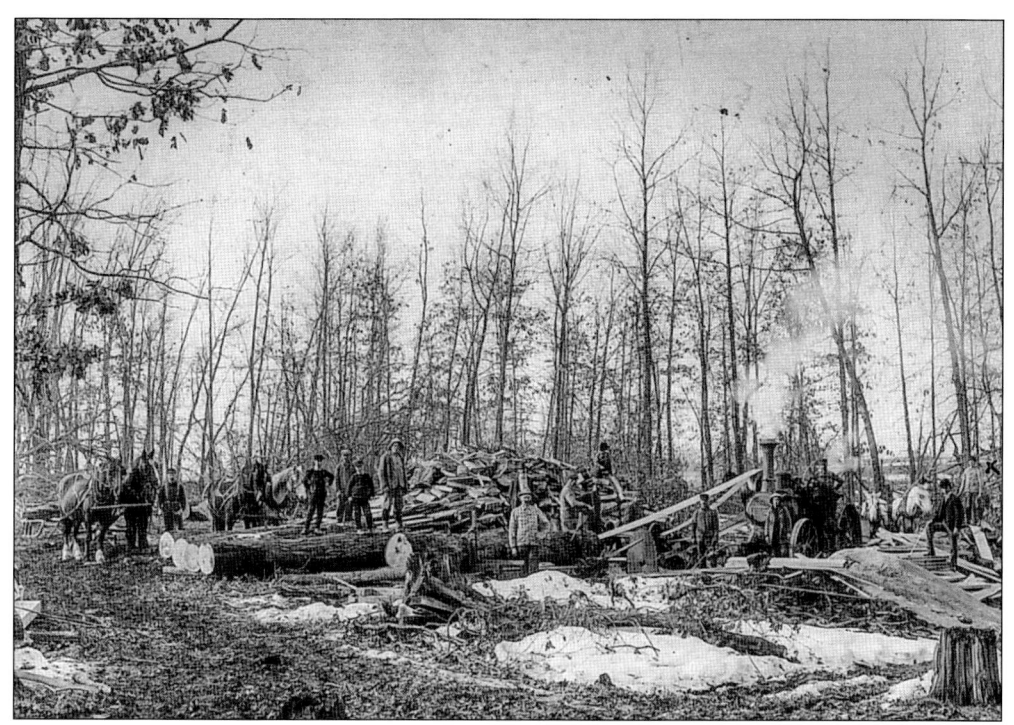

This c. 1901 picture shows a logging sawmill in Ray Moore's woods around the city of Kensington. Charles Tuck and Fred Shefpo were the engineers involved. Will Suthland was the sawyer, and Fred Foote was the setter. (Courtesy of the Lyon Township Library.)

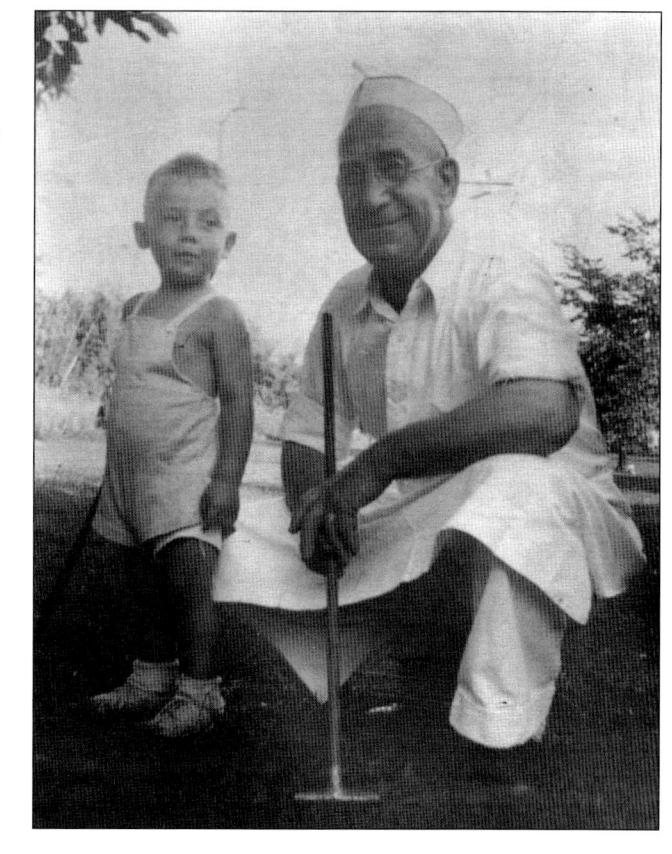

William Kingsley owned and ran the Kingsley Restaurant on Grand River Avenue in New Hudson. It is believed he is shown here with his grandson. (Courtesy of the Lyon Township Library.)

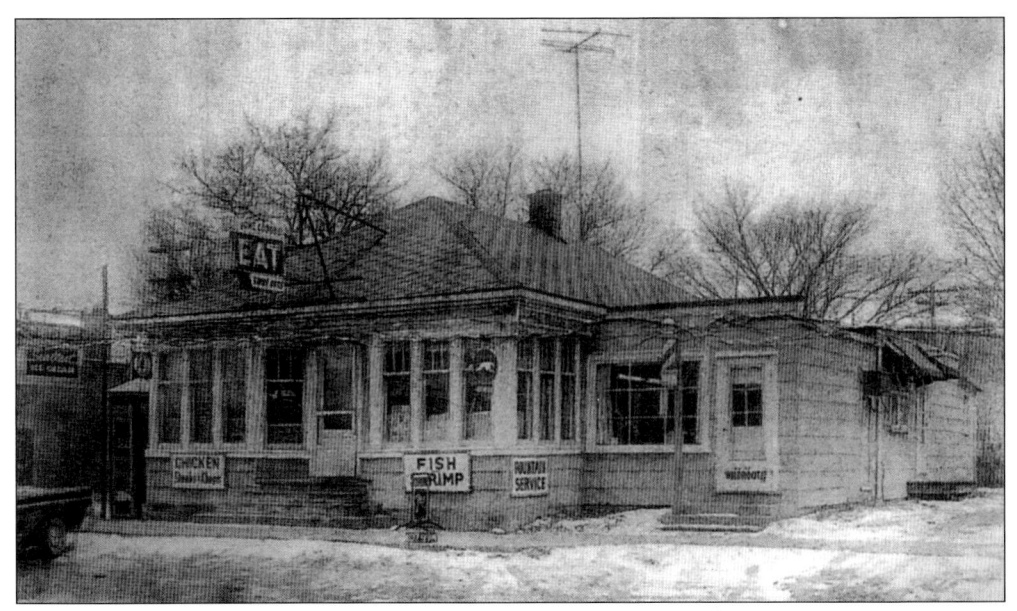

The Kingsley restaurant was one of many on Grand River Avenue in downtown New Hudson. (Courtesy of Miner's Barbershop.)

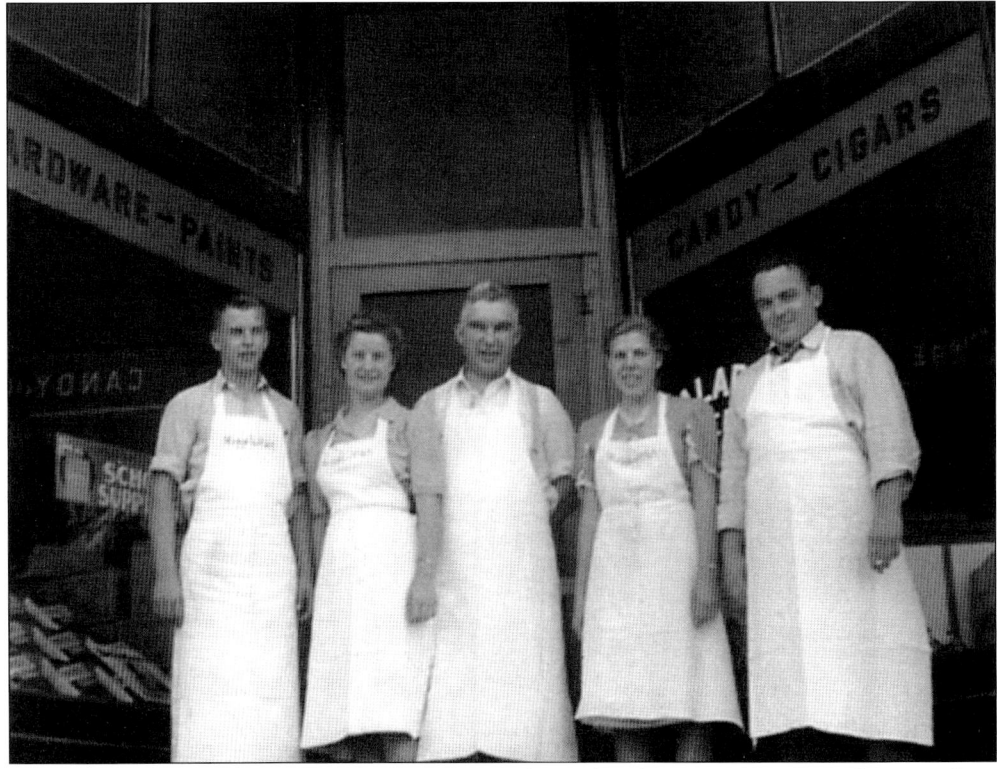

In this picture, taken in 1940, of the Hopp General Merchandise store in New Hudson are, from left to right, Gerald Hopp, the son of owner Henry Hopp; Elsie Tandy Smith, a clerk; owner Henry Hopp; Mary E. Canfield, a clerk; and Jack McKay, the butcher. (Courtesy of Bob Scheets.)

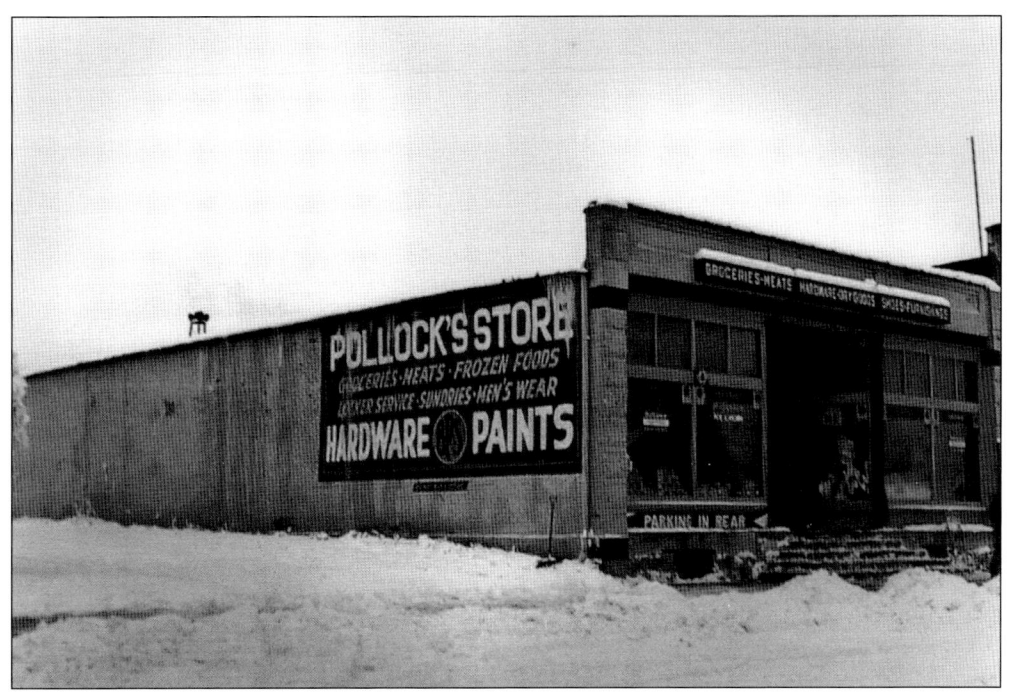

The Pollock general store, pictured around 1944, used to be the Hopp General Merchandise store. It was housed in the former Rice Building. It is currently occupied by BKS Collision. (Courtesy of Bob Scheets.)

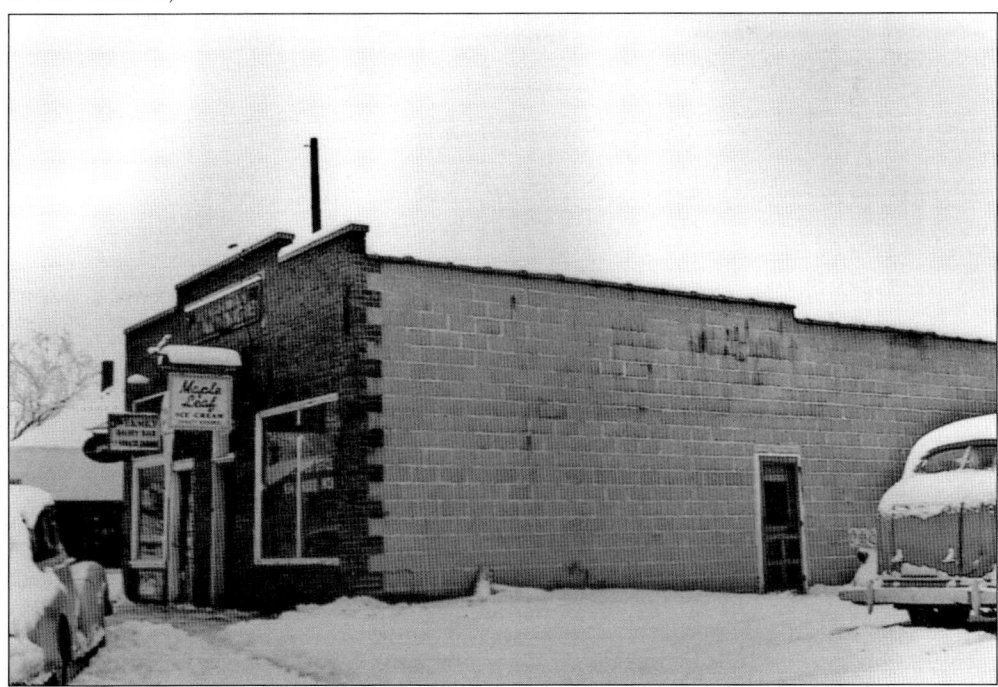

This building in 1943 was located on Grand River Avenue and was next to the Pollock general store. It housed an ice cream store and post office. It also was a Greyhound bus depot and served as a pick-up point for passengers. (Courtesy of Bob Scheets.)

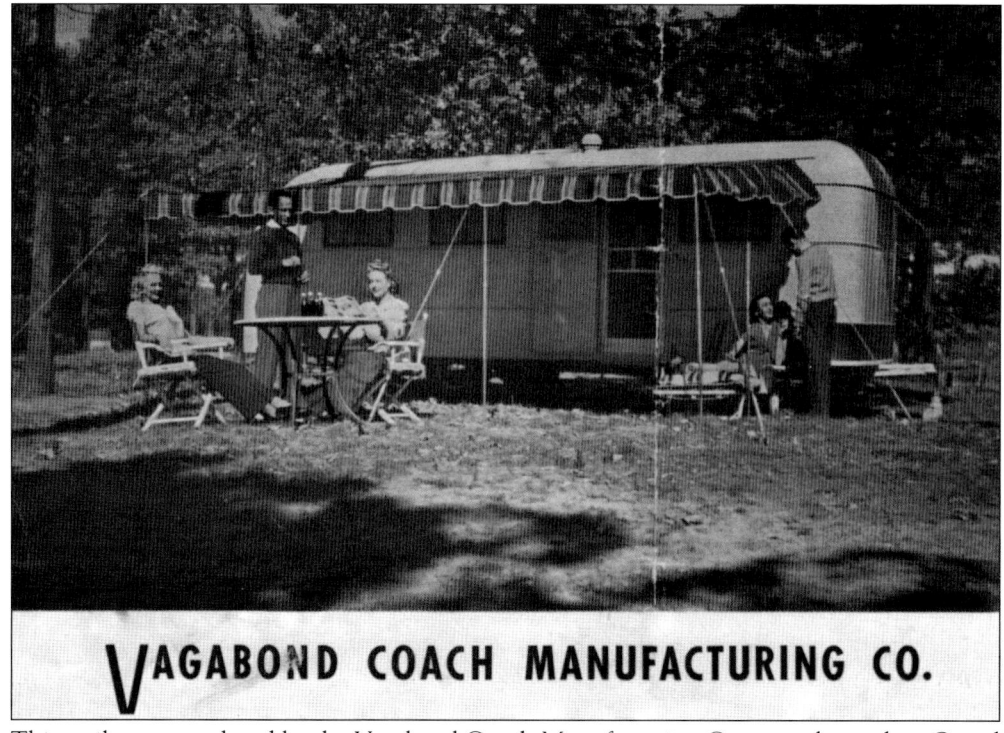

This trailer was produced by the Vagabond Coach Manufacturing Company located on Grand River Avenue. Vagabond was started in 1931 in New Hudson and became one of the premier recreational trailer companies in the country. During World War II, it supplied trailers to house military personnel. (Courtesy of Clinton Cook.)

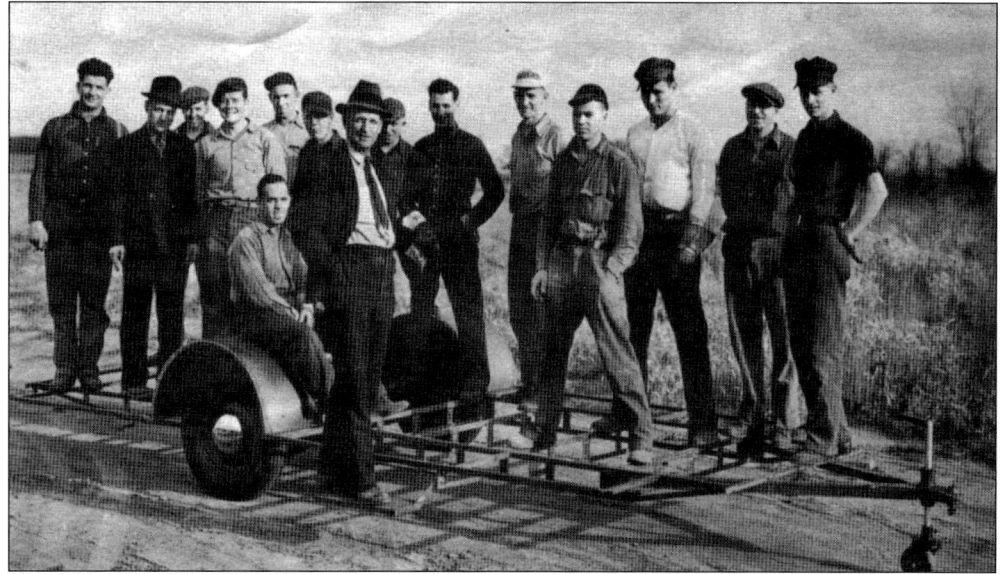

This is part of the workforce of the Vagabond Coach Manufacturing Company around 1941. Pictured are, from left to right, Harvey Childs, George Miles, Lloyd Higby, Donald Davis, Al Stave, Joe Voorheis, Fred Burt, Hap Crawford, Howard Franklin, Harold Metts, John Clark, Hugh MacArthur, Bill McKinley, Frank Arthur, and Tom Cook. (Courtesy of Clinton Cook.)

Four

Agriculture

John Canfield's ancestors arrived in New Hudson from New York State in 1833 and farmed on Milford Road. At one time, the farm was more than 200 acres, and it was primarily a crop farm. They also had a dairy herd. The farm was sold to a land developer in 2001 and a shopping mall now occupies the site. A family history, which details life on the farm from 1918 to 1931, describes a windmill that was used to pump water, a wood range, and a dirt basement to keep food cool in the summer.

In the spring, the fields were plowed by horses and fitted over with a spring-tooth drag to level them off for planting, according to a Canfield family historical account. "For planting, we used grain drills, corn planters and potato planters pulled by horses," the Canfield story said. "We had rollers to roll down the stones and smooth out the grain and hay fields." Crops were rotated to provide different nutrients into the soil.

Potato harvesting was among the fall jobs, and it required using a four-horse team that pulled a potato digger. Potatoes were then picked up by hand. Most potato farmers had 5 to 15 acres to harvest. Sometimes, school would close for a week during potato harvest to allow the young people to help.

Another lifelong resident, Elaine Cash, remembers when New Hudson was a rural community. She was born over 94 years ago on her family's farm. Her dad, George Haack, bought property at Twelve Mile Road and Haas Road around 1915 for the family's dairy farm. Elaine walked a mile and a half each way to the one-room Smith School, at South Hill and Twelve Mile Roads. "Sometimes when the snow was so deep my dad would take us on a sled," she said.

Elaine remembers the family having kerosene lamps to illuminate the darkness of night. Cows and other animals dotted the landscape. The milk was taken to the New Hudson depot and then onto Farmington.

Every Saturday, the Cash family would go into town to the village of South Lyon where they would get groceries and other essentials. They often took time to socialize and attend movies at the theater on Lake Street and North Lafayette Avenue.

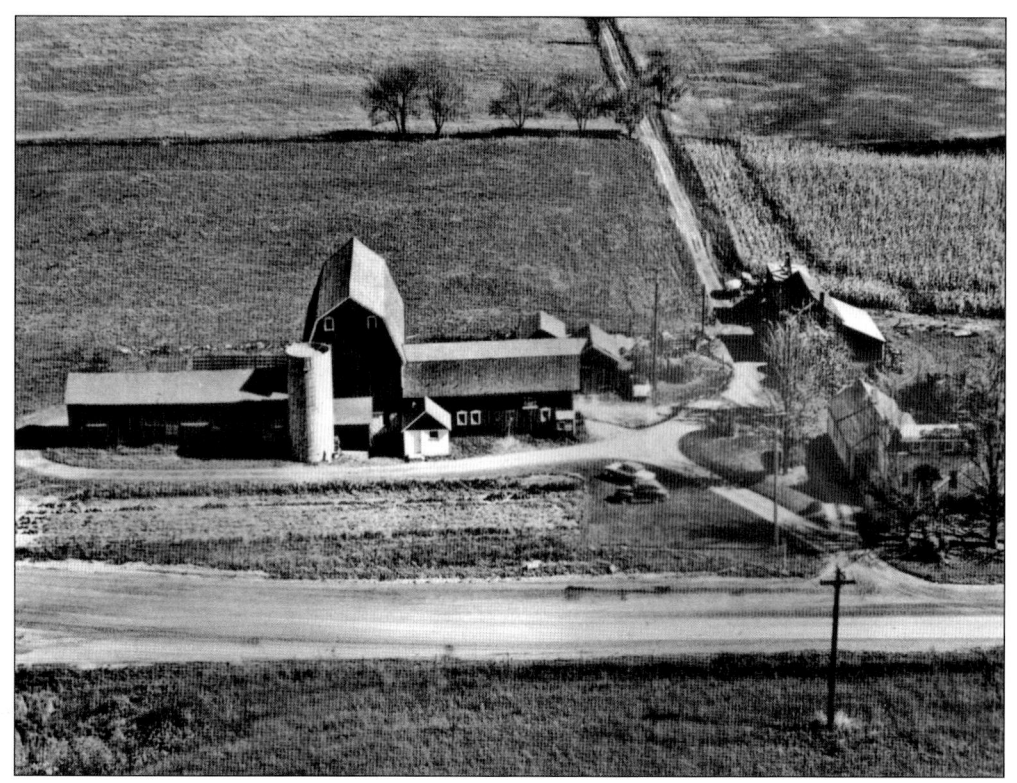

An aerial view of John Canfield's farm on Milford Road is shown in 1953. Canfield's ancestor, William Goldy, arrived in New Hudson from New York around 1830. At one time, the farm was about 200 acres. Canfield also had a dairy herd. A shopping mall now occupies the site. (Courtesy of Doug Canfield.)

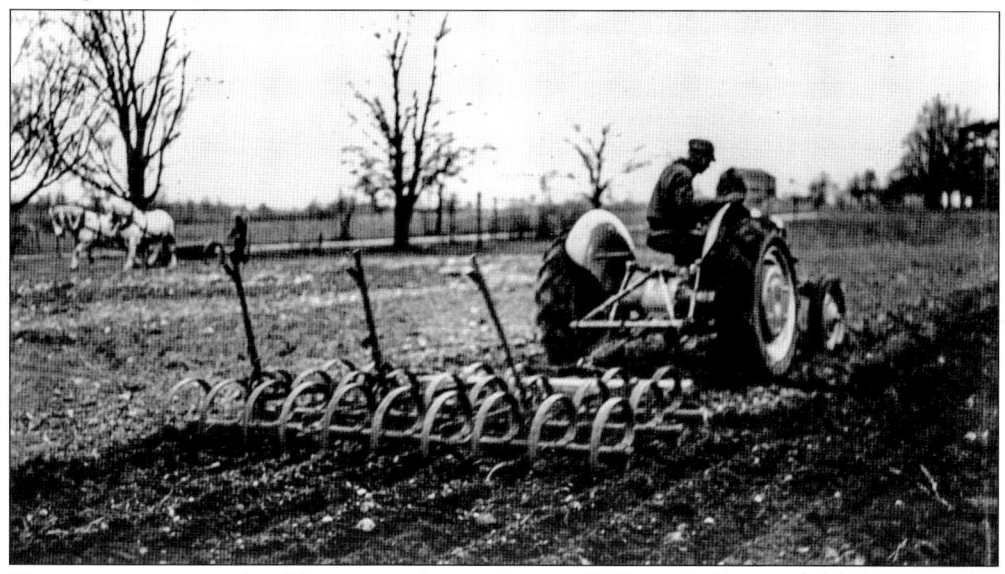

This is a prime example of farming evolution. Prior to William Goldy Canfield obtaining this 25-horsepower 1940 9N Ford tractor, the two horses in the background were the source for cultivating this field on Milford Road. (Courtesy of Canfield family.)

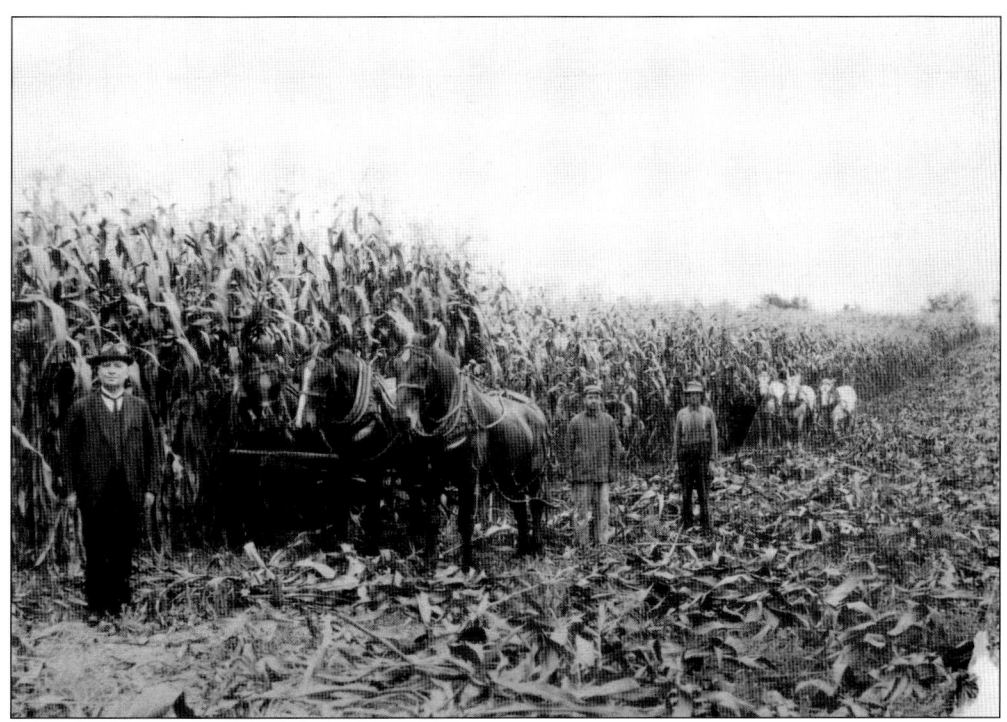

The Pettengill cornfield was on Pontiac Trail and Martindale Roads in New Hudson around 1920. Milo and Erwin Pettengill are shown with their horses. The corn stalks are unusually high. It is believed the man in the foreground was a hybrid corn seed salesman. (Courtesy of Ann Polan.)

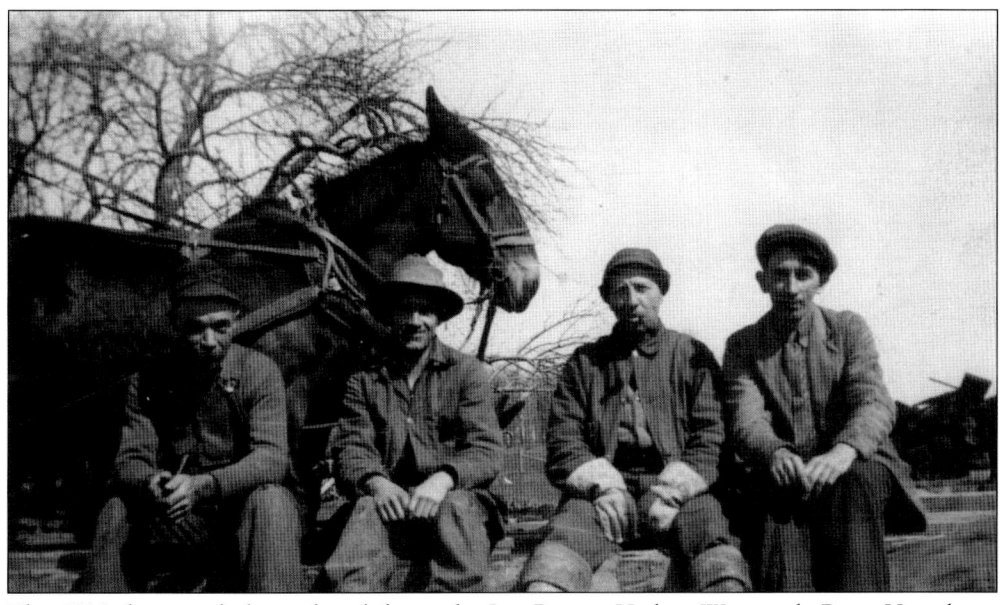

This 1930 photograph shows, from left to right, Leo Bryant, Herbert Westervelt, Rusty Hauteburg, and Millard Elliot on the Hopkins farm, which was located at Old Plank and Pontiac Trail Roads. (Courtesy of Clinton Cook.)

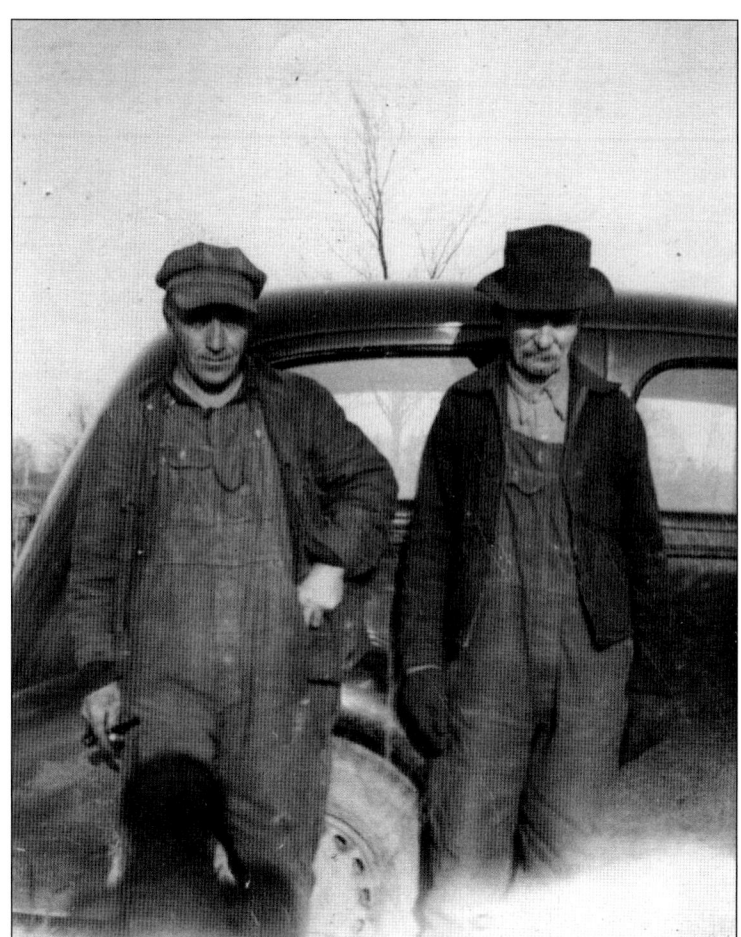

Herbert Hopkins (right) and his son Raymond Hopkins are taking a break on their farm at Pontiac Trail and Old Plank Roads. (Courtesy of Clinton Cook.)

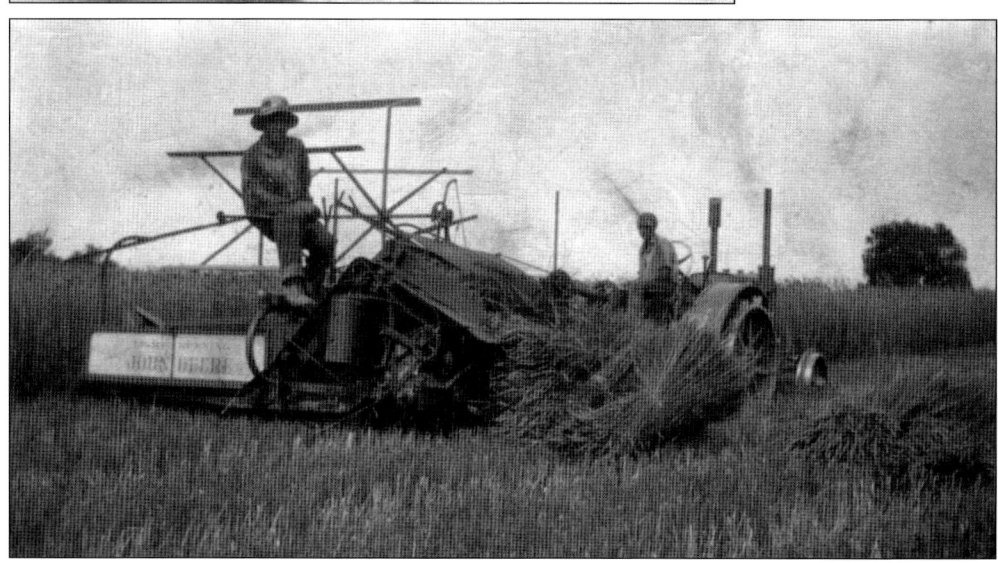

Raymond Hopkins and Edwin Westervelt are shown here at work on the Hopkins farm around 1932. (Courtesy of Clinton Cook.)

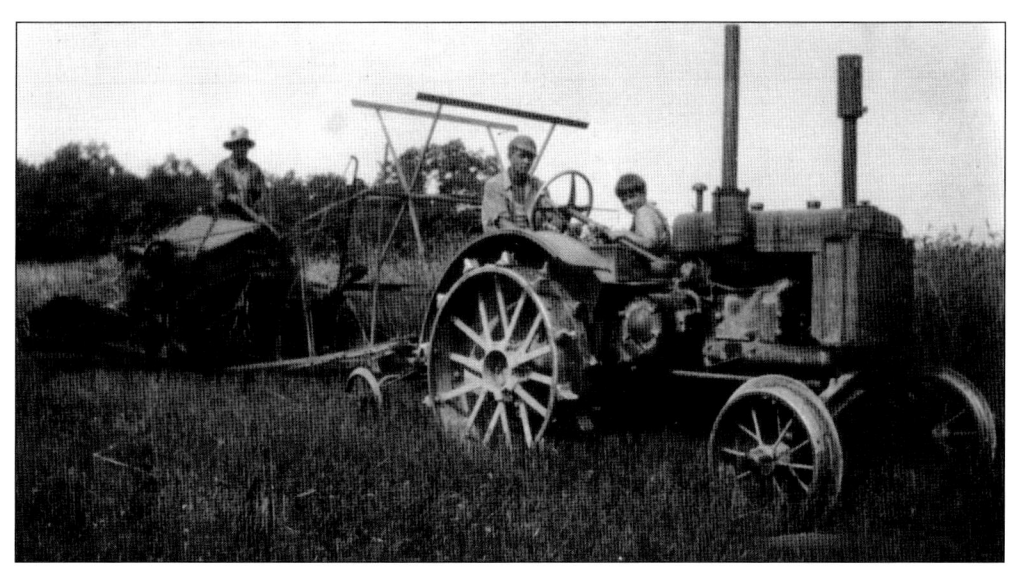

From left to right, Raymond Hopkins, Pete Westervelt, and Bill Westervelt are on the Hopkins farm at Old Plank and Pontiac Trail Roads around 1932. (Courtesy of Clinton Cook.)

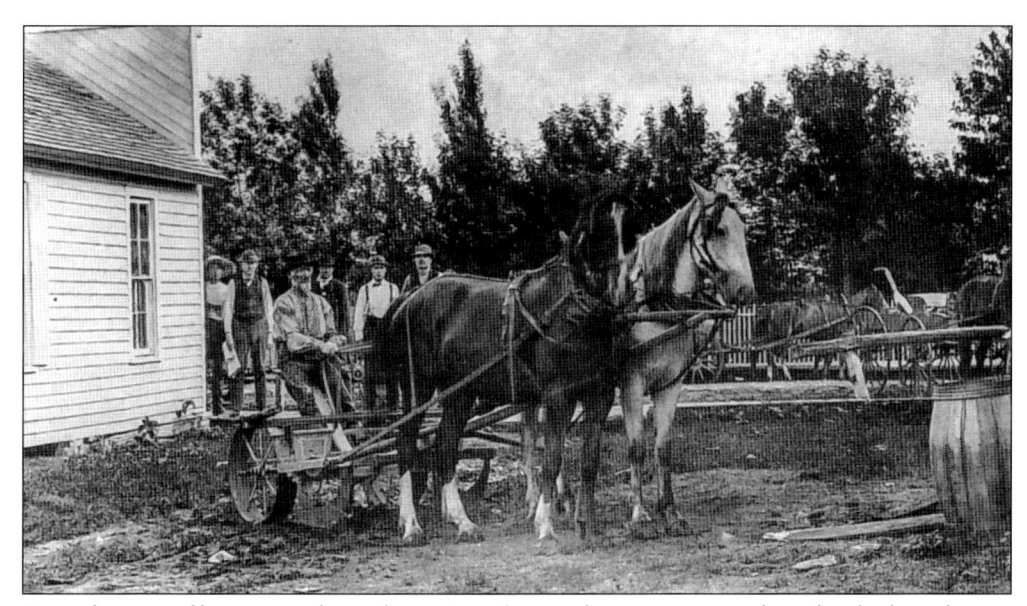

Several teams of horses are shown here. Area farmers have congregated at what looks to be a c. 1890 social event. (Courtesy of the Lyon Township Library.)

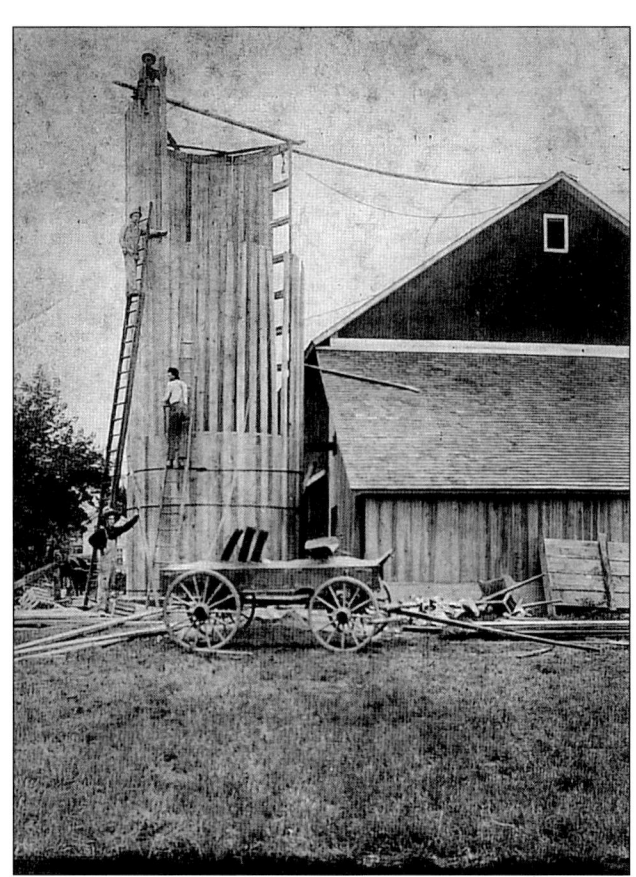

This picture shows construction of a new silo on the George Travis farm on Travis Road in New Hudson. (Courtesy of the Lyon Township Library.)

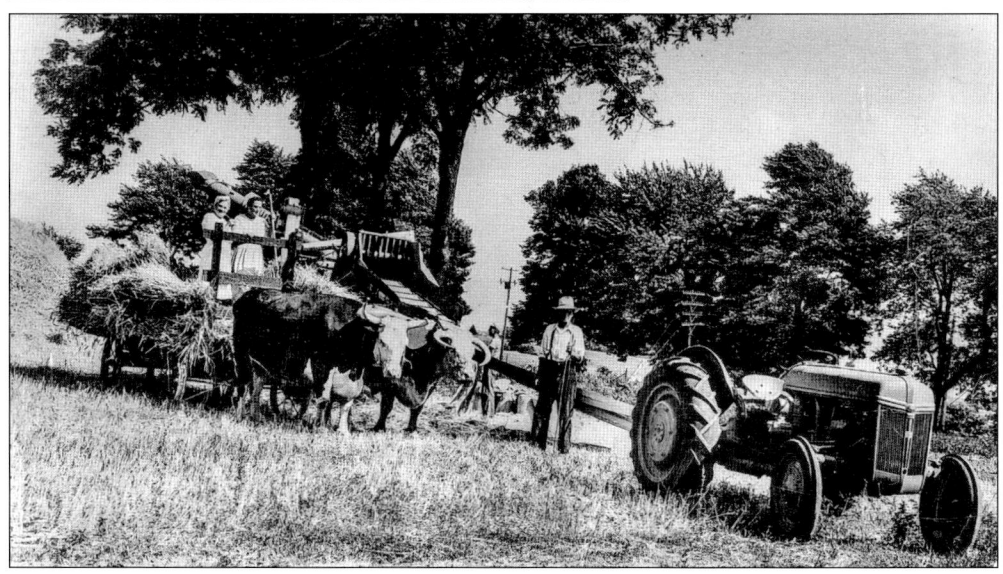

George Travis is seen on his farm with the belt-driven thresher machine powered from a tractor and an oxen-pulled wagon. Commonly, neighbors and friends came out to help during the harvest. The women at the farms where the work was going on churned out hardy meals. (Courtesy of the Lyon Township Library.)

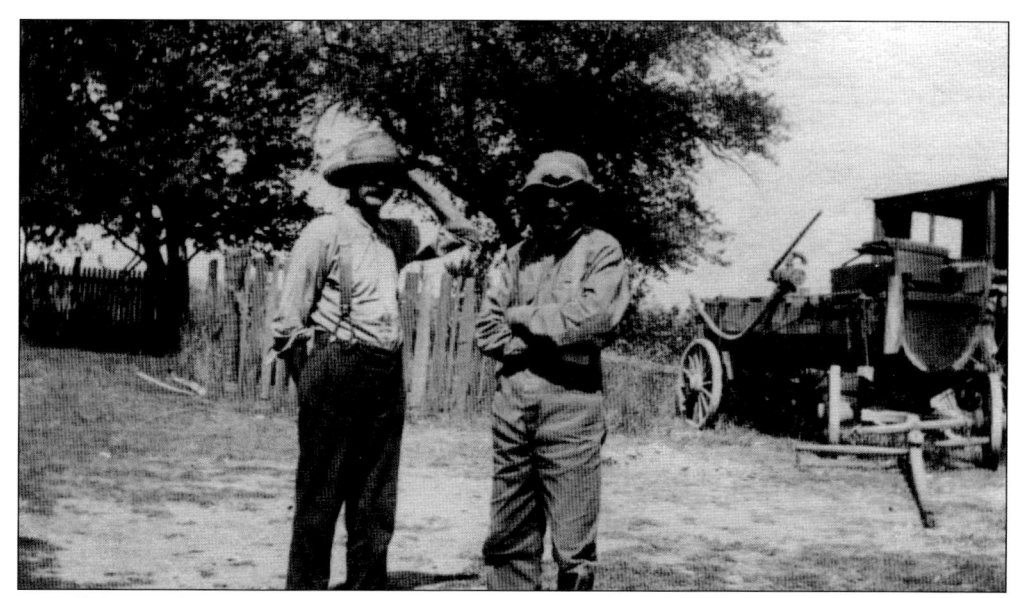

From left to right, Charles Cogger and Frank Renwick are seen on the Cogger farm at Eleven Mile and Martindale Roads. In the background is a water-hauling wagon with a hand pump to draw water from the creeks and wells. The water was transported to the fields to fill the boilers for the steam-driven tractors. (Courtesy of the Lyon Township Library.)

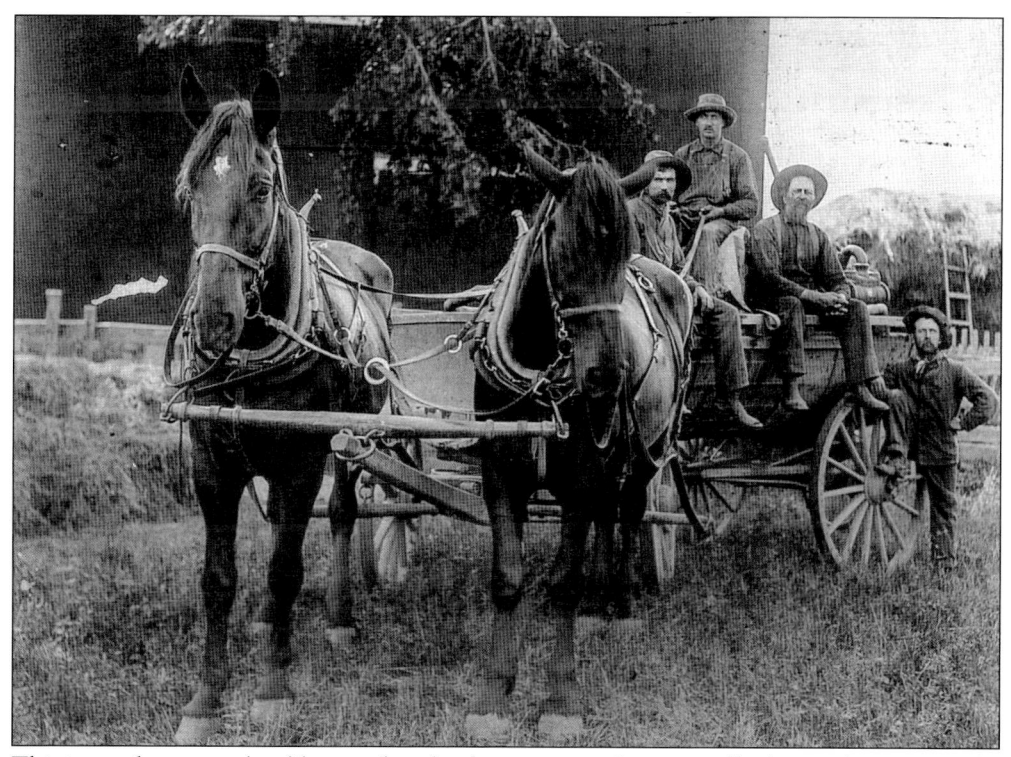

This is another example of farmworkers hauling water in their specially designed wagons to the fields in the township. George Lennox is among the men pictured near Frank Henry's house. (Courtesy of the Lyon Township Library.)

49

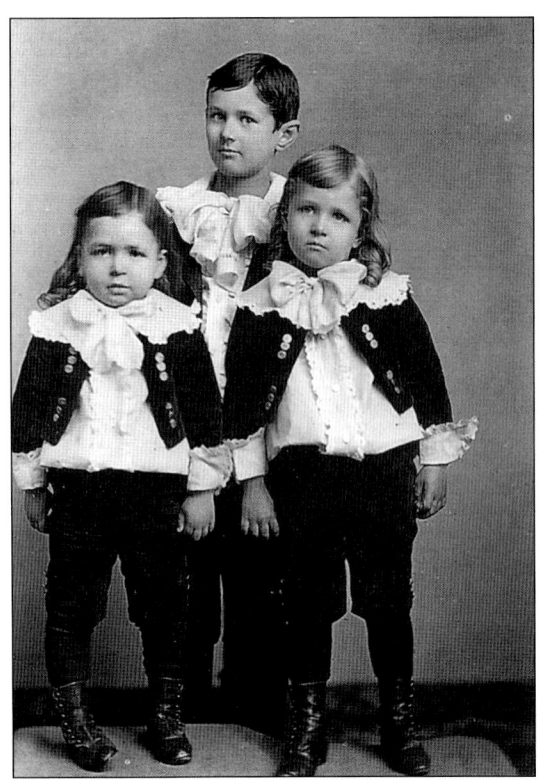

From left to right, young Milo, Rollo, and Erwin Pettengill became the future farmers of the Pettengill farm on Pontiac Trail Road. This photograph was taken around 1900. (Courtesy of Ann Polan.)

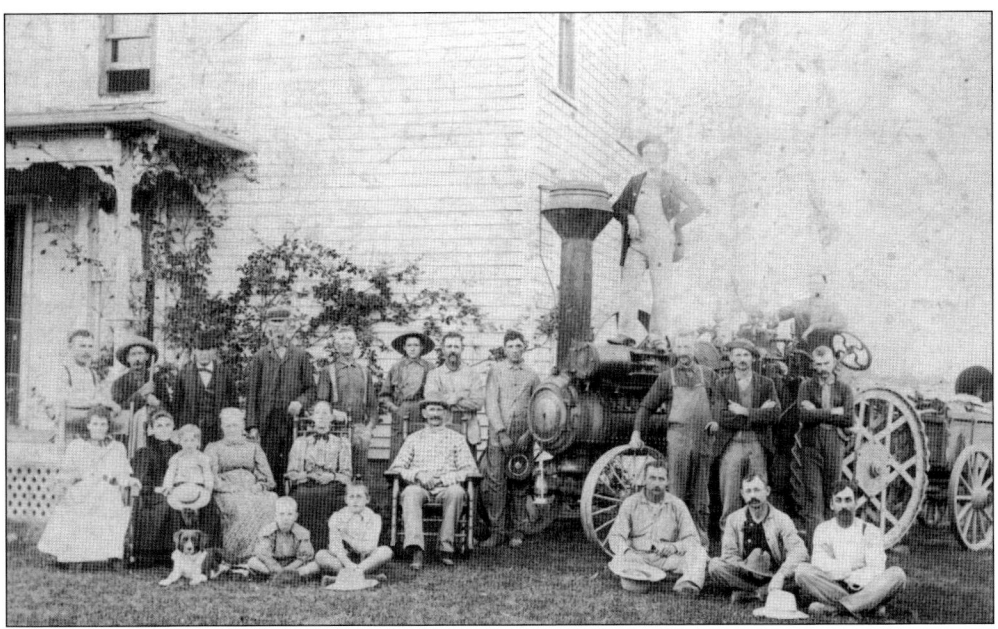

Herbert Hopkins and Adelbert Hopkins join their parents, Calvin and Anna Marie Hopkins, and other family members and neighbors for a photograph. Jim Taylor, a hired hand, is also shown here in the 1880s on the Pontiac Trail Road farm. Calvin Hopkins was a sailor before he became a farmer in Michigan in 1840. He was an eighth-generation descendant of Stephen Hopkins, who arrived on the *Mayflower*. (Courtesy of Ann Polan.)

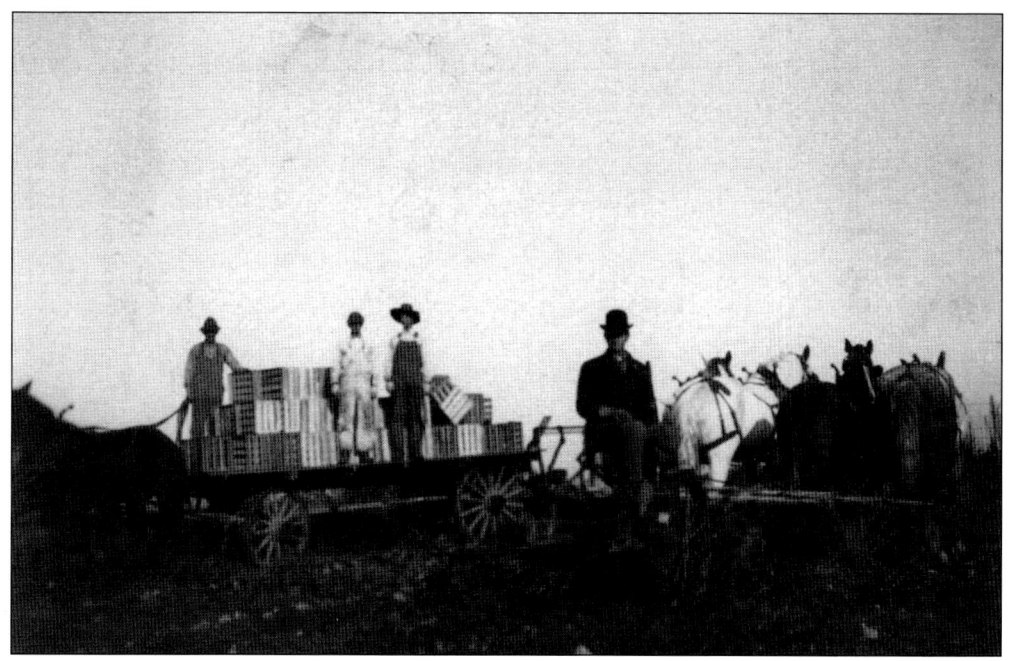

Workers harvest potatoes on the Pettengill farm on Pontiac Trail Road in New Hudson around 1920. The soil, which was sandy, was ideal for potato growing. Included in the picture is Beryl Hopkins Pettengill (standing on wagon, center). Note the farmer in a bowler hat and tie. (Courtesy of Ann Polan.)

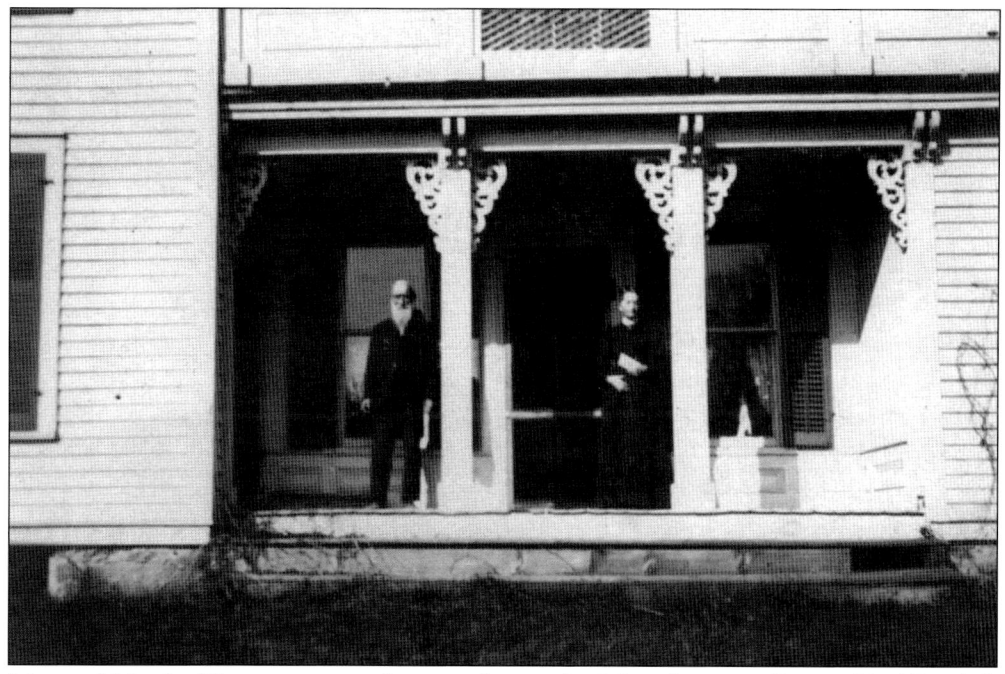

John and Martha Thomas are seen here on the porch of their home on Pontiac Trail Road. It later became the Pettengill farm. (Courtesy of Ann Polan.)

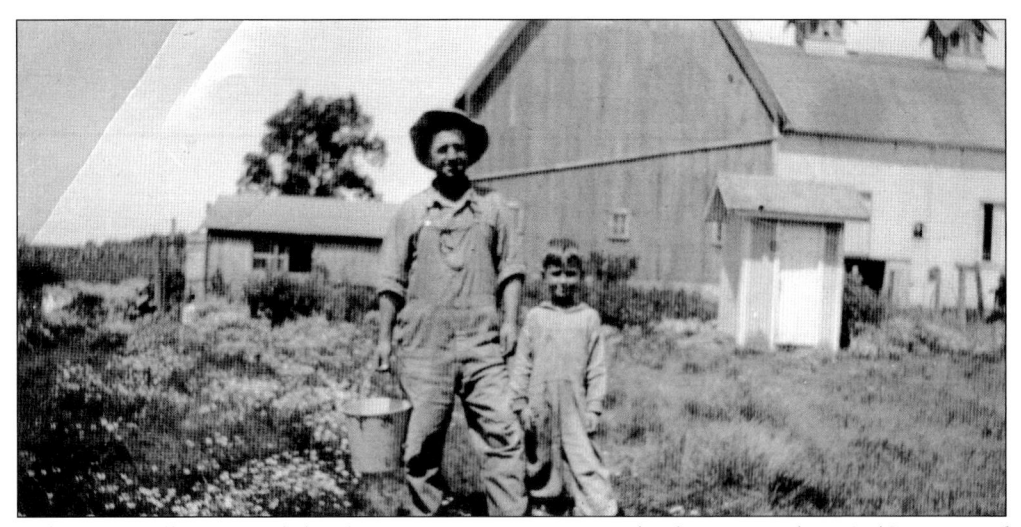

Milo Pettengill poses with his foster son Junior Craig on the farm around 1920. (Courtesy of Ann Polan.)

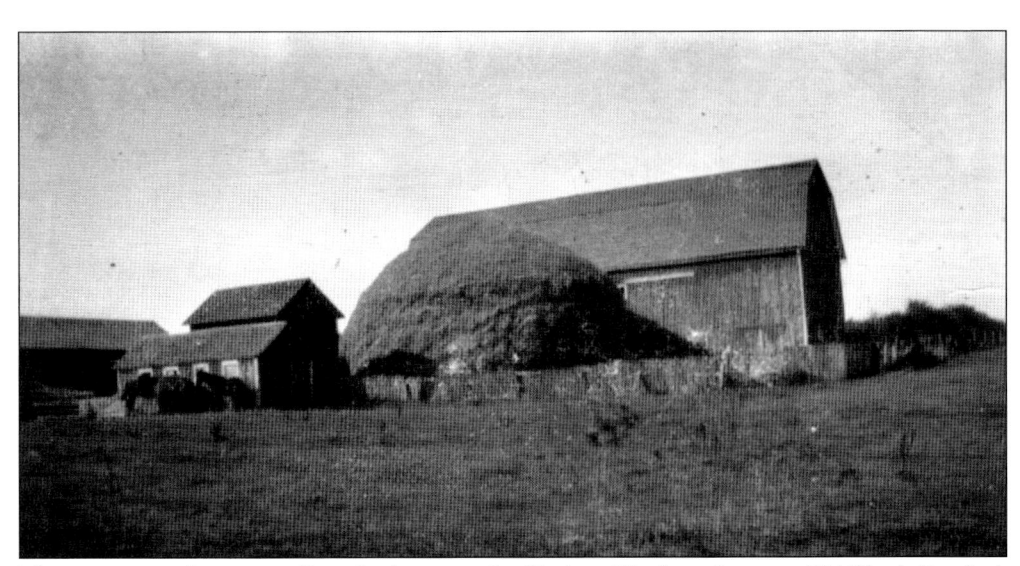

The straw was almost as tall as the barn on the Herbert Hopkins farm on Old Plank Road. A threshing machine removed the grain off the stalk. (Courtesy of Ann Polan.)

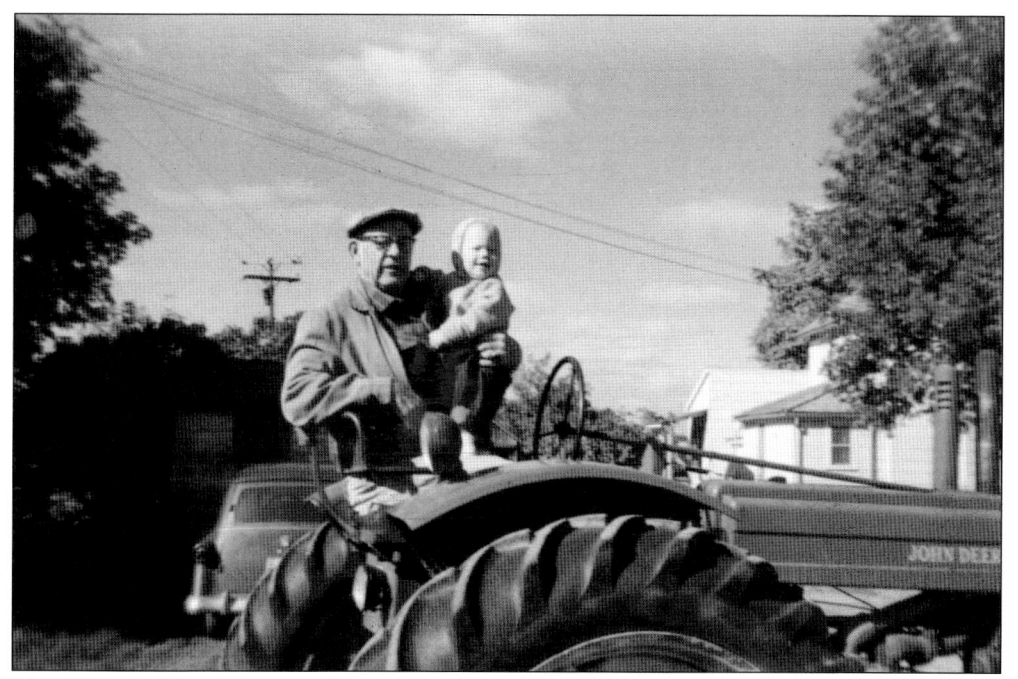

Max Butterfield, with his grandson Richard Fairfield, takes time to get his picture taken around 1961 on his Grand River Avenue farm. The Butterfield home was said to be the first brick house built in the township. (Courtesy of Richard Fairfield.)

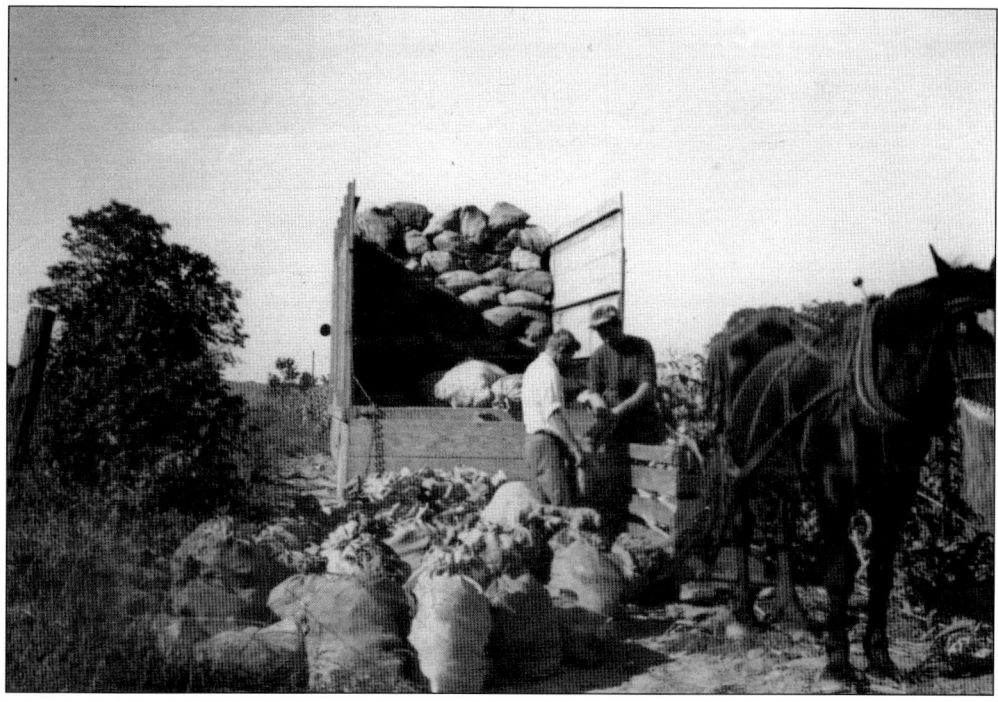

Ray Raney (left) and Don Burton bag sweet corn for market in October 1951 on Raney's Ten Mile Road farm. The horse's name was George. The men packed five dozen ears of corn per bag. (Courtesy of the Raney family.)

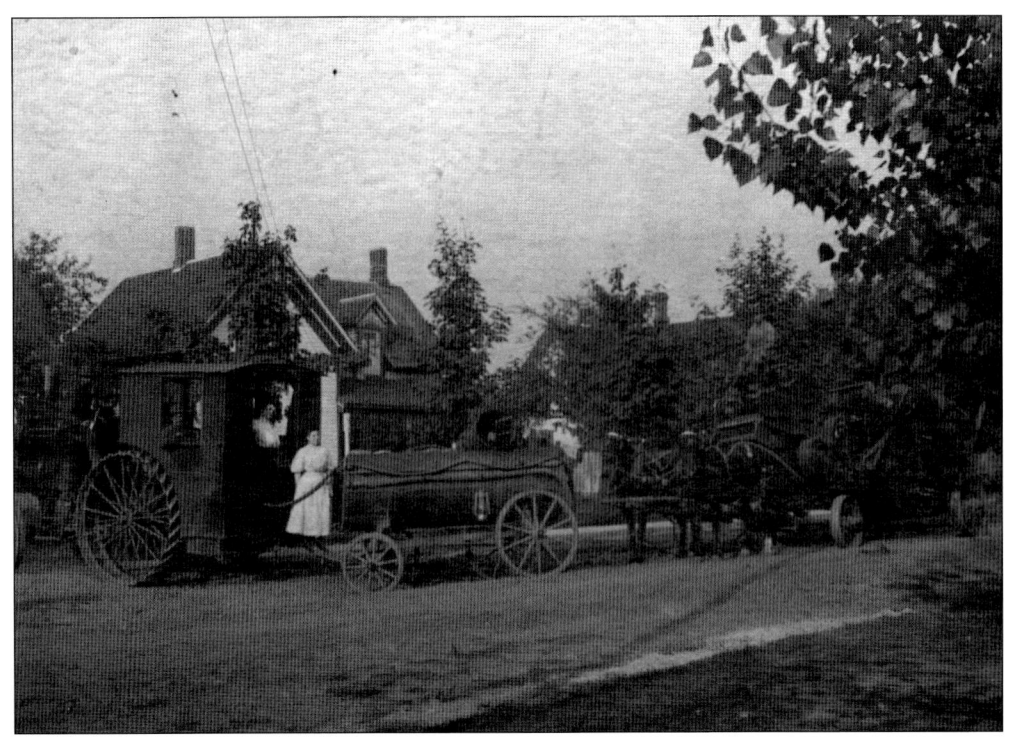

Adelbert Hopkins sits on a thresher with other unidentified people on the steel-wheeled steam-driven tractor. He is entering Herbert Hopkins farm on Old Plank Road around 1920. (Courtesy of Ann Polan.)

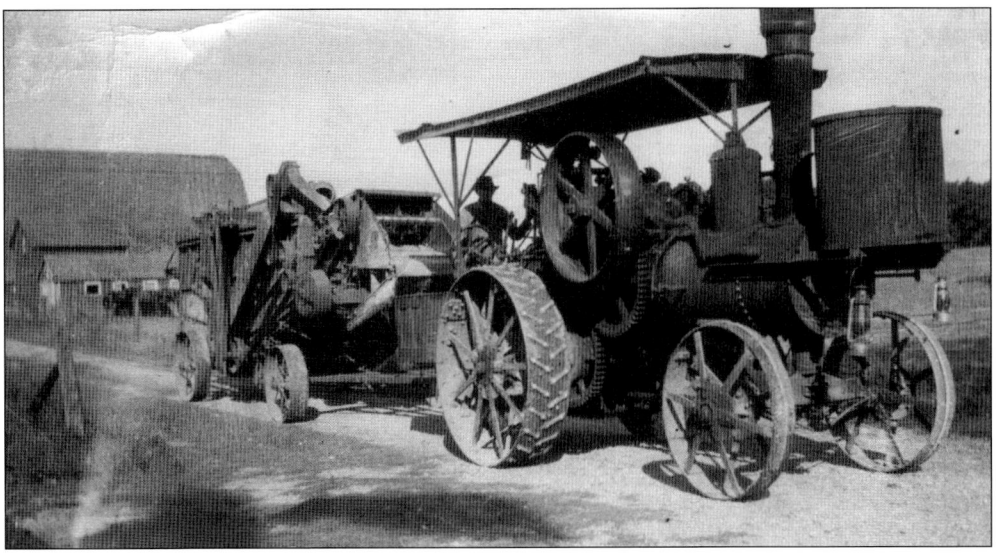

Adelbert Hopkins pulls a threshing machine as he leaves his brother Herbert's farm on his way to a field. This equipment was expensive and not many farmers could afford to buy their own. Adelbert Hopkins provided his threshing machine for his neighbors and others in the community around 1920. (Courtesy of Ann Polan.)

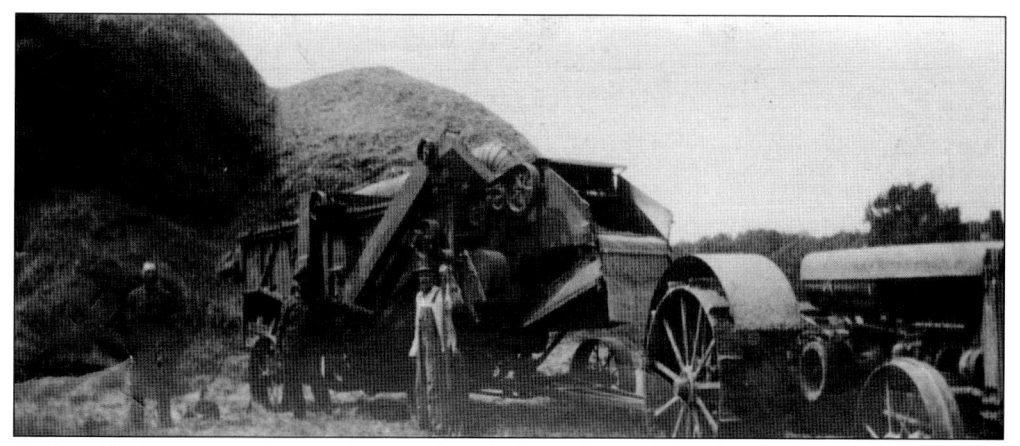

Herbert Hopkins is seen here with an unidentified hired hand. This threshing machine separated grain from the stalk on his New Hudson farm. (Courtesy of Ann Polan.)

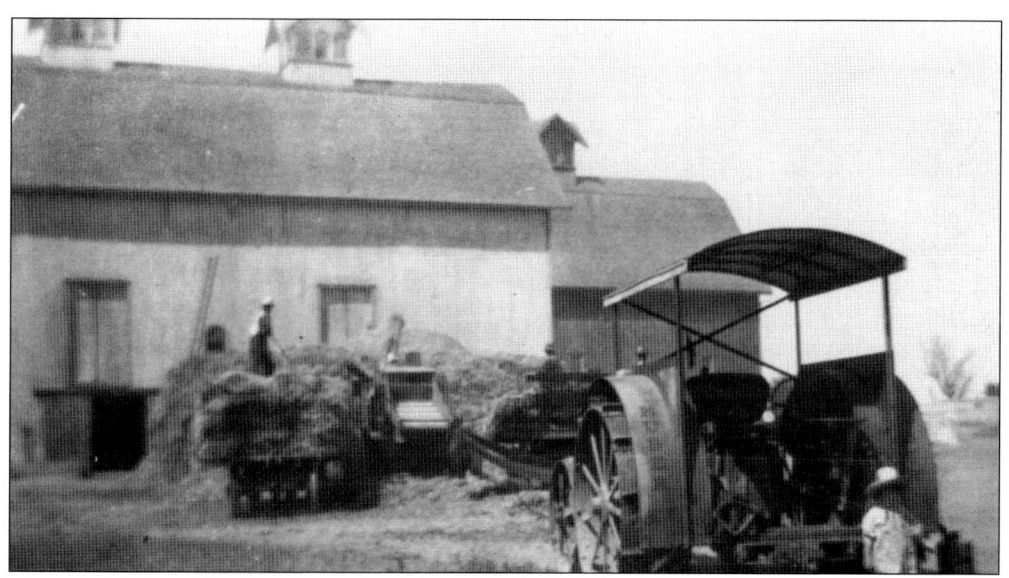

This shows Hopkins's threshing machine at the Pettengill farm around 1930. A barn owned by Erwin Pettengill is to the right. It was torn down in 2014. (Courtesy of Ann Polan.)

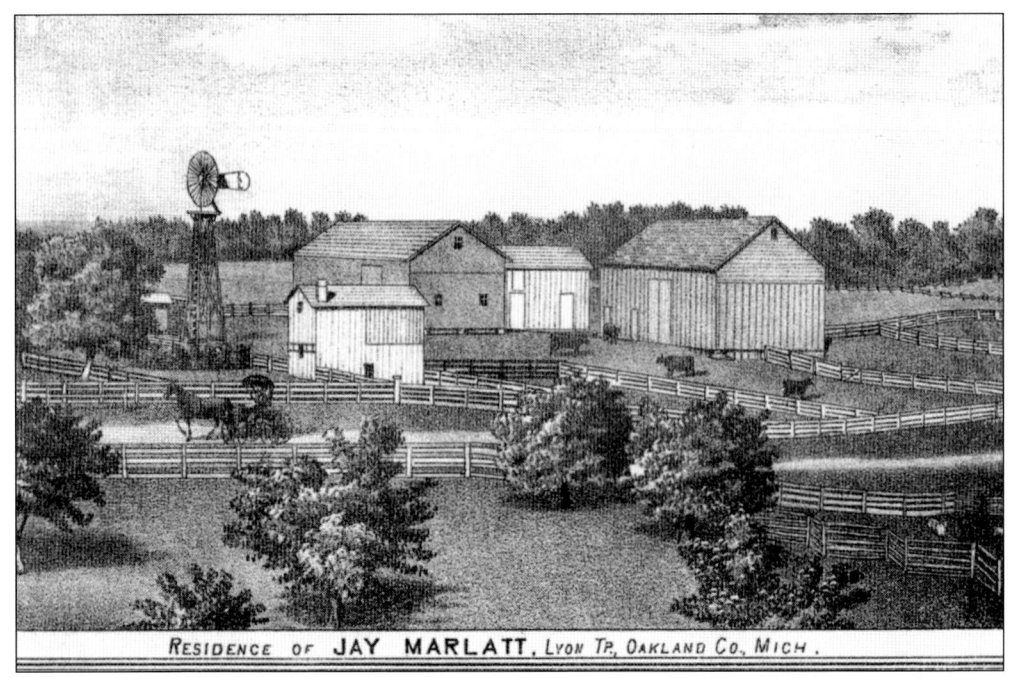

This is an etching of the Jay Marlatt farm on Grand River Avenue at Old Plank Road in New Hudson. The family farm was started by Jay's father, Phillip Marlatt. Jay was born September 12, 1826, and married Sarah Baker February 22, 1875. (Courtesy of Lyon Township Library.)

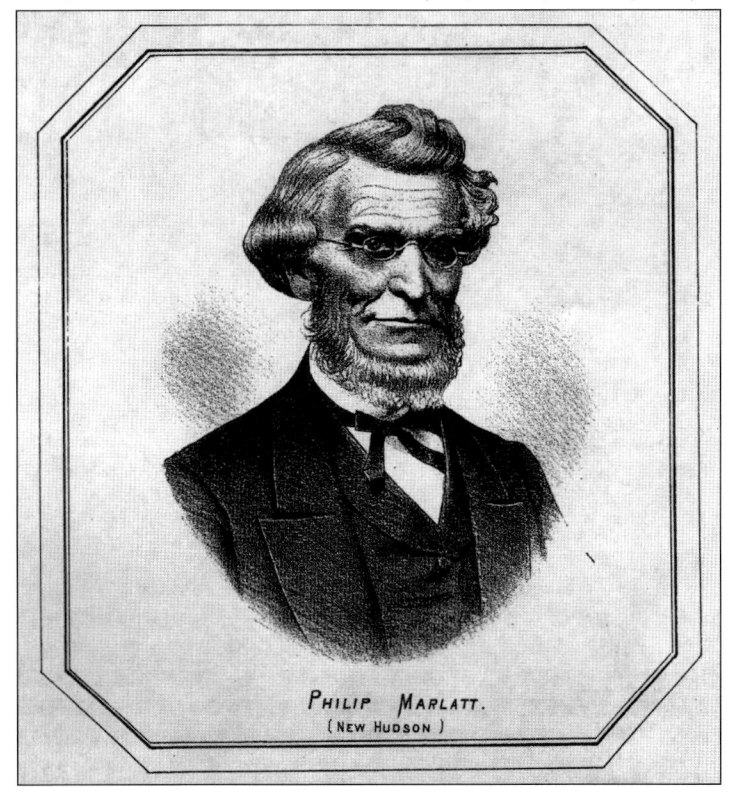

Phillip Marlatt came to Lyon Township from East Farmington, Michigan. He was born in Schoharie County, New York, in 1798. He came to Michigan in 1825. He bought property on Old Plank Road where his descendants farmed for generations. He was among the first postmasters in Farmington. (Courtesy of the Lyon Township Library.)

SARAH A. MARLATT.   JAY MARLATT.

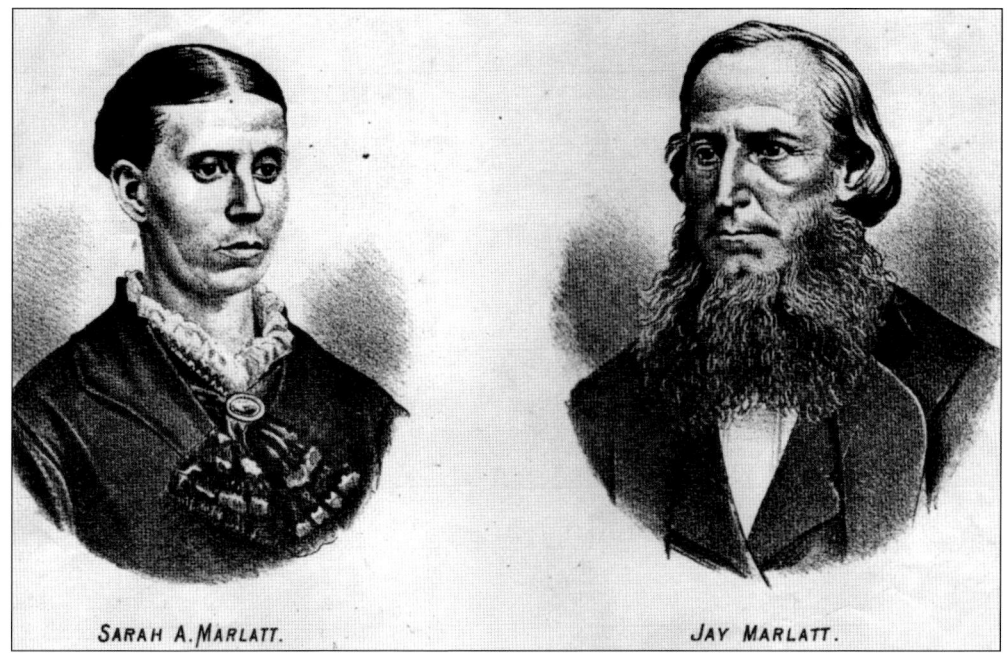

This photograph shows Sarah and Jay Marlatt. Sarah was born in 1836. She was a widow and had two children, Lewis and Lucy Baker, when she married Jay Marlatt. He died tragically in 1887. Sarah is beloved by her descendants who use her recipes still to this day. She was famous for hickory nut cake, sugar cookies, and molasses cookies. (Courtesy of Oakland County.)

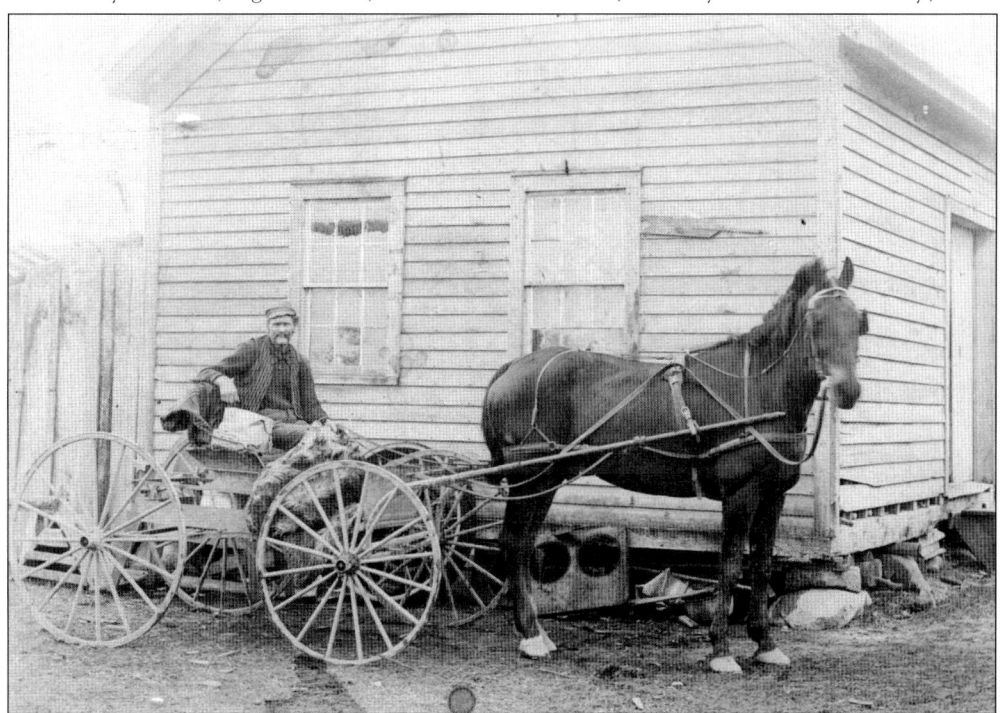

Jim Taylor worked for Adelbert Hopkins on Hopkins's farm on Old Plank Road. (Courtesy of Ann Polan.)

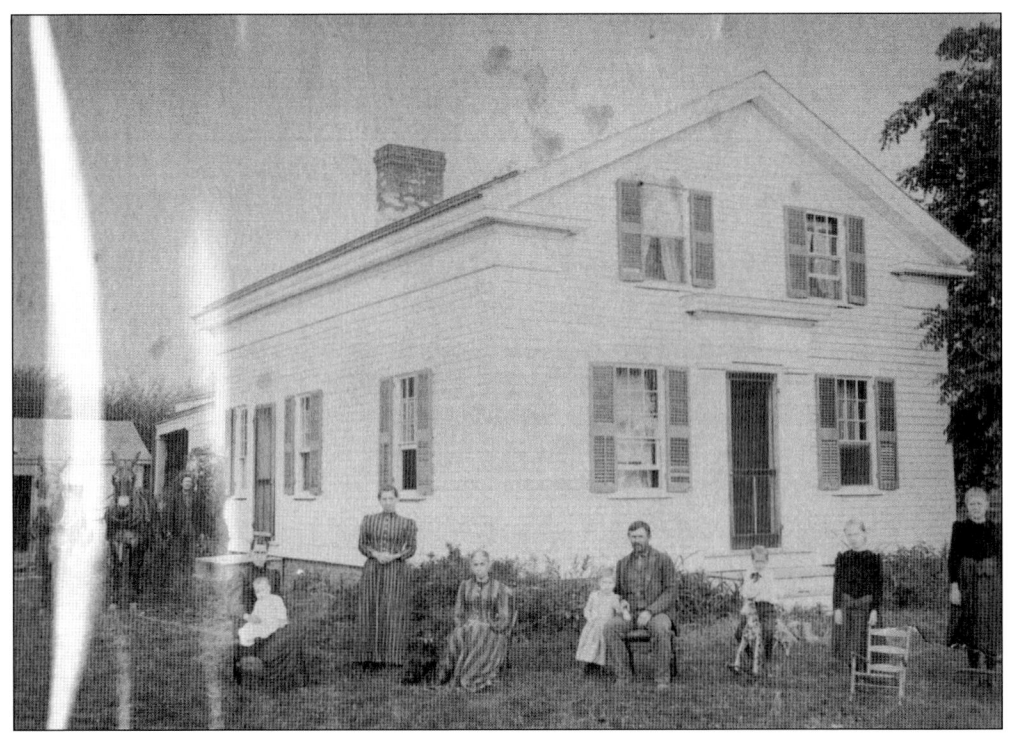

This is a picture of the Marlatt farmhouse on the west side of Old Plank Road around 1894. Pictured are, from left to right, farmhand Jim Taylor, Lucy Hopkins with baby Hazel, an unidentified woman, Sarah Marlatt, Adelbert Hopkins, Ben Hopkins, Clair Hopkins, Sadie Hopkins, and Blanche Hopkins. (Courtesy of Ann Polan.)

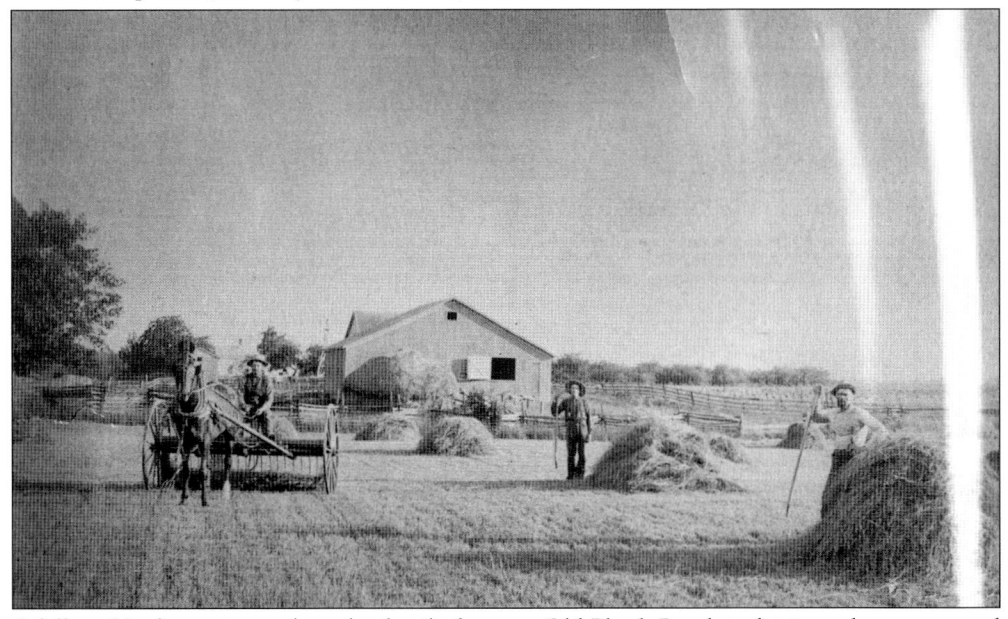

Adelbert Hopkins, pictured on the family farm on Old Plank Road, is driving a horse-powered hay rake. Jim Taylor, on the far right, and an unidentified hired hand are also shown around 1892. (Courtesy of Ann Polan.)

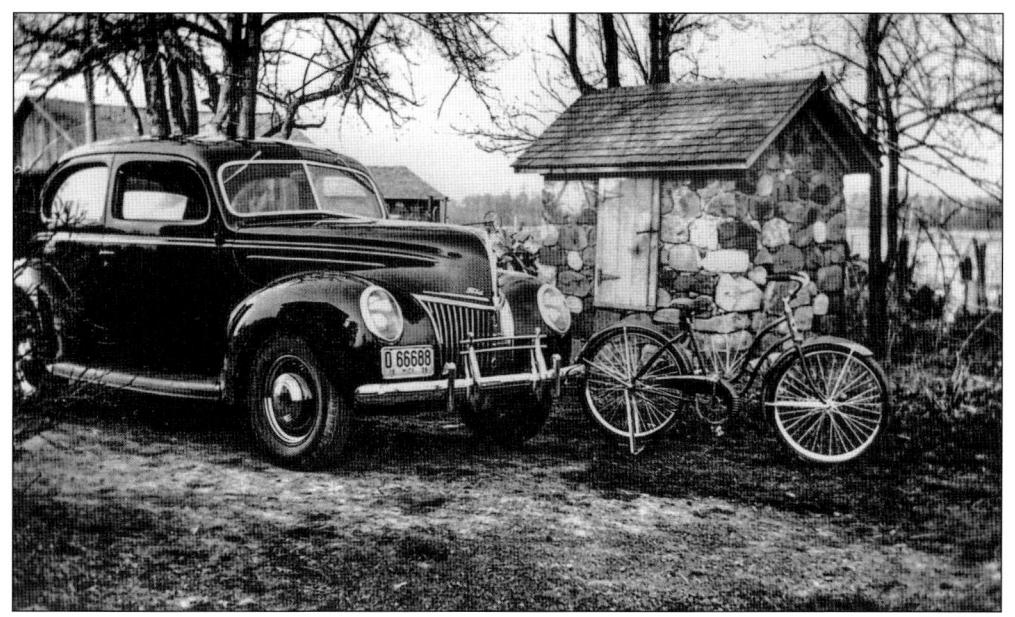

This 1939 two-door Ford sedan is parked on the Canfield farm, located on Milford Road. It stands next to a smokehouse that was used to prepare meat. (Courtesy of the Canfield family.)

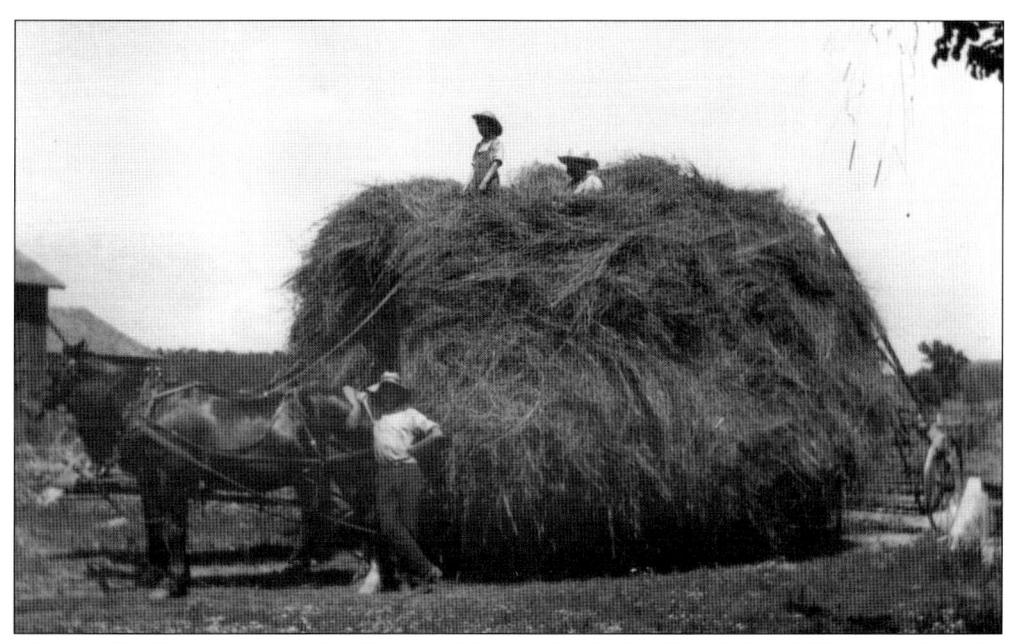

John Canfield leans on his mules. His sister Mary E. Canfield and his father, William G. Canfield, are on top of the hay wagon. A loading machine, pictured at the back of the haystack, elevated the hay to the top of the stack. (Courtesy of the Canfield family.)

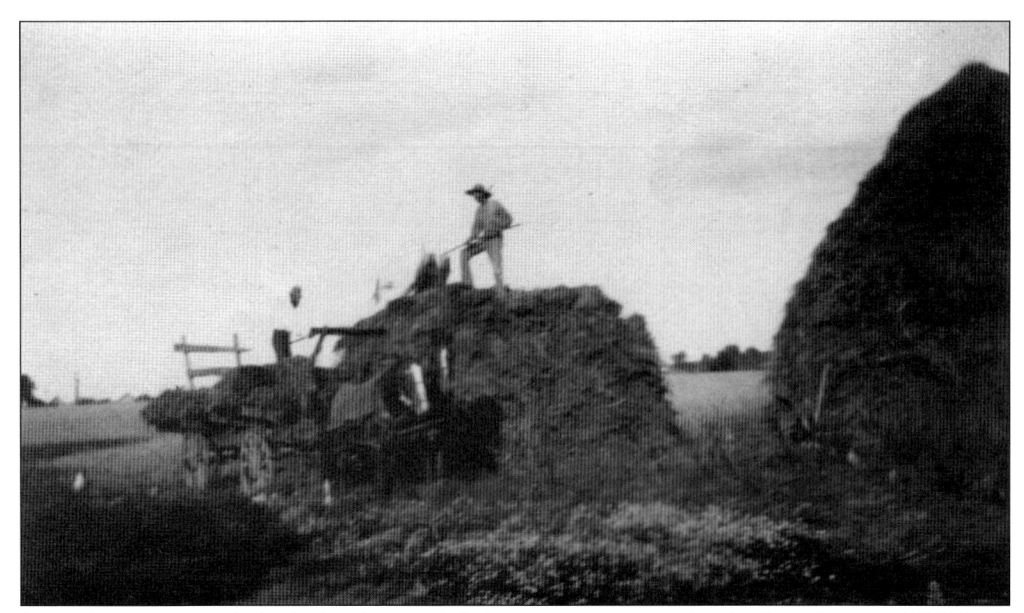

Loose hay is manually loaded with a pitchfork onto a wagon at the Hopkins farm on Old Plank and Pontiac Trail Roads. As shown in the previous picture, elevators were sometimes used to replace the hand method. (Courtesy of the Hopkins family.)

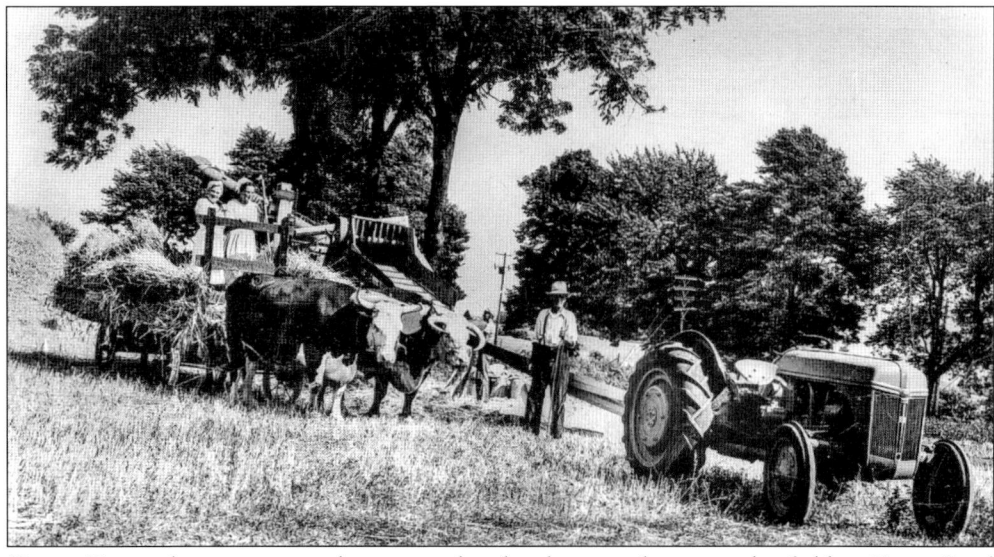

George Travis, shown wearing a hat next to his threshing machine, is in his field on Travis Road in New Hudson around 1920. As was common in those days, women helped in the harvesting. The oxen, shown pulling the hay wagon, were later replaced at many farms by tractors. (Courtesy of the Lyon Township Library.)

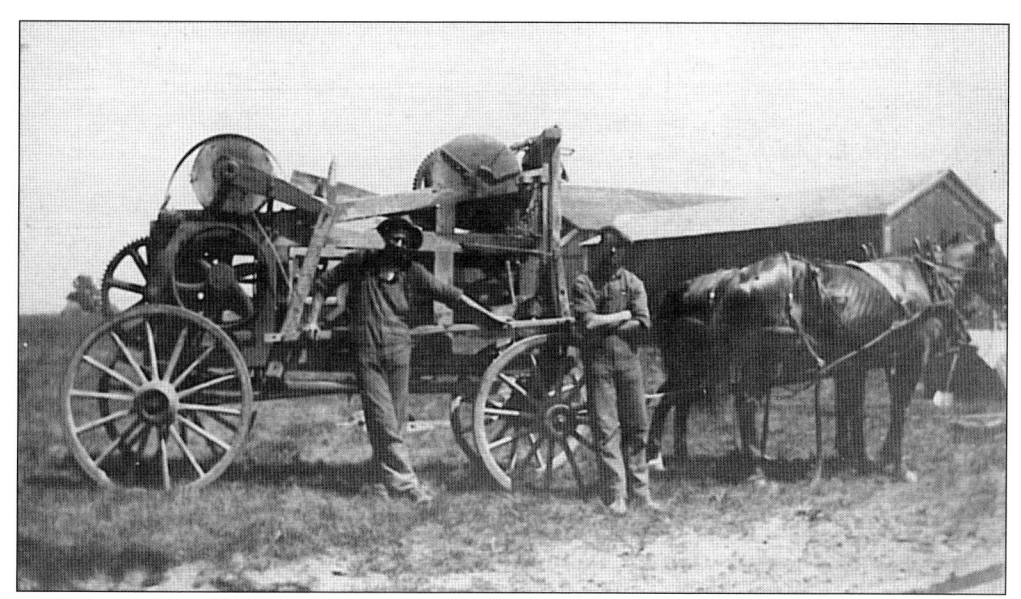

It is believed this well-digging equipment was used throughout the township around 1880. (Courtesy of the Lyon Township Library.)

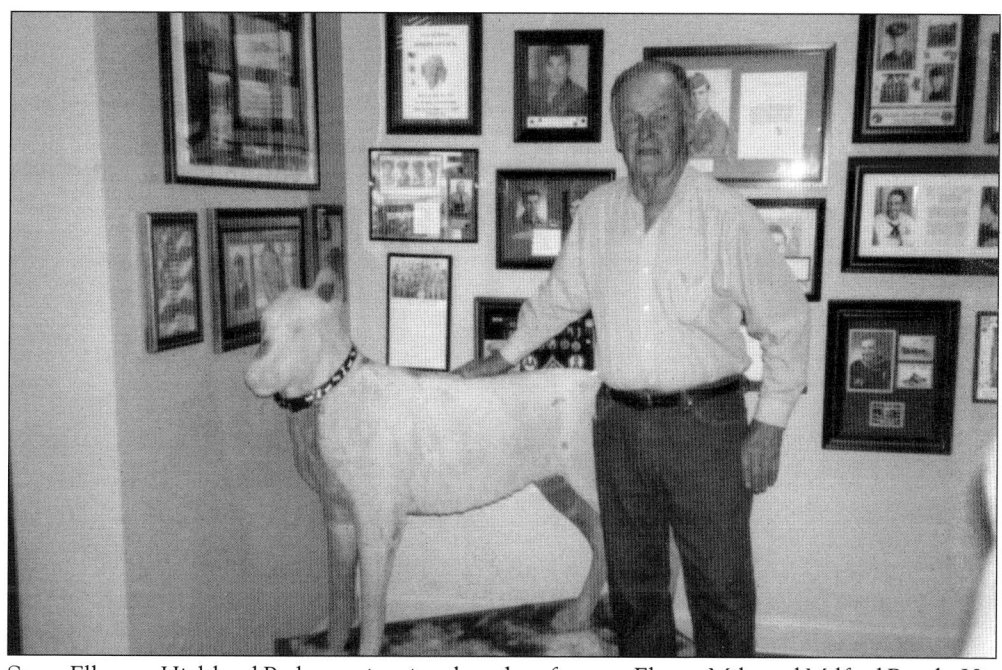

Steve Elkow, a Highland Park veterinarian, bought a farm on Eleven Mile and Milford Roads. His brother Cornell farmed in Wisconsin. Steve convinced him to move to Lyon Township. Local folklore has it that Cornell loaded two railroad boxcars full of furniture, farm equipment, and livestock. They reportedly took a break in Chicago to milk the cows. They unloaded the animals in South Lyon and marched them to the Elkow property. The family started a dog cemetery on Milford Road where the bronze dog pictured stood on a granite monument. It was stolen but was recovered. Phil Elkow, Cornell's son, is shown here with the dog, now protected, at Abbey Park, a senior living facility in New Hudson. (Courtesy of Jane and Jack Purslow.)

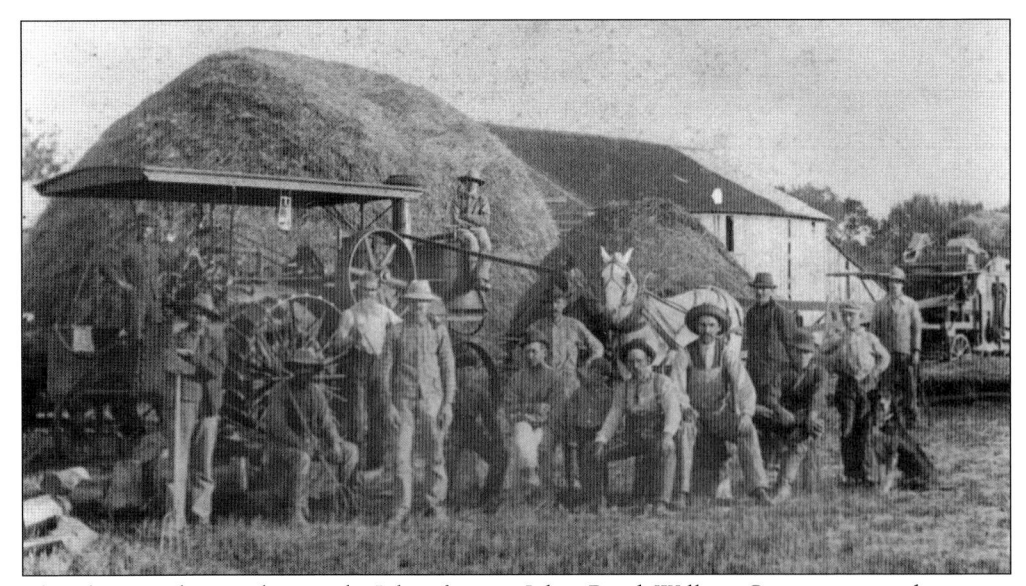

This photograph was taken on the Johns farm on Johns Road. William Case is seen on the steam-fired tractor, which is connected with a belt to the threshing machine. Fred Everett is shown on the tractor water tank, Elmer Jones is standing in front with a plaid work jacket, and Theron Smith is on the far right with the horses around 1895. Smith had a hardware store in South Lyon in the 1920s. The farm became a public golf course known as Godwin Glens in 1970. In 1988, it was sold and renamed Walnut Creek Golf Course when it became privately owned. (Courtesy of the Raney family.)

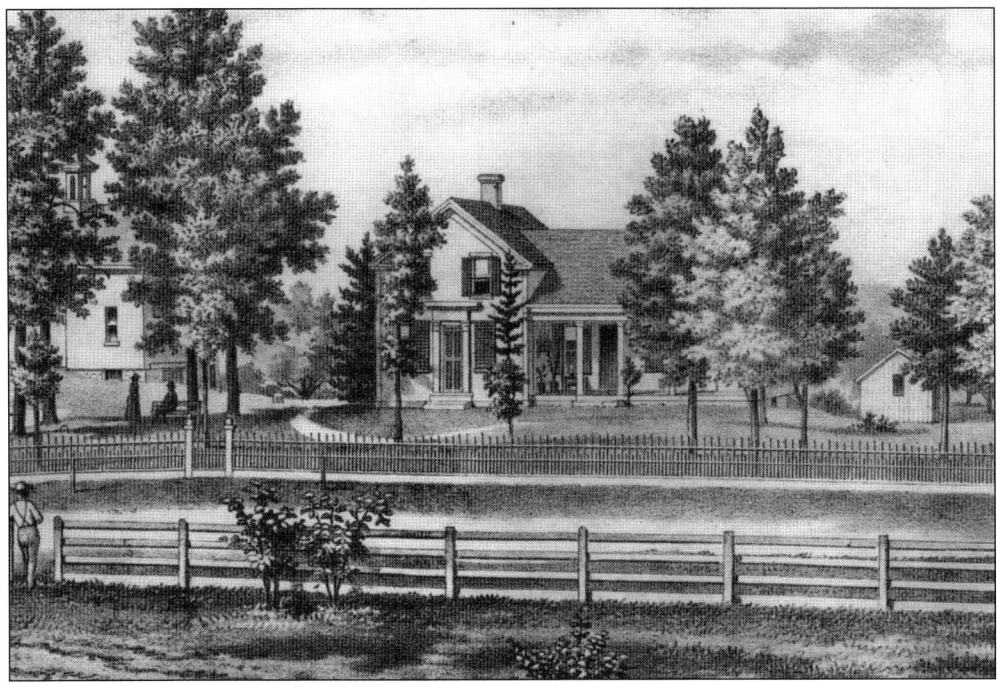

This is an etching of the Whipple farm on Nine Mile and Currie Roads around 1800s. This house is presently occupied by Bob and Dolores Seccombe. The Whipple family was associated with the South Lyon Hotel in the village of South Lyon. (Courtesy of the Lyon Township Library.)

An early-1920s Lyon Township map shows the 1,100 acres owned by Charles E. Sorensen, a senior executive at Ford Motor Company. Albert Kessler managed this land, which was called Cesor farms. (Courtesy of Roy Cash.)

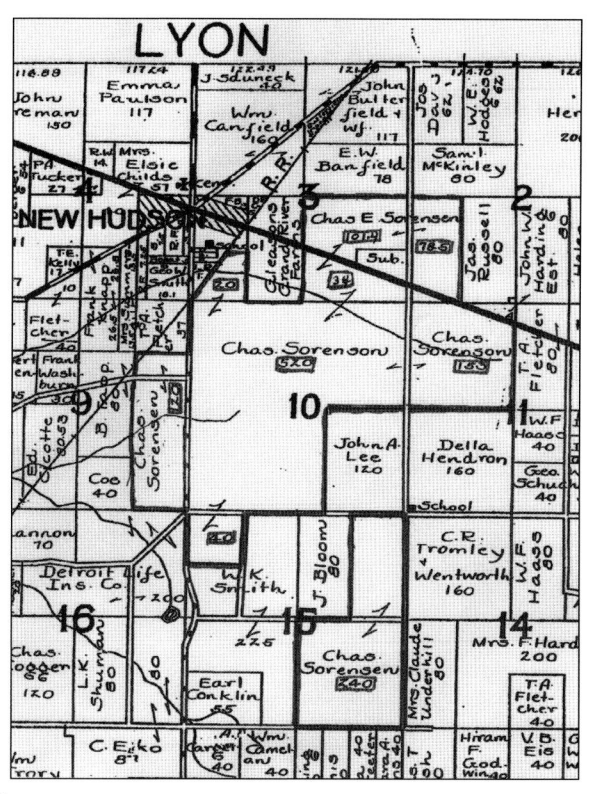

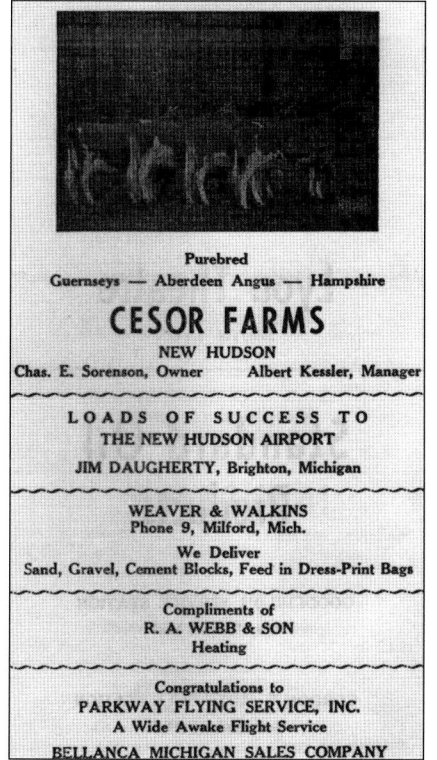

Cesor farms is advertised in a 1947 booklet commemorating the dedication of the Edward G. Knapp Airport on Pontiac Trail Road in New Hudson. In addition to farmland in Lyon, Sorensen owned farm property in the township of Farmington. That farm was only used for milking cows. The cows were milked three times daily. (Courtesy of the Canfield family.)

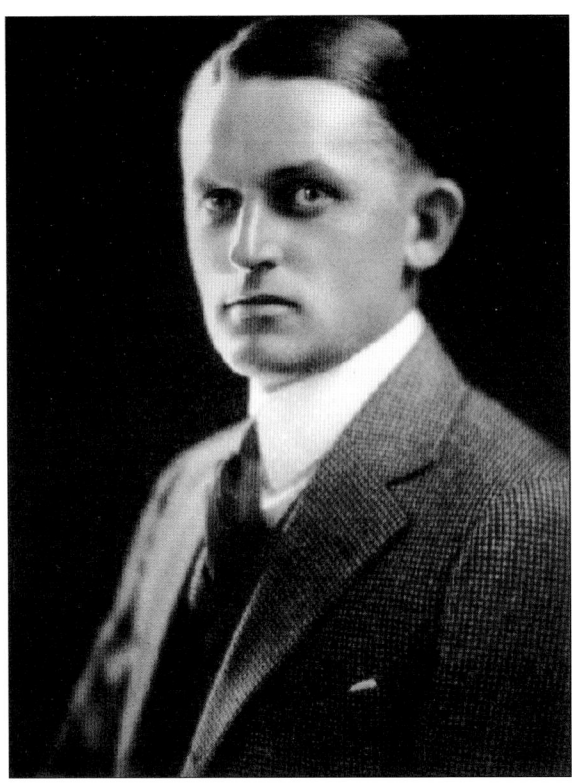

Charles E. Sorensen was said to be second in command to Henry Ford at Ford Motor Company. He was in charge of the company's car production. He was instrumental in developing the production process for the World War II B-24 bomber plane at the Willow Run Plant. His contribution increased the production of the B-24s from one a day to one an hour. (Courtesy of The Henry Ford.)

Charles E. Sorensen is seen here with Henry Ford and his son Edsel Ford at Greenfield Village with two unidentified men during the early years of World War II. (Courtesy of The Henry Ford.)

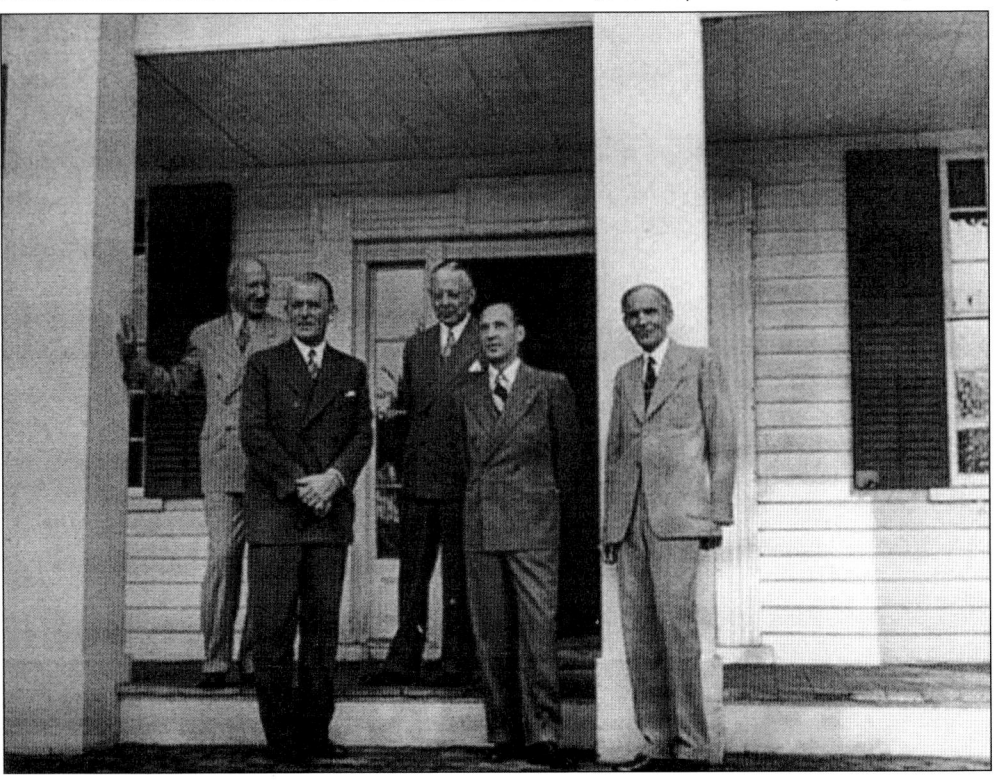

Charles E. Sorensen retired from Ford Motor Company in 1944. He went on to become the president of Willys Overland Motors in Toledo, Ohio. The company produced wartime jeeps. This letter invited government officials to his New Hudson farm to demonstrate how jeeps could be used for farm applications. (Courtesy of Roy Cash.)

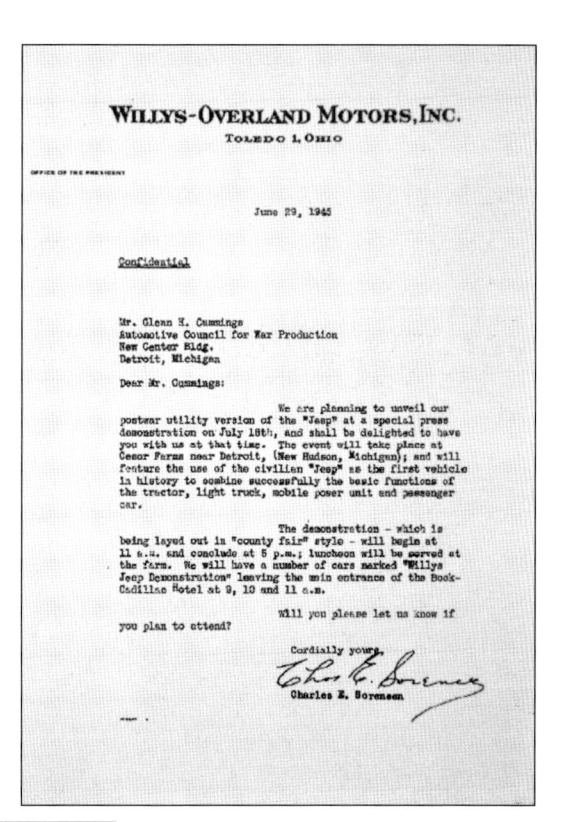

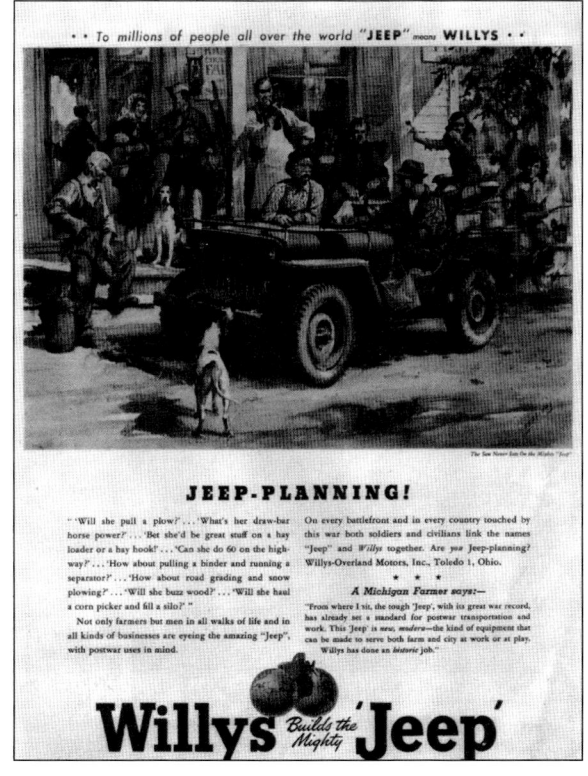

This *Saturday Evening Post* advertisement shows the use of a jeep as an agricultural machine to replace the tractor. (Courtesy of Willys Overland Motors, Inc.)

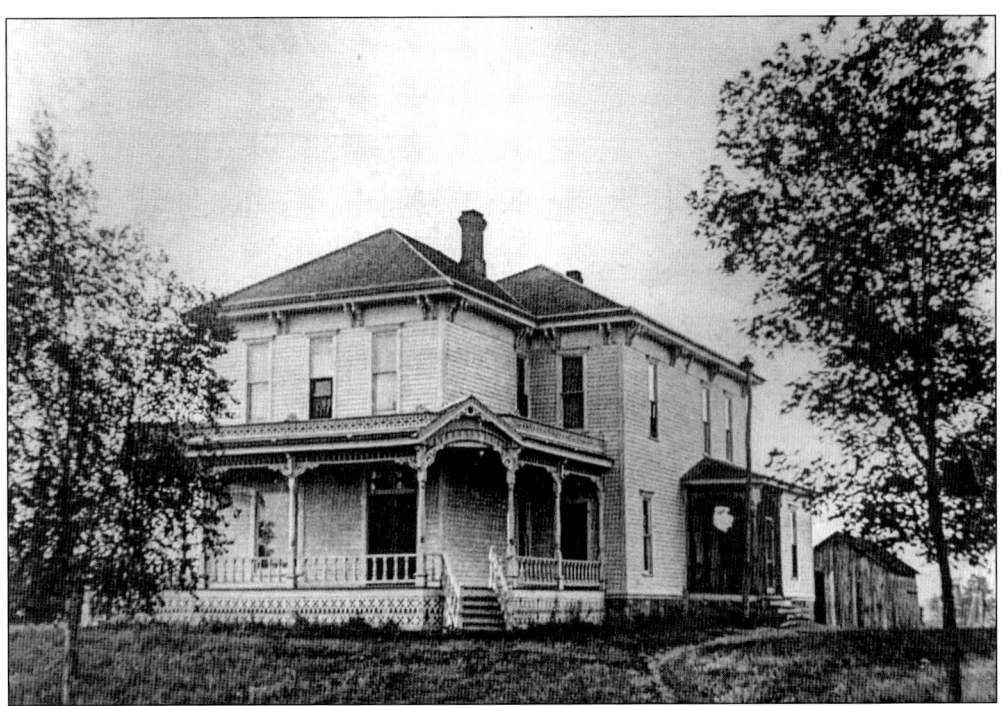

The home of William K. Smith was on Locust Road and was built before 1870. He served as township supervisor from the 1940s to the 1970s. Smith preceded his father, William Kingsley Smith, who served as supervisor from the 1920s to the 1930s. At one time, the Smith family farmed more than 425 acres between Eleven and Twelve Mile Roads. (Courtesy of the Lyon Township Library.)

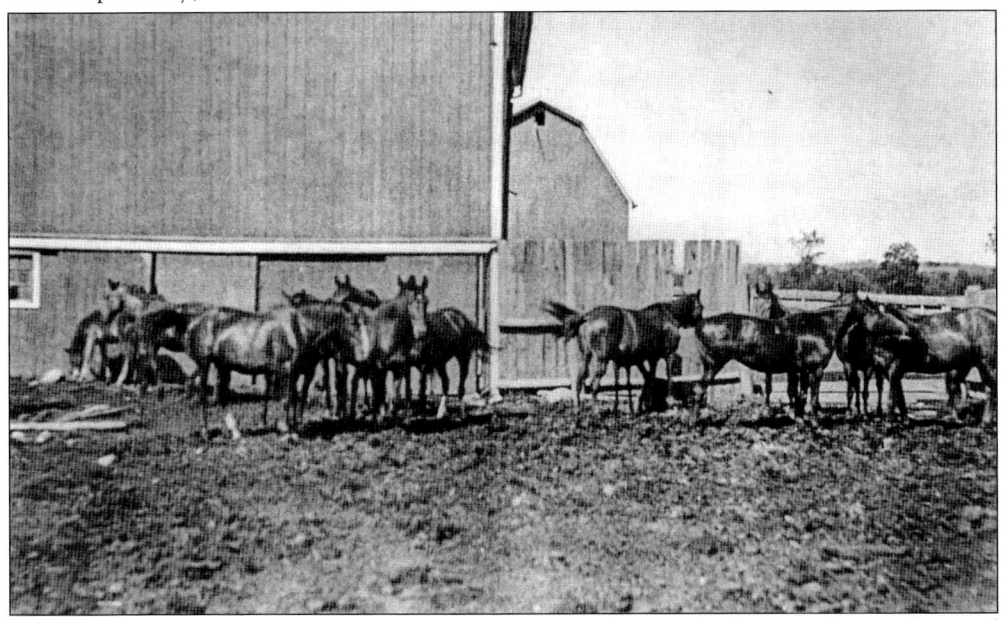

William K. Smith's barnyard contained horses that were sold as matched pairs and were often used for pulling buggies, according to family members. It is also reported his horses pulled the hearse for Phillip's Funeral Home in the village of South Lyon. (Courtesy of the Lyon Township Library.)

Five

SCHOOLS

The first New Hudson school was a log building constructed in 1836 on South Milford Road. Thomas Bogart taught the students in classes held four months in the summer and four months in the winter.

At one time, there were six one-room schoolhouses in Lyon Township, including Bullard School, at Eleven Mile and Martindale Roads; Wilson School, at Ten Mile and Griswold Roads; Smith School, at Twelve Mile and South Hill Roads; Blackwood, at Nine Mile and Currie Roads; Lowell, on Kent Lake Road and Grand River Avenue; and the Wood School, at Eight Mile and Pontiac Trail Roads.

The New Hudson School was erected in 1866 on three acres of land. It served the community until April 13, 1921, when it burned down. Fortunately there were no injuries; the devastating fire was early in the morning when no one was inside the building. After the fire, schoolchildren attended classes at Maccabee Hall on Grand River Avenue. The school went through two renovations—first it was a two story building with red brick. It is currently a one-story structure and was renamed Dolsen Elementary.

By about 1947, the consolidation of rural schools started, and eventually these schools were abandoned, and the pupils were bused to schools within the South Lyon Consolidated School District.

Currently, two school districts serve the township—South Lyon Community Schools and Northville Community Schools.

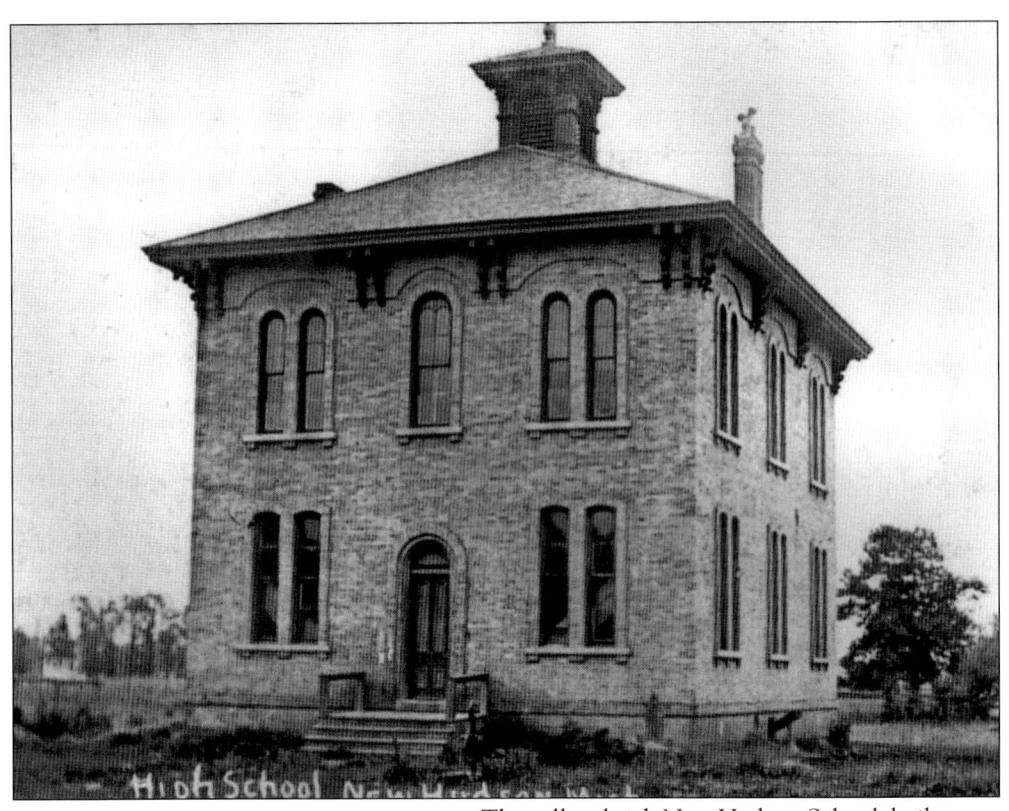

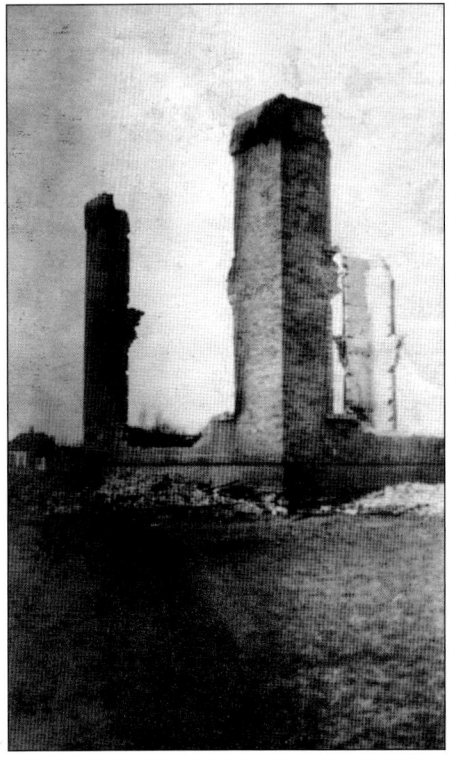

The yellow-brick New Hudson School, built around 1866, housed all grades and was located on South Street, currently named Rice Street. Questions from a Salina, Kansas, eighth-grade final exam in 1895 were likely similar questions used in the New Hudson School. Questions covered grammar, history, geography, and orthography; for example, "Name the parts of speech and define those that have no modifications." (Courtesy of the Lyon Township Library.)

Brick columns are all that remained of the New Hudson School after it was destroyed by fire in April 1921. During a 1998 interview with local historian and author John Bell, prominent farmer John Canfield said, "My mother and I were watching out our window from our house on Milford Road and we saw the building burn." John Canfield graduated from New Hudson School in 1934. (Courtesy of the Canfield family.)

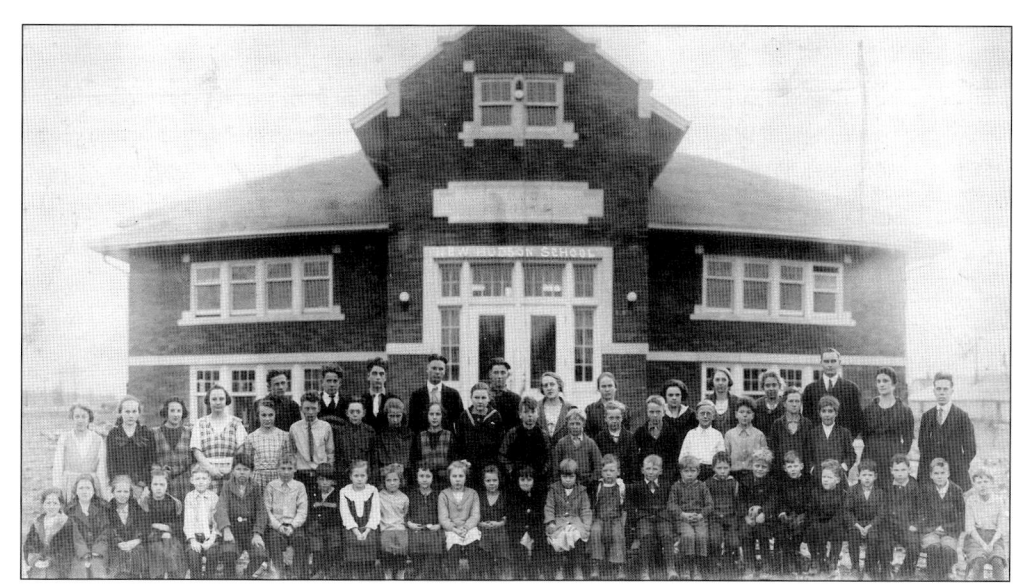

This is the New Hudson School in 1924 with its redbrick facade. A basement room was used as the first township library around 1960. The library was relocated to the township hall on Pontiac Trail Road when the school needed the space. (Courtesy of the Lyon Township Library.)

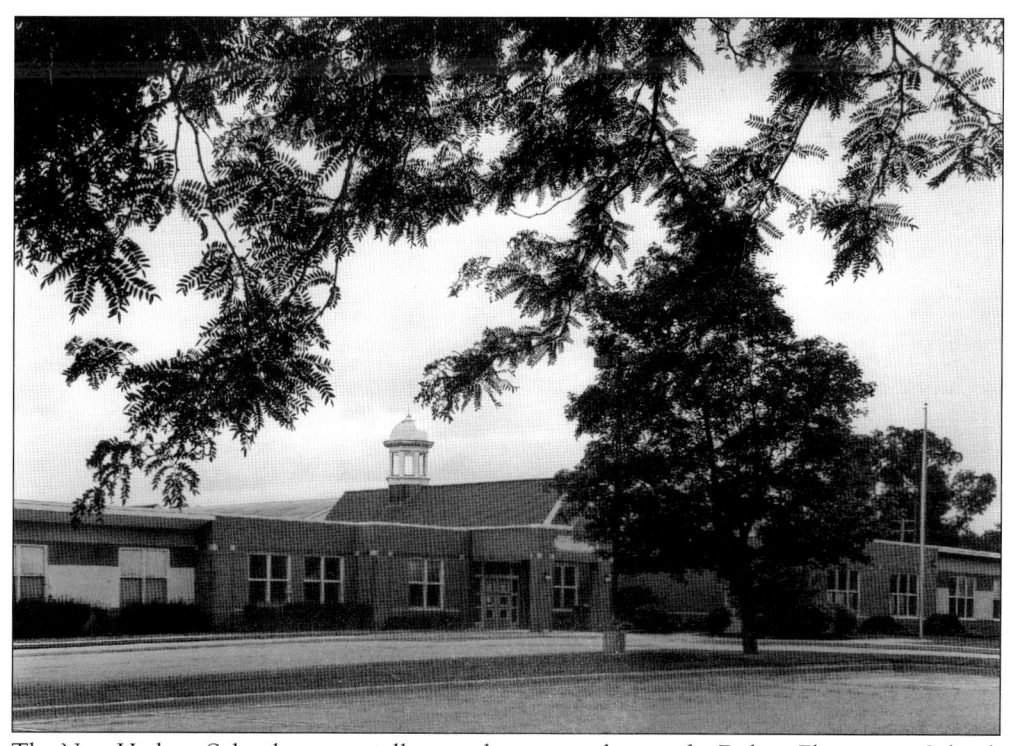

The New Hudson School was partially torn down to make way for Dolsen Elementary School. (Courtesy of Jane and Jack Purslow.)

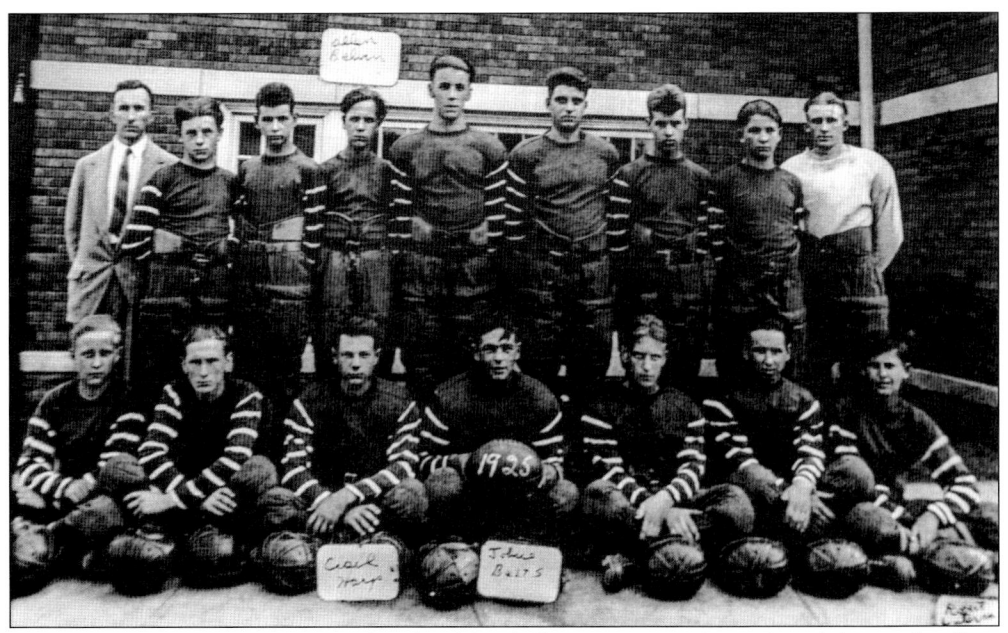

This is the 1925 New Hudson High School football team. Pictured are, from left to right, (first row) Sherman Templeton; Dale Renwick; Ciel Harp; Jamie Belts, team captain; George Miles; Herbert Majori; and Robert Luttermaser; (second row) a Mr. Hath, school superintendent; Wilber Losing; Bob Cash; Allen Baldwin; Ted Bryant; Clayton Chiles; Floyd Cash; Harvey Chilek; and a Mr. Worden, team coach. (Courtesy of the Lyon Township Library.)

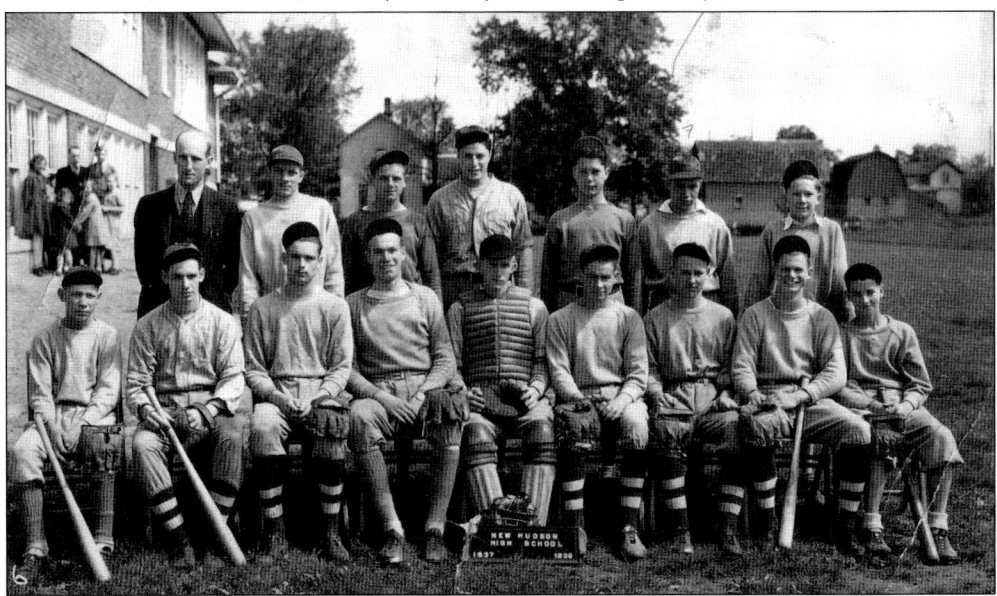

This is the 1937–1938 New Hudson High School baseball team with coach George Veldman. Veldman also coached the basketball and football teams. In 1939, the football team won the Oakland, Livingston, and Washtenaw Tri-County League championship. Next to the coach is Dallas Fletcher, who was an all-star athlete and lettered in three sports. Clayton Rickard is in the first row, third from right. Fletcher and Rickard were later business partners and operated the Haas Lake Park. (Courtesy of the Lyon Township Library.)

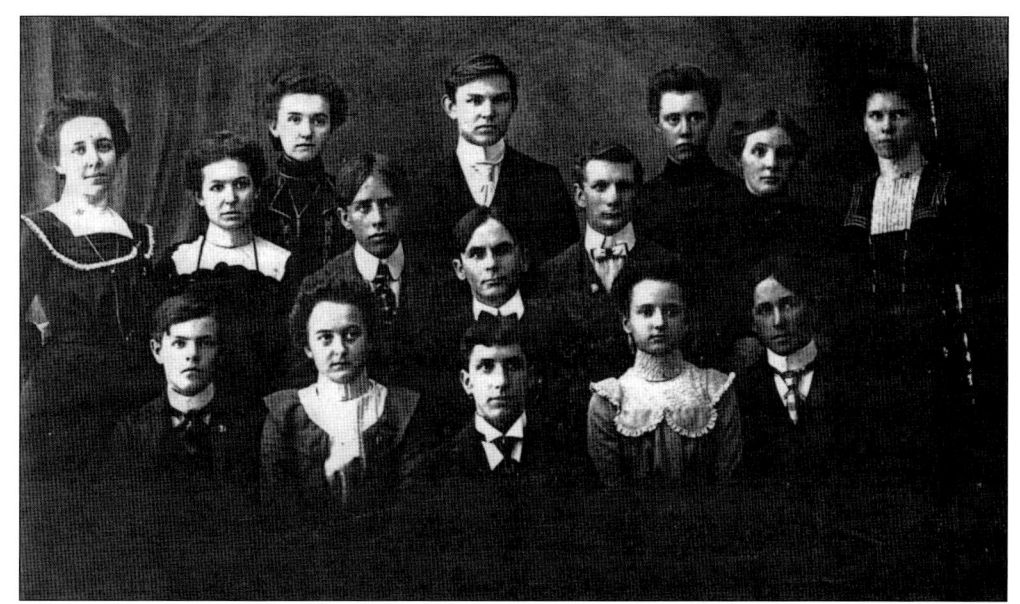

This is the New Hudson School graduating class of 1899–1900. Pictured are, from left to right, (first row) Forrest Harding, Goldie McKinley (Banfield), Alfred LaFever, Edith Taylor (Munn-Gale), and Charlie Taylor; (second row) Iva Dodge, Vivac Fielding, Prof. John Galbraith, Larned Rice, and Dulah Bunn (Taylor); (third row) Elsa Higby (Sinclair), LuLu Sinclair (Harding), Will Sdunek, Sadie Hopkins, and Leda Weeks (Tapp). (Courtesy of the Lyon Township Library.)

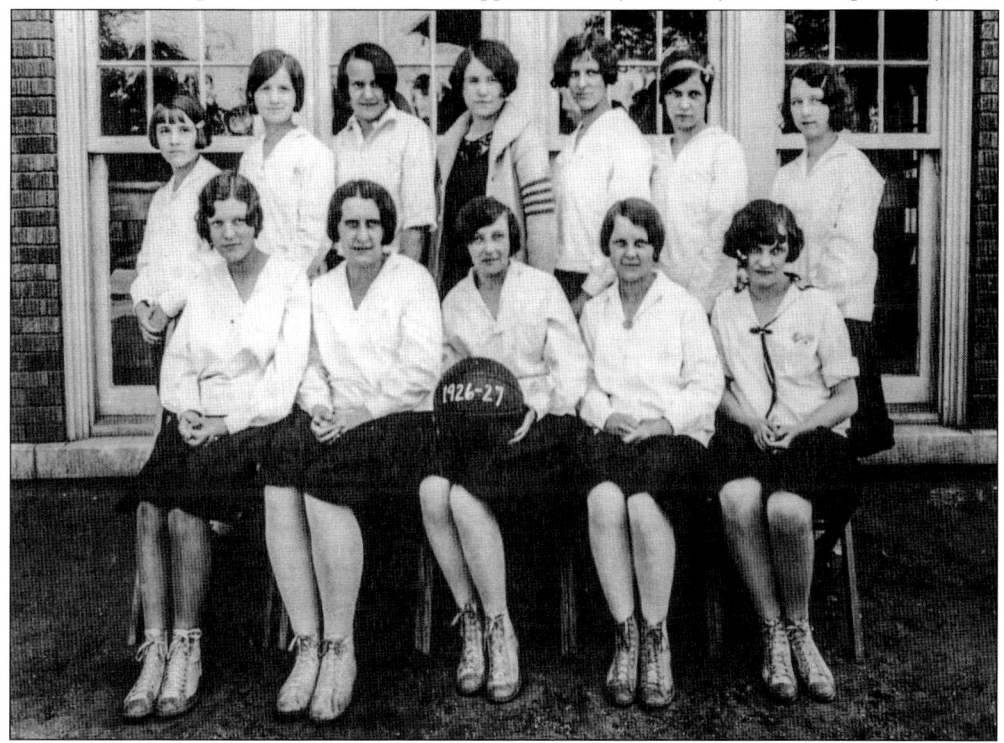

In 1927, the New Hudson School had a girls' basketball team. The New Hudson School was known for its accomplished sports teams for both genders. (Courtesy of the Lyon Township Library.)

71

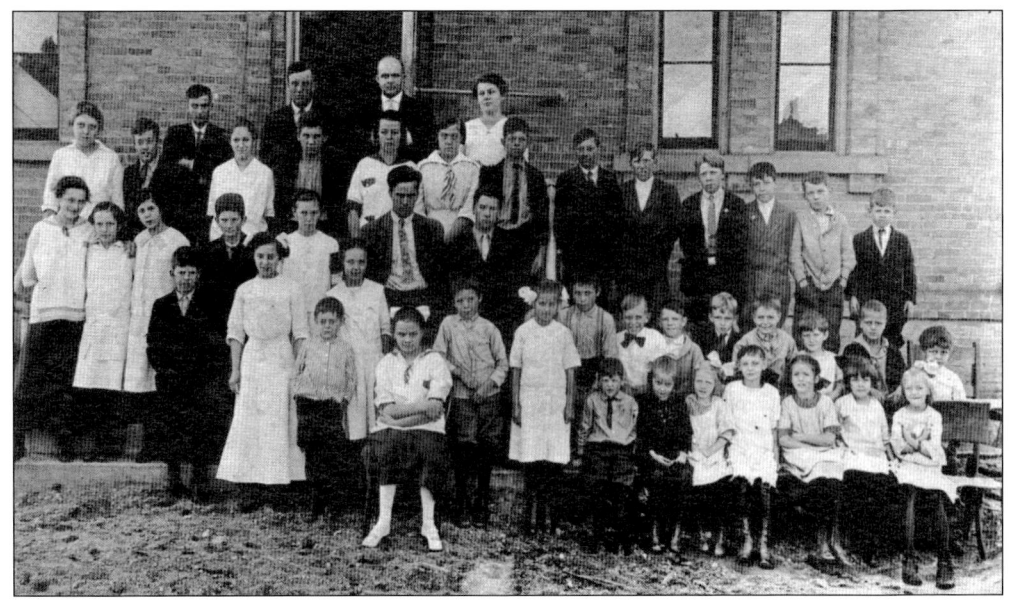

The students of the New Hudson School are pictured here. The following students are seen in this image: Rollo Pettengill, Gert VanAmberg, Orville O'Leary, Dale Renwick, Hazel VosBurg, Harriet Hodges, Jessie Arthur, Orpha Bunn, Beryl Hopkins, Merle Renwick, Nota Chatfield, Thurman Bunn, Reg Smith, Margaret Smith, Don Smith, Dulah Shear, Arthur Travis, Hazel Davis, Doris Hopkins, Floyd Tapp, Art Smith, Carl Smith, Floyd Pettengill, Frank Arthur, Clayton Brock, and two teachers. (Courtesy of the Lyon Township Library.)

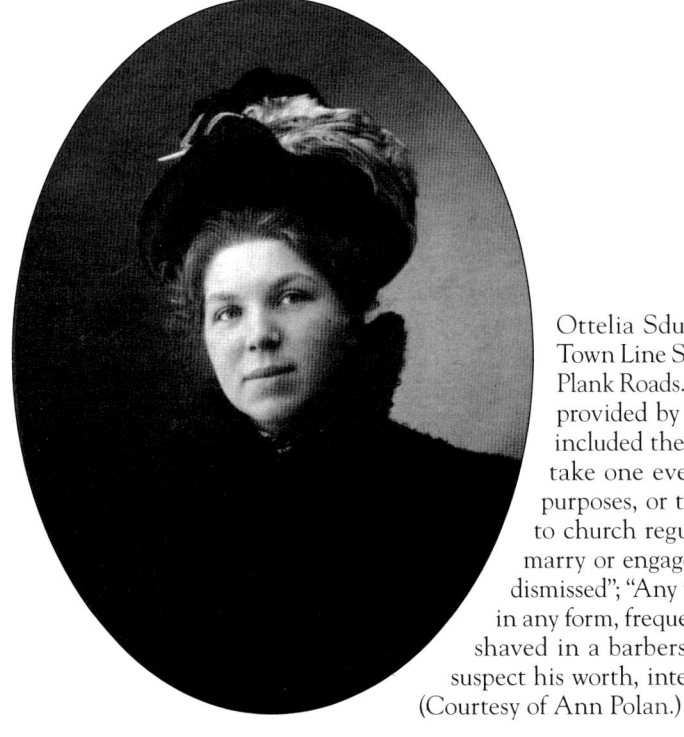

Ottelia Sdunek, born in 1880, taught at Town Line School on Pontiac Trail and Old Plank Roads. Some rules for teachers in 1872, provided by Greenfield Historical Village, included the following: "Men teachers may take one evening each week for courting purposes, or two evenings a week if they go to church regularly"; "Women teachers who marry or engage in unseemly conduct will be dismissed"; "Any teacher who smokes, uses liquor in any form, frequents pool or public halls, or gets shaved in a barbershop will give good reason to suspect his worth, intention, integrity, and honesty." (Courtesy of Ann Polan.)

The Bullard School, seen here c. 1930, was located on Eleven Mile, east of Martindale Road. (Courtesy of the Lyon Township Library.)

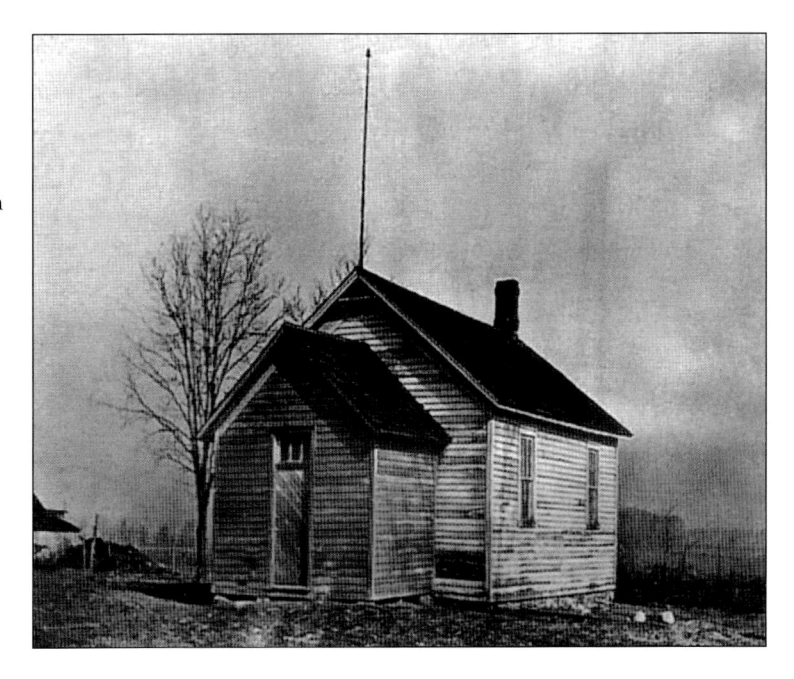

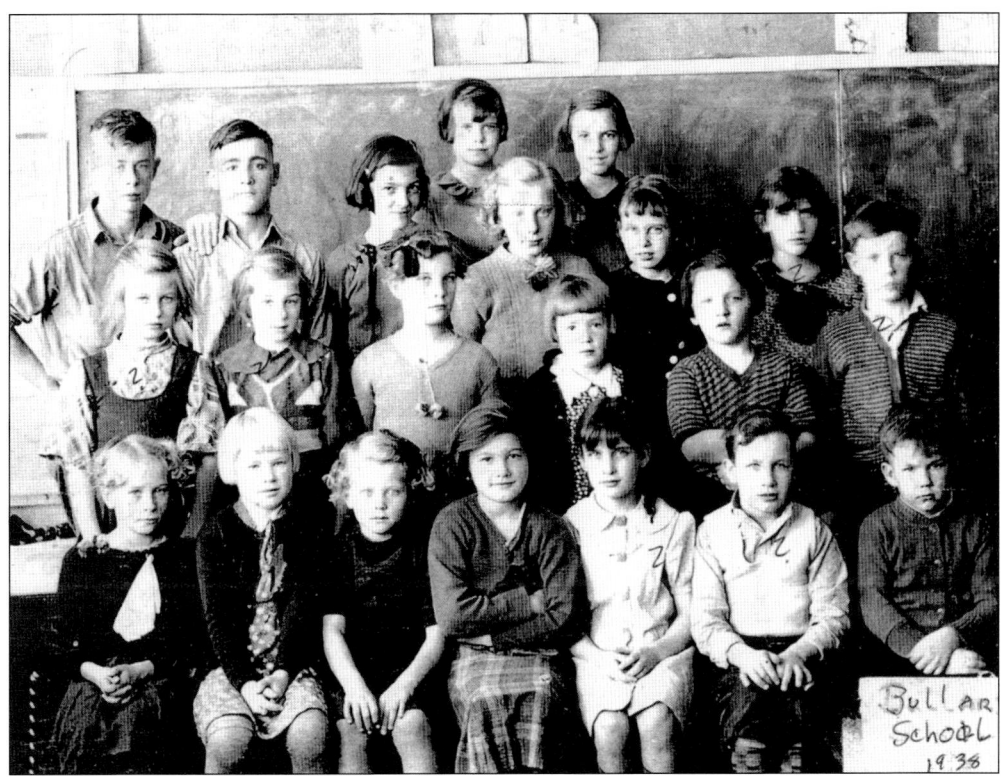

Many of the students from the Bullard School class of 1938 are unidentified. However, some are identified as follows: Bette Drum (Haack), Gloria Elkow, Dolores Wydell (sitting), Mag Morton, Barbara Drum (Chapman), Ramona Elkow, Nancy Bourns, D. Bourns, Pat Morton, and Ruth McCrory. (Courtesy of the Lyon Township Library.)

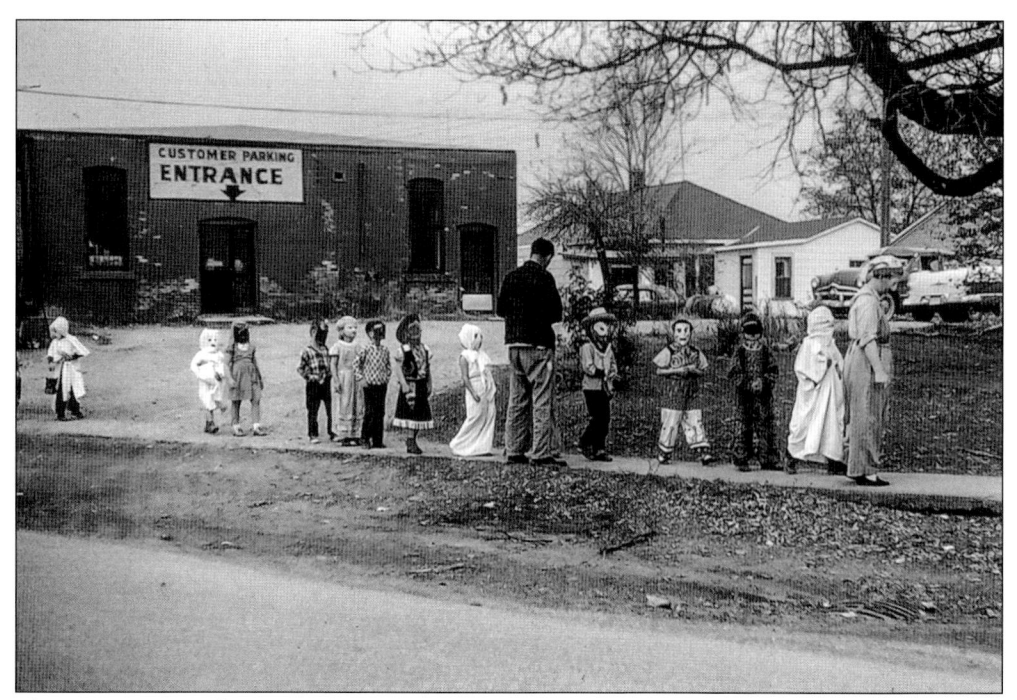

This picture was taken near the end of the Halloween parade on Milford Road around 1949. The background shows the customer entrance to the general merchandise store on Grand River Avenue. (Courtesy of Doug Canfield.)

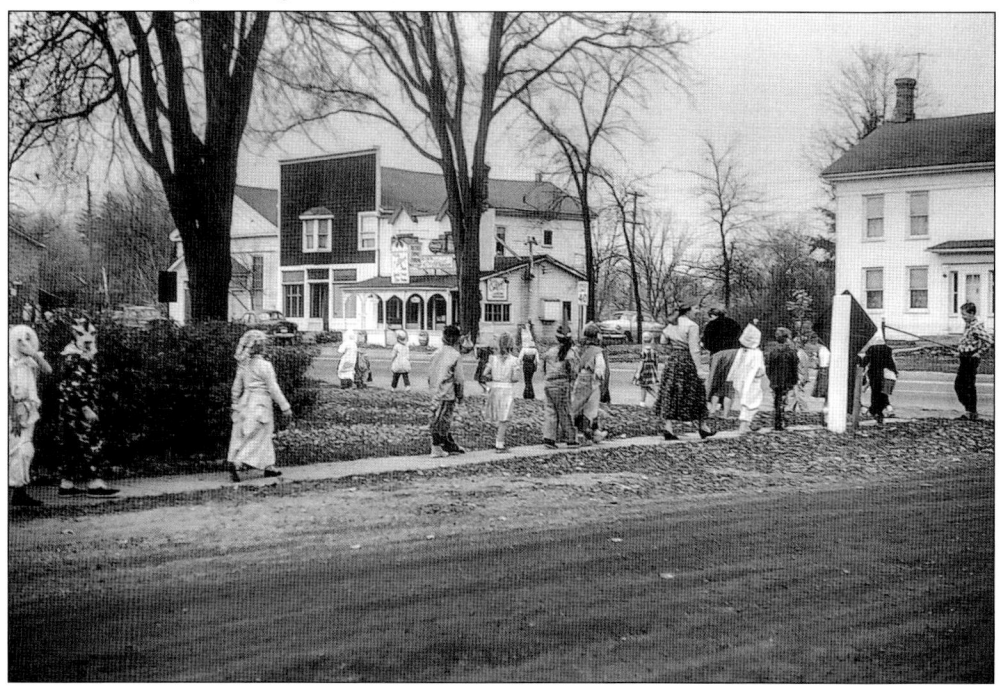

One of the traditions at Dolsen Elementary School was the annual Halloween parade. Students wore handmade costumes and showed off their designs as they walked toward Grand River Avenue. (Courtesy of Doug Canfield.)

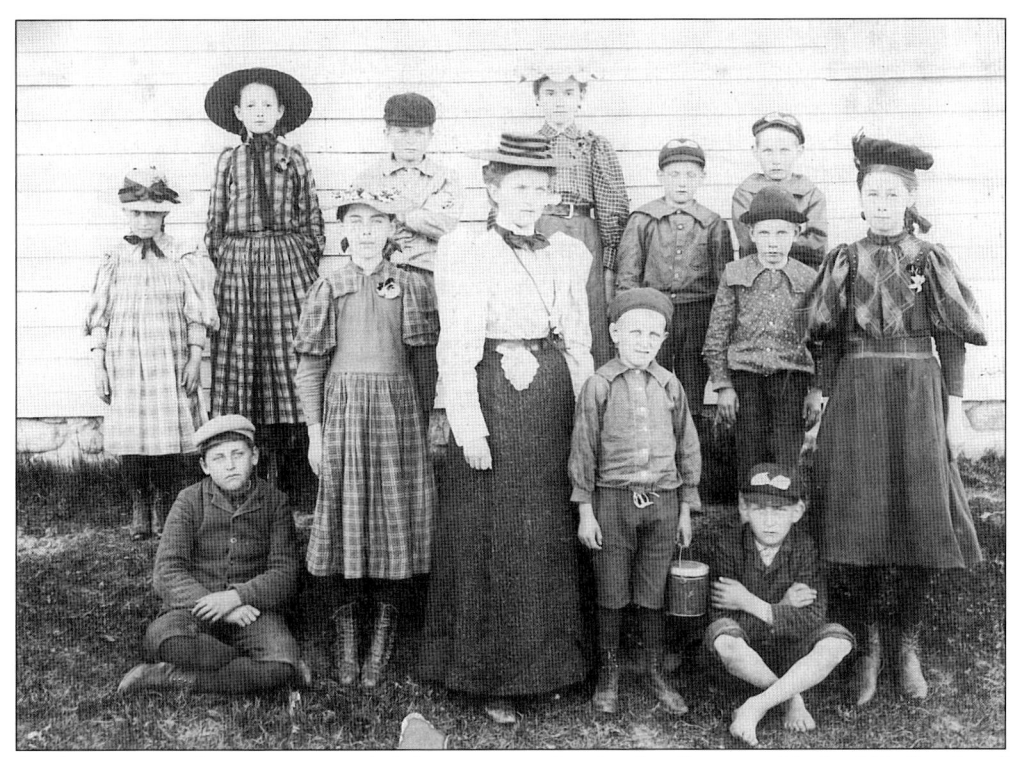

Students seen in this picture attended the one-room Smith schoolhouse on Twelve Mile Road and South Hill Road around 1895. Some of the students are Ava Miles, Edith Munn, Lulu Harding, and Veina Underhill. In the evenings, the earliest school buildings were often used for spelling bees, debate clubs, antislavery and temperance lectures, religious meetings, and singing schools. Husking bees and apple paring bees were among the other social diversions. (Courtesy of Lyon Township Library.)

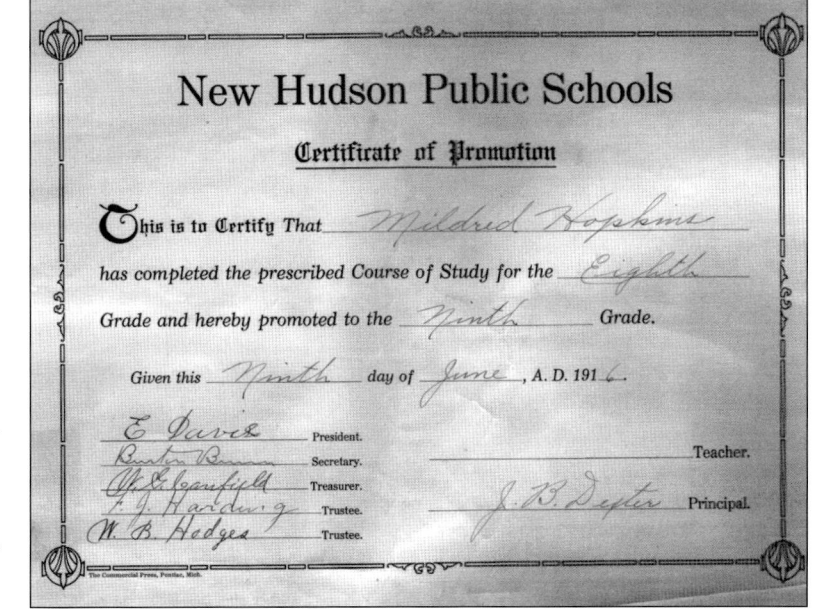

A certificate of promotion from the New Hudson Public Schools was issued to Mildred Hopkins in June 1916. It was signed by J.B. Dexter, principal. (Courtesy of Ann Polan.)

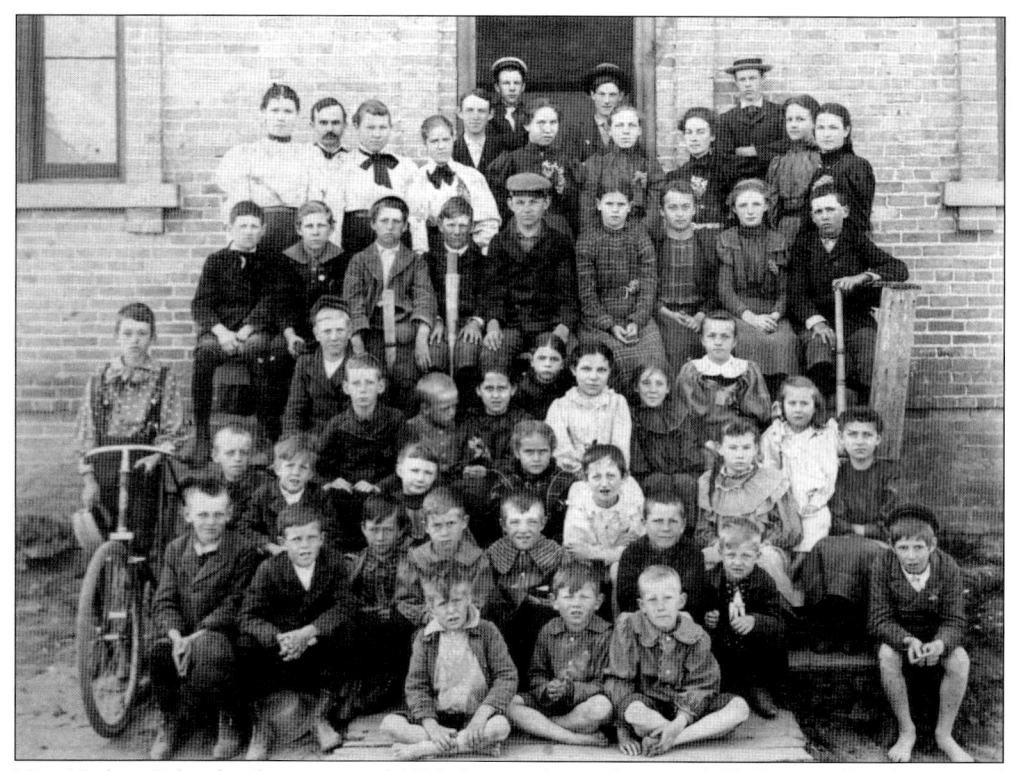

New Hudson School is shown around 1914. Among the students are Milo Pettengill and Doris and Mildred Hopkins. Many of the children came from farms, and if weather permitted, they attended school barefoot. Some of the teachers are seen in the back row. (Courtesy of Ann Polan.)

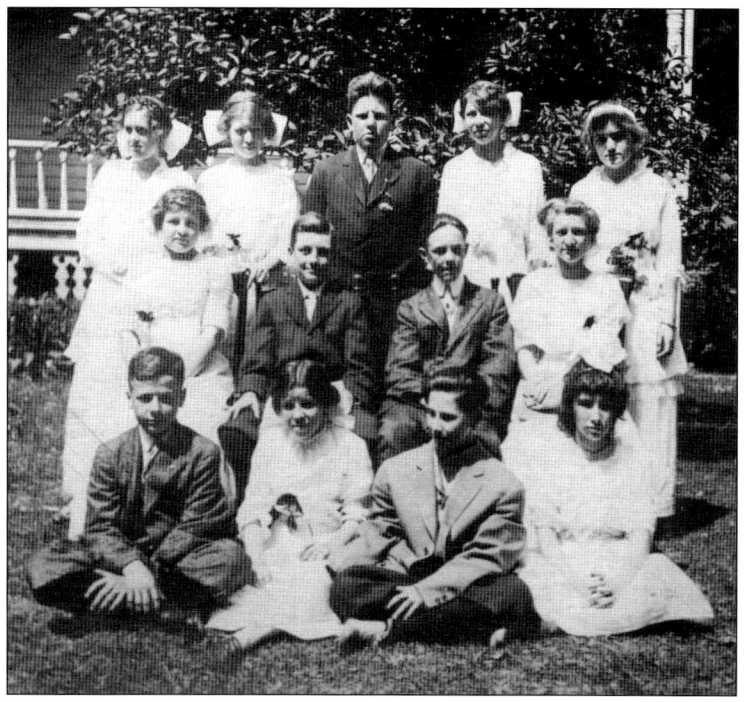

These high school students include Thelma Bond, Lucien Lovewell, Kathleen Kahl, Dorothy Kalmbach, Stella Rogman, Robert McCrory, Harold Fawcett, Lillian Burley, Clarence Brangar, Thelma Anderson, Carvell Phillips, and Florence Kuhn. (Courtesy of the Lyon Township Library.)

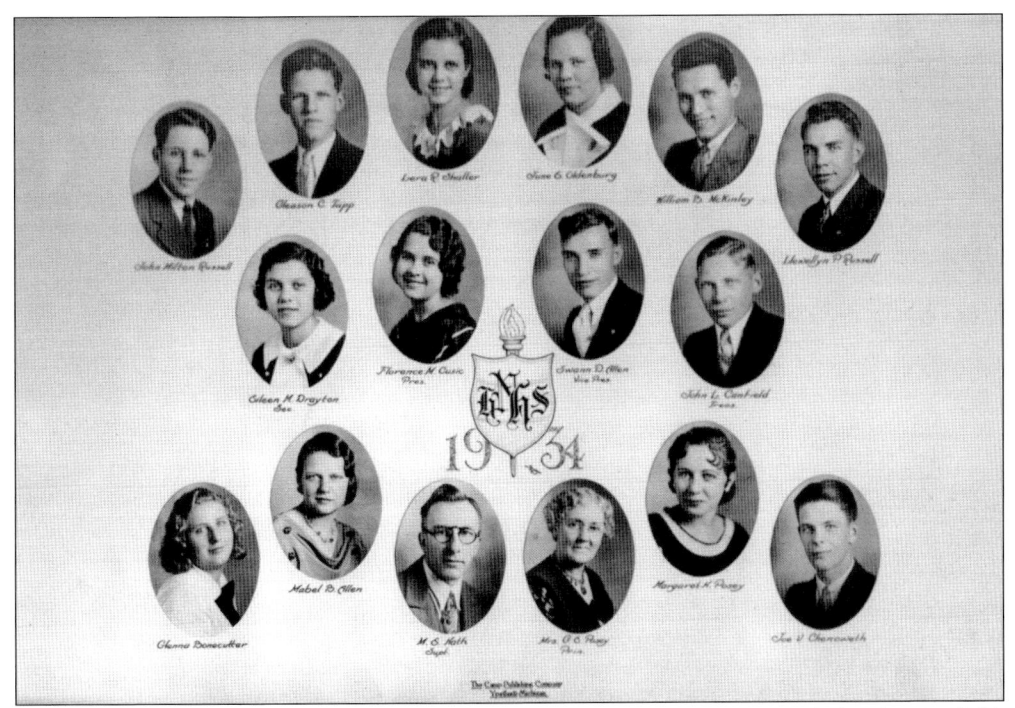

This is the 1934 graduating class of New Hudson High School. The students include John Canfield, a prominent farmer; Gleason Tapp, an area banker, and Bill McKinley, who operated the Knapp Airport. (Courtesy of the Canfield family.)

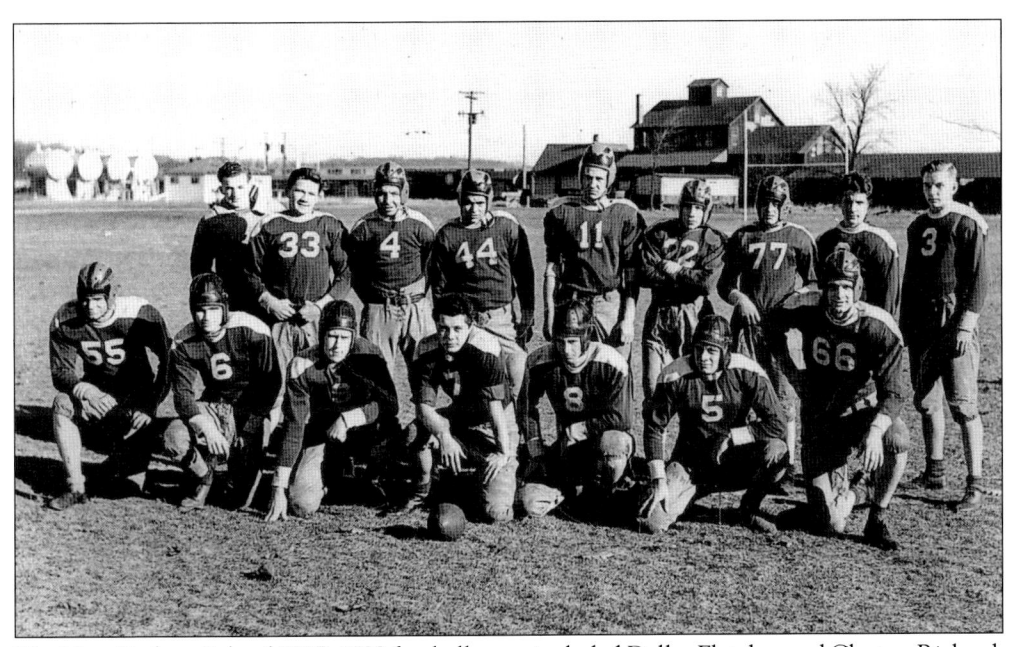

The New Hudson School 1937–1938 football team included Dallas Fletcher and Clayton Rickard. The New Hudson feed mill and train depot are in the background of the football field. (Courtesy of the Lyon Township Library.)

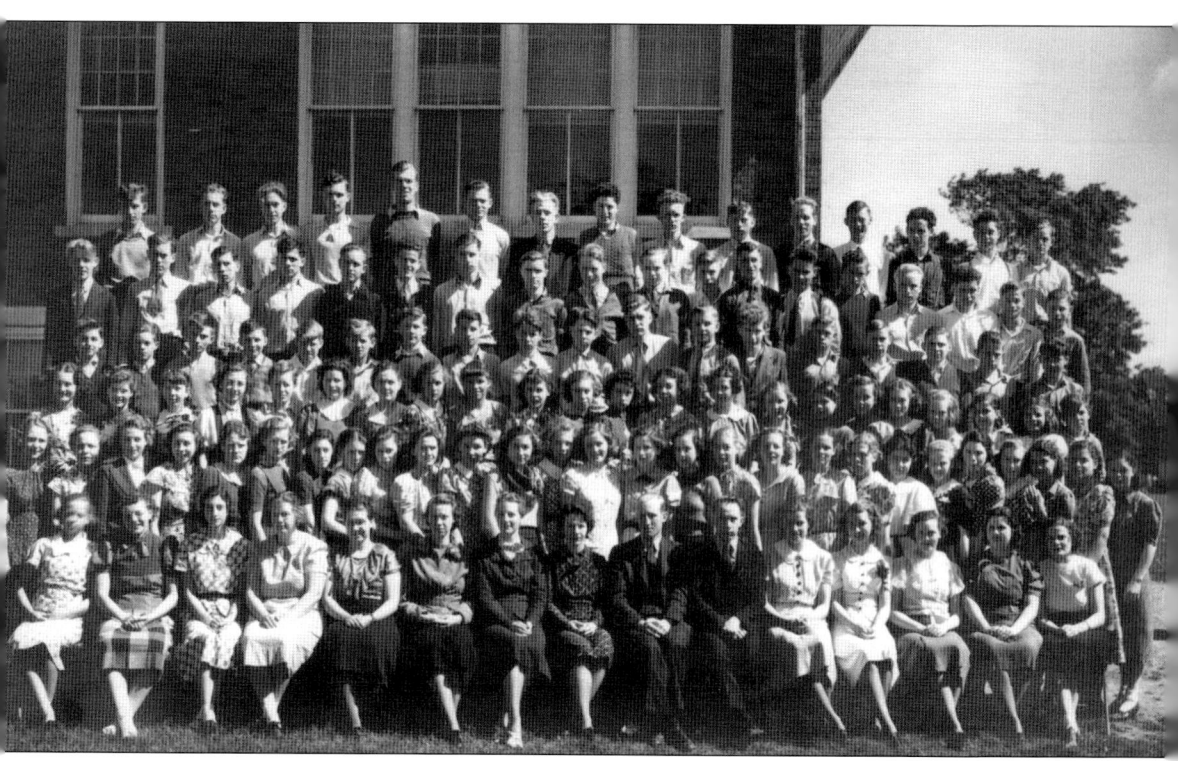

New Hudson High School students in 1938 are, from left to right, (first row) Kathern Pulaskey, Almedia Galloway, H. Rickenbacker, Jean Hern, Rose Hagerman, a Miss Hollebrands, a Miss Anderson, a Mrs. Knapp, a Mr. Veldman, a Mr. Kongas, Bernice Owsiak, Helen Hopp, Dorothy Stewart, Ethel Wilt, and Dorothy Vettes; (second row) Dorothy Johnson, Myrtle Johnson, Luella Brock, Jeanne Gord, V. McMichael, Bettie Nicholson, Rella Mae Chamberlain, Thelma Chenoweth, Lillian McLoy, Marion Darlington, Lillian Moore, Lillian Morrow, Emily Gooding, Glenna Jean Schuman, Lorraine Pettengill, Dora Mae Darlington, Patricia Scheer, Gladys Moore, Virginia Fletcher, Mary E. Canfield, Cecelia Westervelt, Marion Franklin, Elaine Haack, Gertrude Schneider, Evelyn Haack, Thelma Burt, and Myrtle Dickinson; (third row) Helen Butcher, Mary Womack, Bessie Loehne, Betty Lee, Ethel Slabaugh, Almedia Wilt, Geraldine Vettes, May Luttermoser, Esther Powelson, Arbutas Moore, Norma Hath, Margaret Davis, Evelyn Bondie, Virginia Kelly, Jean Moynihan, B. Welch, Dorothy Brocklehurst, Clara Schneider, Thelma Dickerson, Annabell Bowers, Esther Luttermoser, and Leon Edmundson; (fourth row) James Morrow, Charles Butcher, Richard Gorlich, James Jacklin, R. Goers, Norman Luttermoser, Harry Loehne, John Cash, Raymond Russell, Marion Fletcher, Paul Kunzog, Gerald Hopp, Robert Morse, Laverne Franklin, James Brocklehurst, Lewis Bogart, Arthur Templeton, and Harry Cusic; (fifth row) Kenneth Edmunson, John Schneider, William Villerot, Dallas Fletcher, Arthur Richter, John McLoy, Harold Lee, Bill Moynihan, Ralph Hopkins, Charles Gooding, Leonard Goers, Erwin Powelson, Donald Cash, Thomas Kelly, Fred Wagner, Arthur Wilt, A. Lyman, and Thurman Bowers; (sixth row) D. Richter, Herschel McGary, Earl Anderson, Forrest Jacobs, Charles Weiss, Gussie House, Lawrence Wagnitz, Alfred Morris, Ralph Coleman, Delbert Musoff, Clarence Wagnitz, William Leczel, Gene Hurst, Elmer Loehne, and Richard Luttermoser. (Courtesy of the Lyon Township Library.)

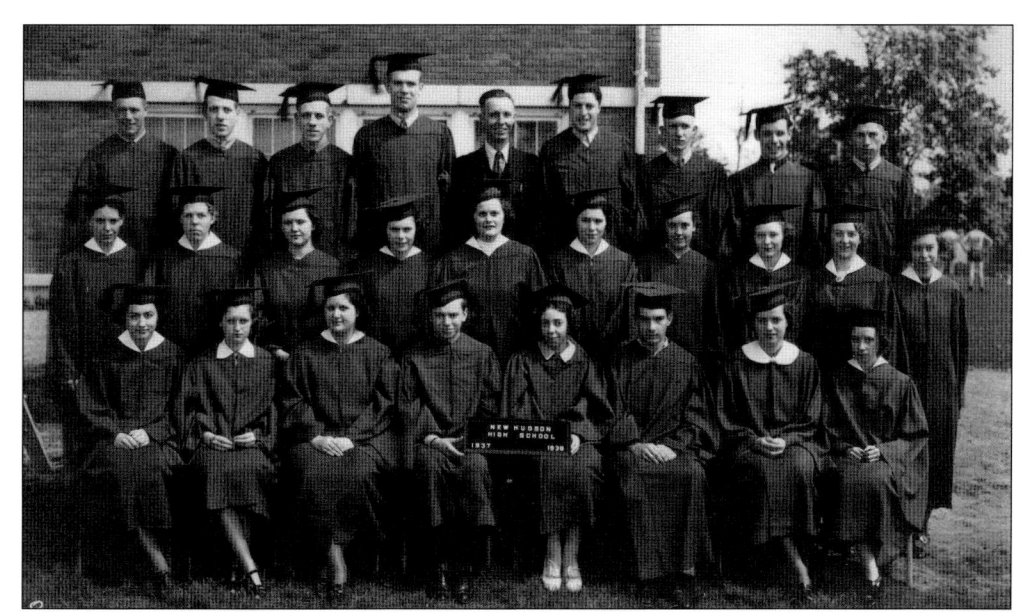

The senior graduating class of 1938 includes, from left to right, (first row) Lillian Morrow, Betty Nicholson, Ethel Wilt, Charles Gooding, Evelyn Bondie, Robert Brocklehurst, Bernice Oswiak, and Margaret Davis; (second row) Thelma Chenoweth, Mary E. Canfield, Mary Darlington, Lillian McLay, Dorothy Vettes, Elaine Haack, Dorothy Stewart, Dorothy Johnson, Luella Brock, and Norma Hath; (third row) Ralph Hopkins, Clarence Wagnitz, Lawrence Wagnitz, Charles Weiss, J.H. Jacklin, Alfred Morris, Ralph Coleman, Jean Hurst, and Delbert Musoff. (Courtesy of the Canfield family.)

Dallas Fletcher was a high school letterman in three sports, football, basketball, and baseball. This all-around athlete was also a boxer. Fletcher and high school buddy Clayton Rickard went on to form a partnership and opened Haas Lake summer park. Fletcher lived in his family home on Grand River Avenue and Haas Road. (Courtesy of the Fletcher family.)

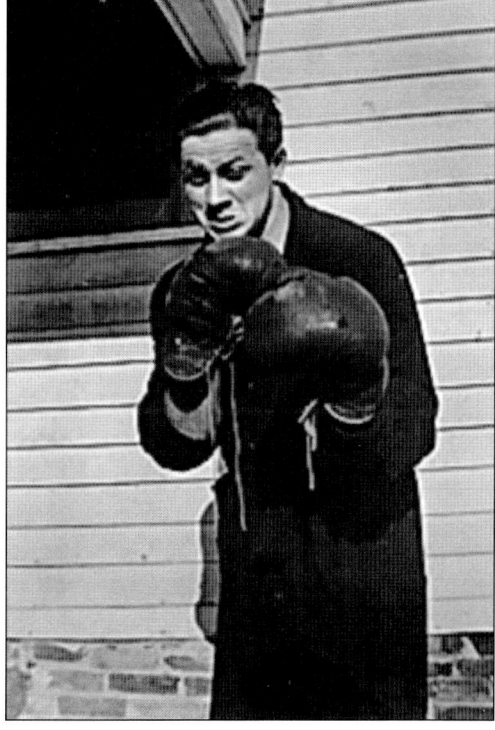

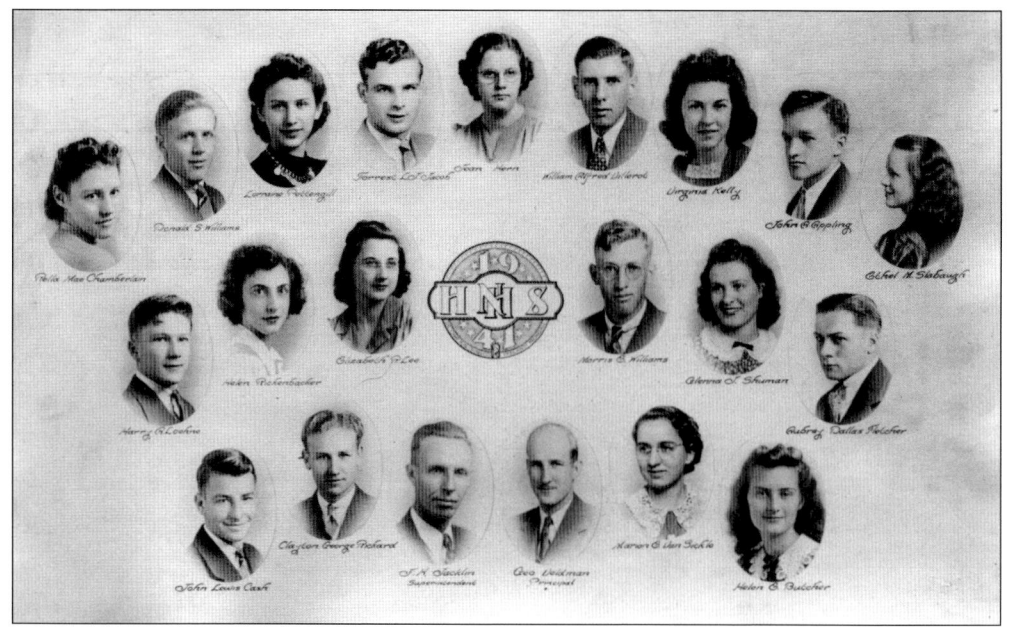

This is the 1941 graduating class of New Hudson High School. Pictured are, from left to right, (first row) Rolla Mae Chamberlain, Donald S. Williams, Lorraine Pettengill, Forrest L.J. Jacob, Jean Horn, William Alfred Villerot, Virginia Kelly, John A. Appling, and Ethel Slabaugh; (second row) Harvey Loehne, Helen Rickenbacker, Elizabeth Lee, Morris Williams, Glenna J. Shuman, and Aubrey Dallas Fletcher; (third row) John Cash, Clayton Rickard, Supt. J.H. Jacklin, Principal George Veldman, Marion Van Sickle, and Helen Butcher. (Courtesy of the Lyon Township Library.)

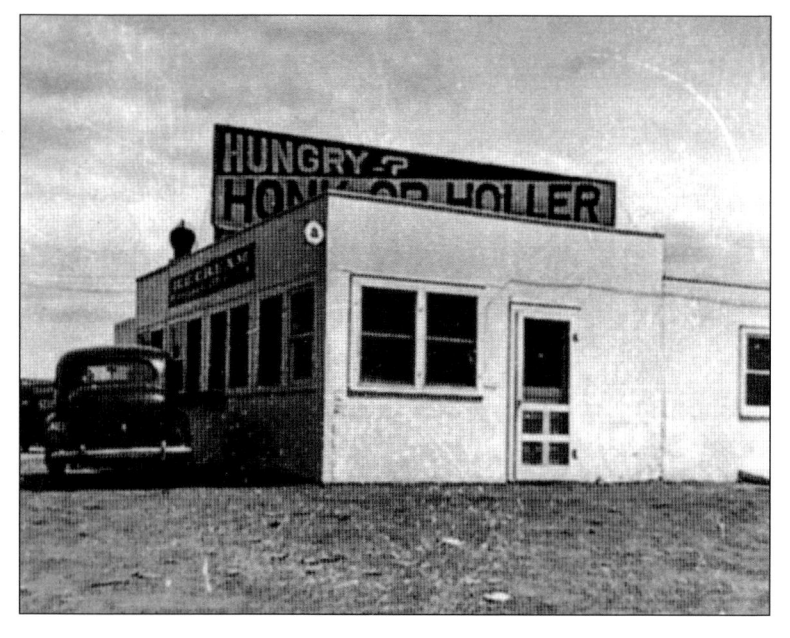

Hilltop was a favorite restaurant and hangout for students in the 1940s. The sign out front said, "Hungry? Honk or Holler." It was located at Grand River Avenue near Martindale Road. It was also used as a truck stop when Grand River Avenue was traveled extensively before the I-96 expressway. (Courtesy of the Powelson family.)

80

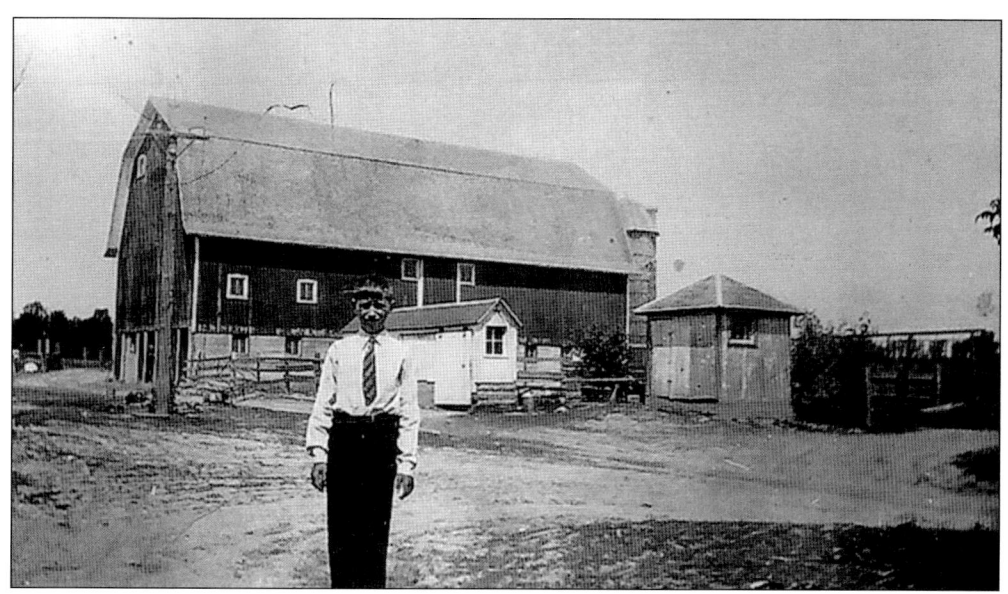

A Mr. Powelson stands on his father's farm, which was just below the Hilltop restaurant. The former restaurant operated in 2014 as a party store. (Courtesy of the Powelson family.)

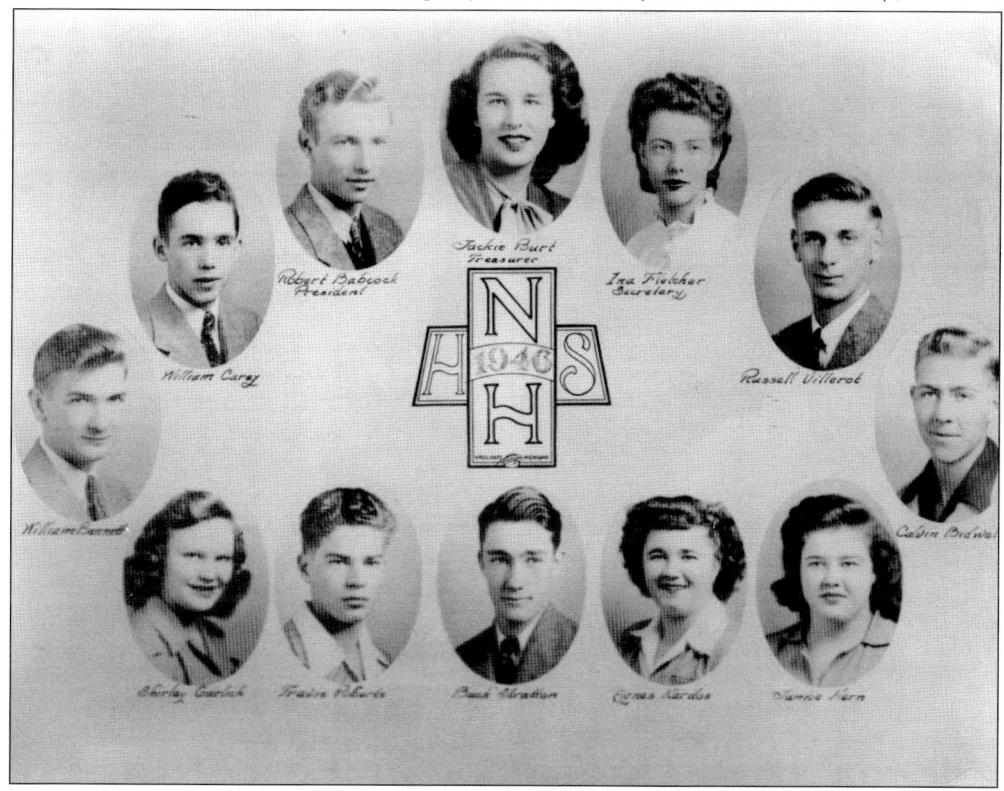

William Carey and class treasurer Jackie Burt were students in the 1946 graduating class of New Hudson High School. They later married. Jackie Burt's grandfather founded a buggy manufacturing shop in New Hudson. Her father was among the founders of the Vagabond Coach Manufacturing Company. (Courtesy of the Canfield family.)

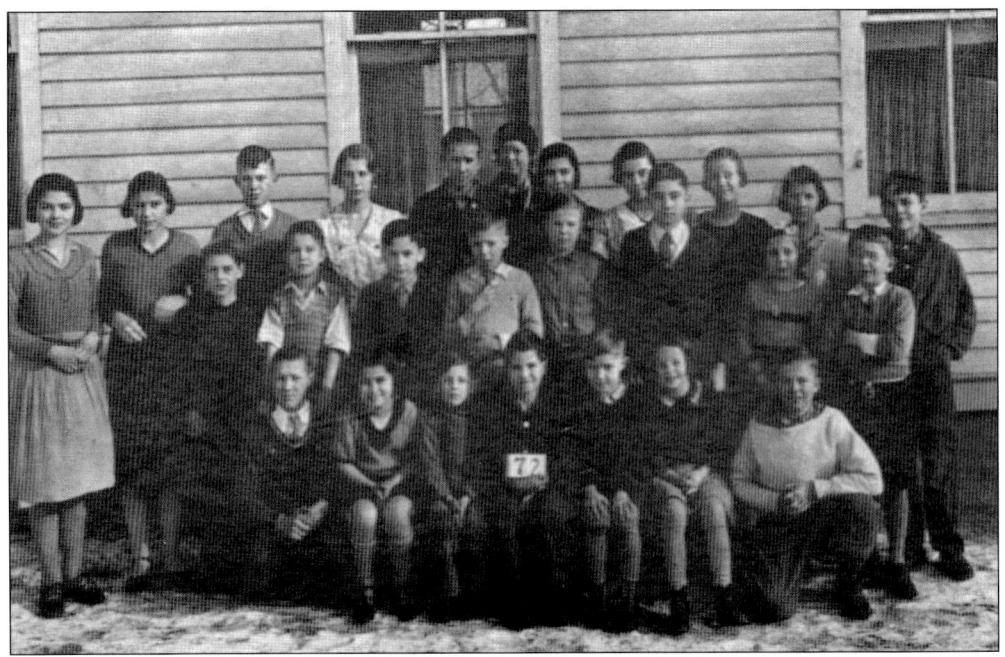

This is the 1934 class of the one-room Stone School at Ten Mile and Napier Roads. It was located on the limits of the township of Novi, but many Lyon Township residents attended the school. Included in the picture are Lucy, Lawrence, Donald, Avis, and Esther Bidwell. (Courtesy of Ann Polan.)

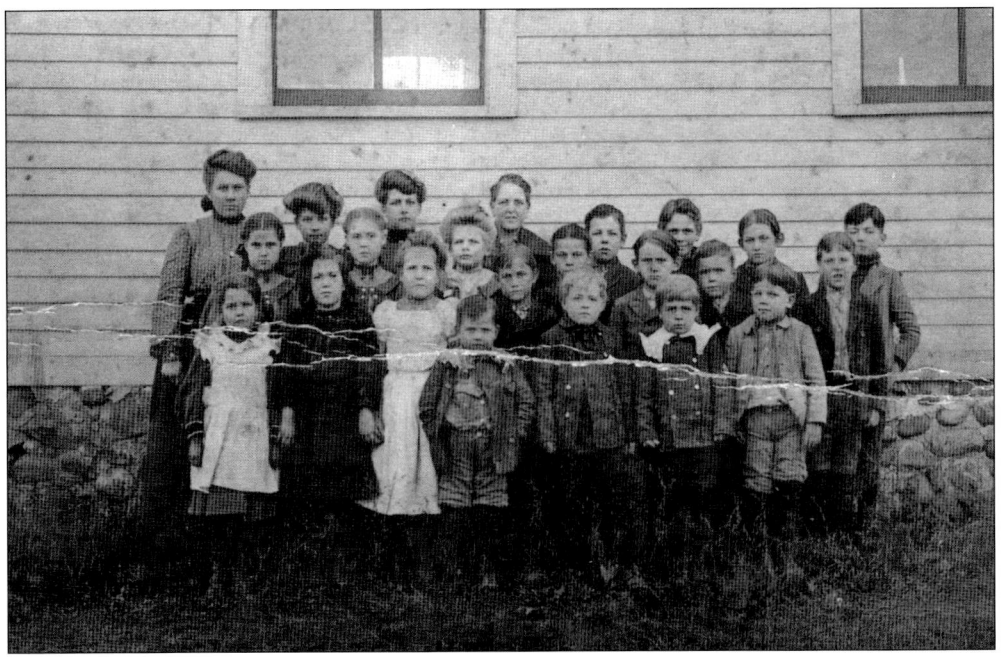

The one-room Town Line School on Old Plank and Pontiac Trail Roads was also located outside of the township boundaries; however, children from the surrounding communities attended the school. Included in this c. 1905 photograph are Beryl Hopkins (Pettengill), Hazel Hopkins (Bidwell), and Ben Hopkins. (Courtesy of Ann Polan.)

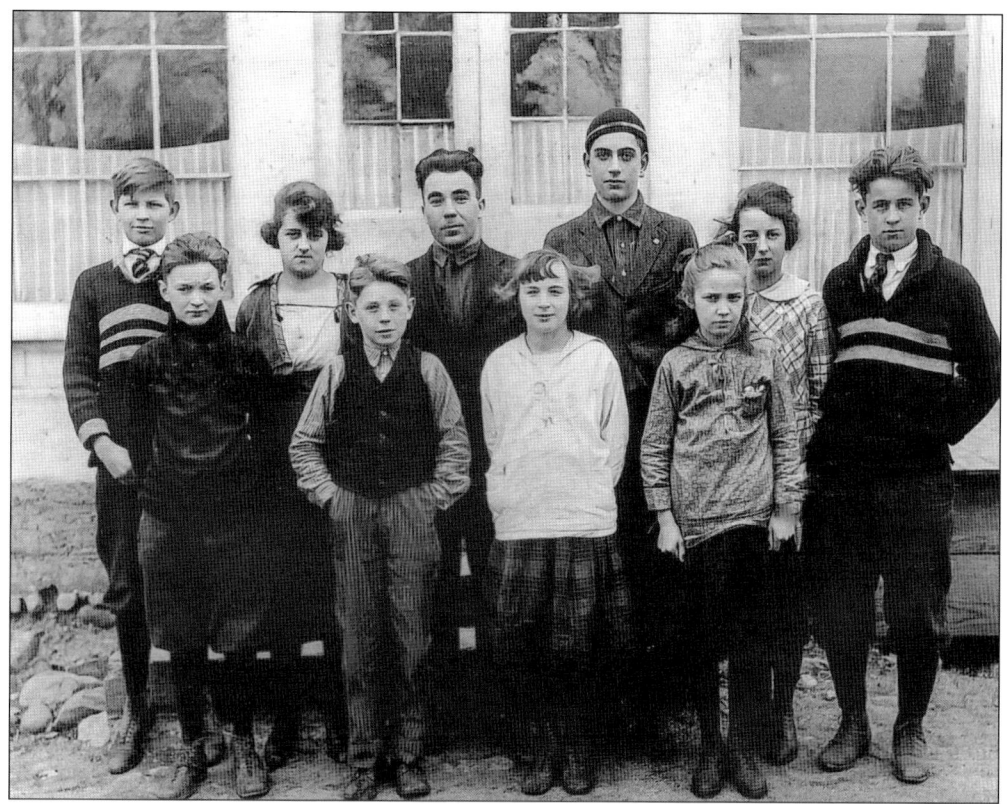

It is believed these students used this building when the New Hudson School was burned down in April 1921. Students were shifted from place to place while a new school was constructed. Another structure that was used was Maccabee Hall. (Courtesy of the Lyon Township Library.)

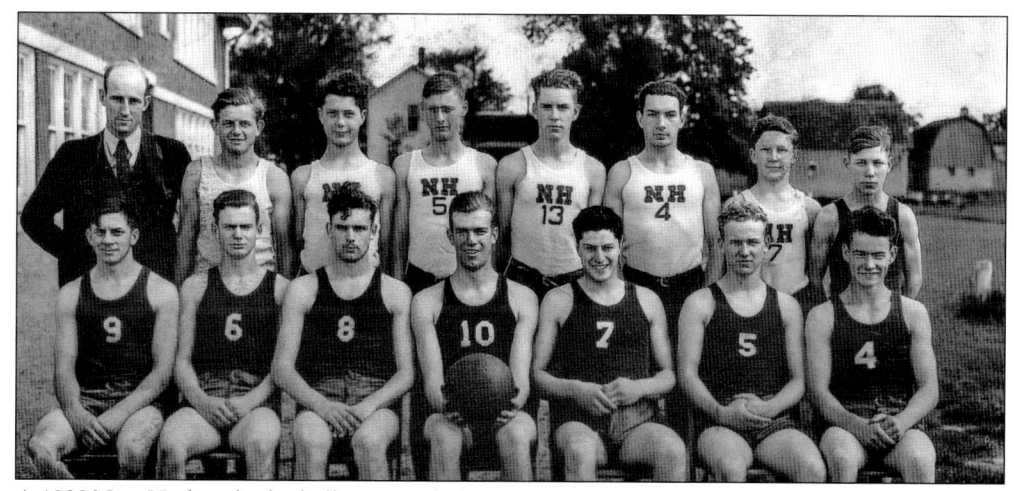

A 1938 New Hudson basketball team included (first row) varsity members Dallas Fletcher, Gussie House, Forrest Jacobs, Charles Wild, Alfred Mores, Clayton Rickard, and Donald Cash; (second row) Coach Veldman and junior varsity members Dick Luttermoser, Elmer Loehne, Wally Letsel, Hershal McGory, Bob Brocklehurst, Harry Loehne, and Thurman Baneas. (Courtesy of the Fletcher family.)

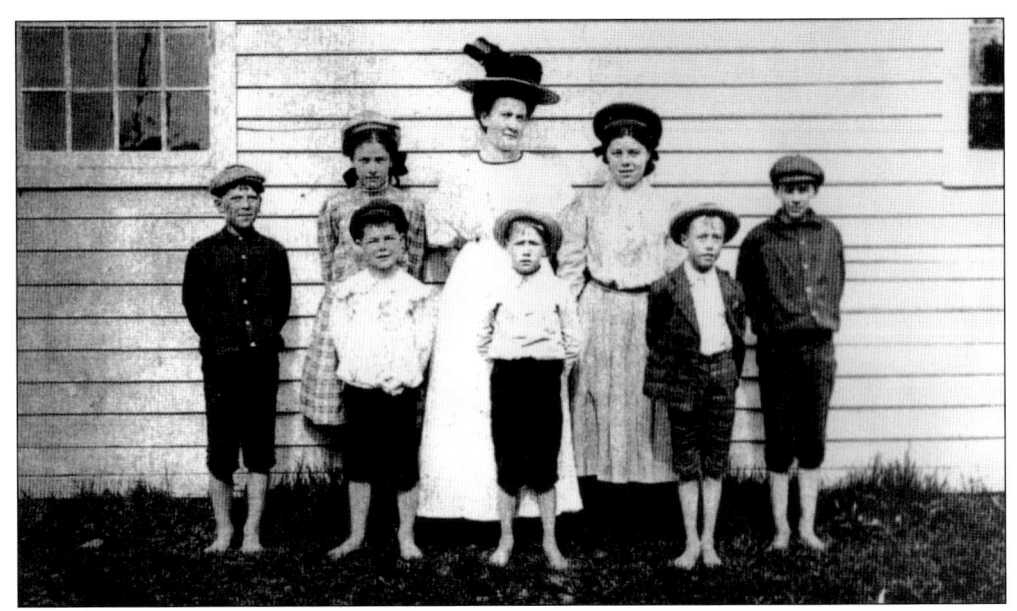

Smith School students in 1909 took their annual photographs alongside of the one-room schoolhouse on Twelve Mile and South Hill Roads. All of the students could not be identified. The first row includes, from left to right, Reginald Hugh Smith, his brother Donald Kingsley Smith, and Frank Harold Taylor, who lived on a Haas Road farm. In the second row is a Miss Hathaway, teacher. (Courtesy of the Lyon Library.)

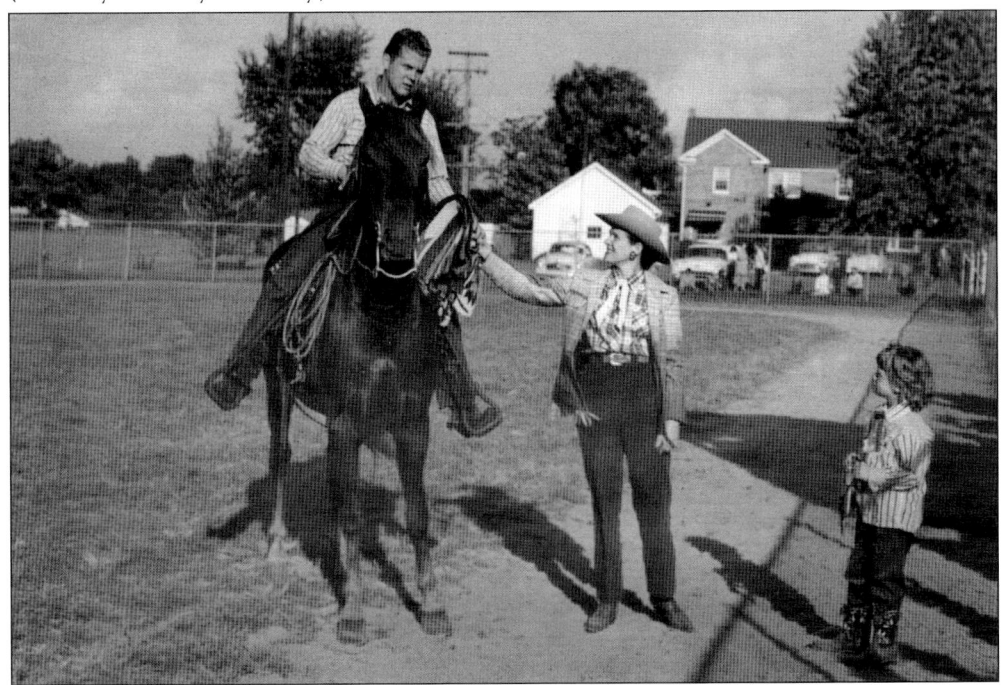

Lyon Township was once known as the horse capital of Michigan. Horse exhibitions were held on this Nine Mile and Pontiac Trail Roads farm around 1955. Exhibitors like Eddie Earehart (shown here) received ribbons for their performances. Millennium Middle School is now on the site. (Courtesy of Patty Frigon.)

Minty E. Hath was the superintendent of New Hudson School around 1925. He was very popular, and in addition to teaching, he coached athletic teams. Hath lived on Milford Road. He could see the school from his house and could keep an eye on the site. (Courtesy of the Lyon Township Library.)

This picture shows New Hudson School in 1872. Some typical rules of the era included the following: "Respect your schoolmaster"; "At the end of the class, wash your hands and face"; "Wash your feet if they are bare"; "Bring firewood into the classroom for the stove whenever the teacher tells you to"; "If the master calls your name after class, straighten out the benches and tables"; and "Sweep the room, dust and leave everything tidy." (Courtesy of Greenfield Historic Village and the Lyon Township Library.)

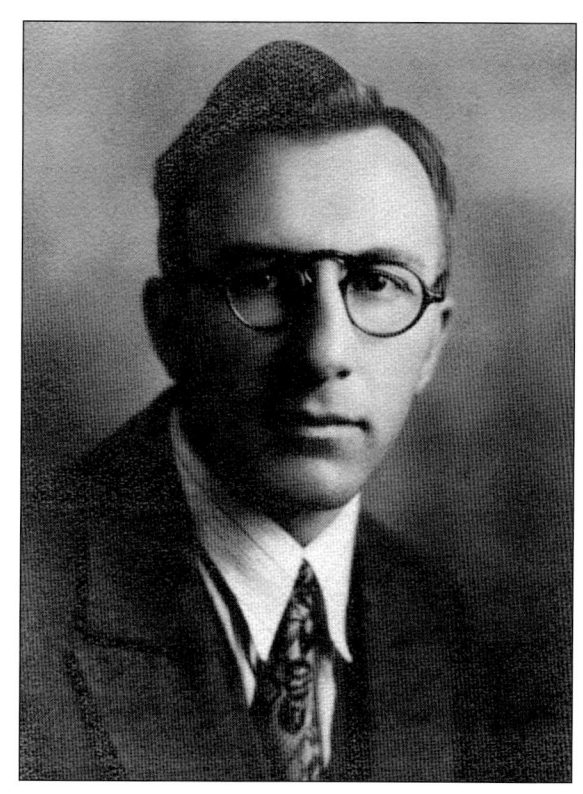

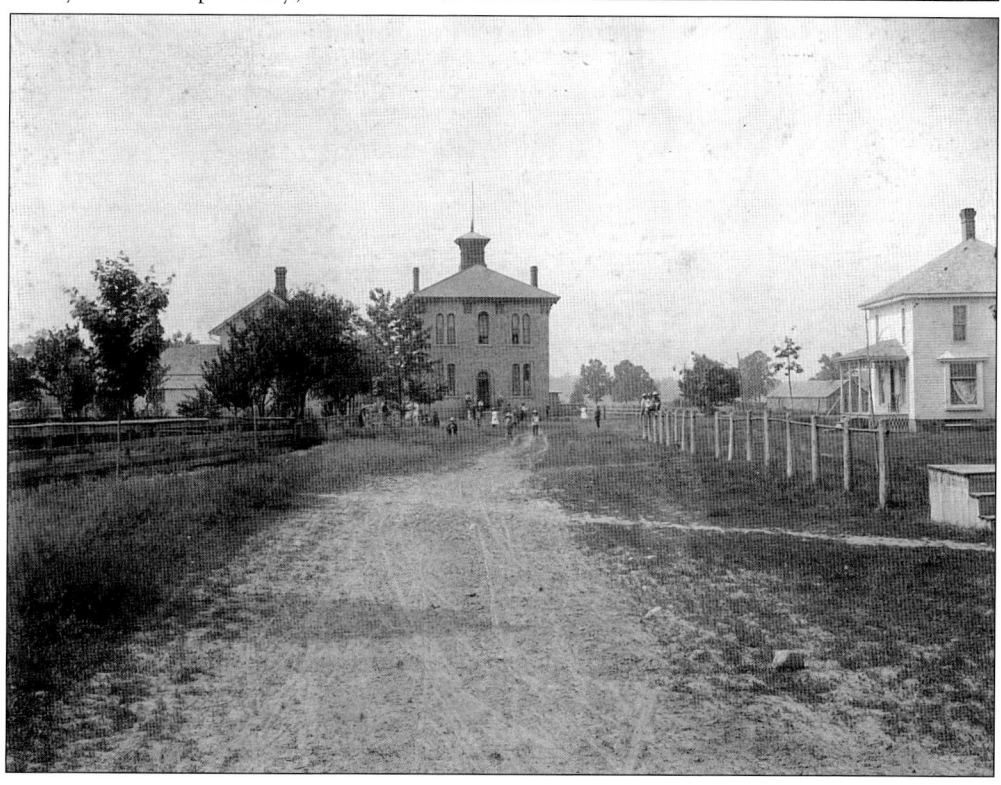

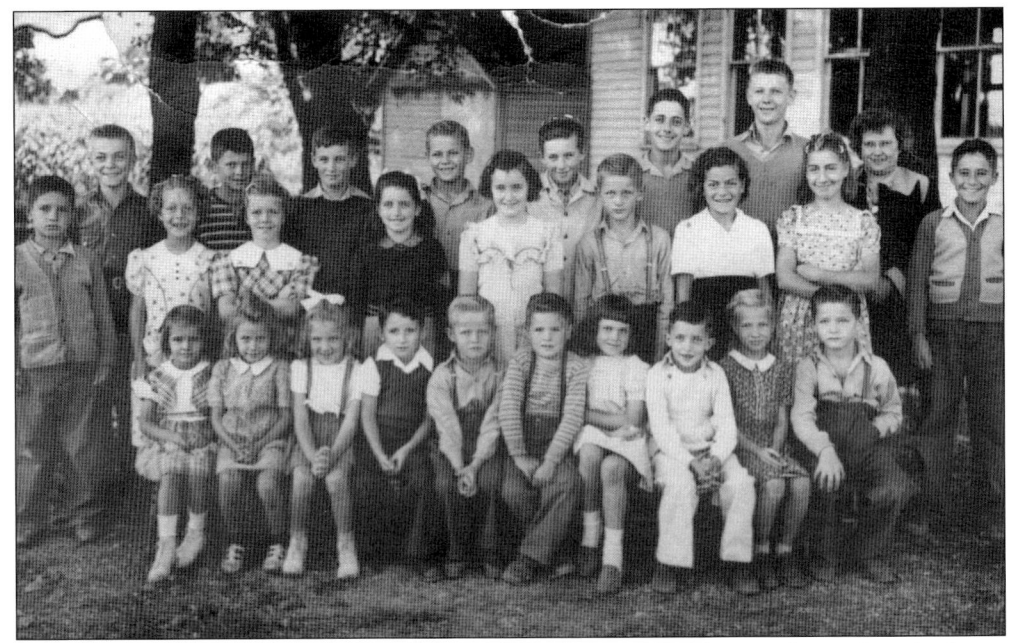

Stone School in 1948 was at Napier and Ten Mile Roads. Although it was located on the limits of Novi and Lyon Township, many children from the township attended the school. A church is now located at the site. Some of the students pictured here are Ann Bidwell, Virginia Slaybaugh, Dorene Bidwell, Neil Jones, Bob Jones, and Terry Slaybaugh with their teacher Ruby Bunn. (Courtesy of Ann Polan.)

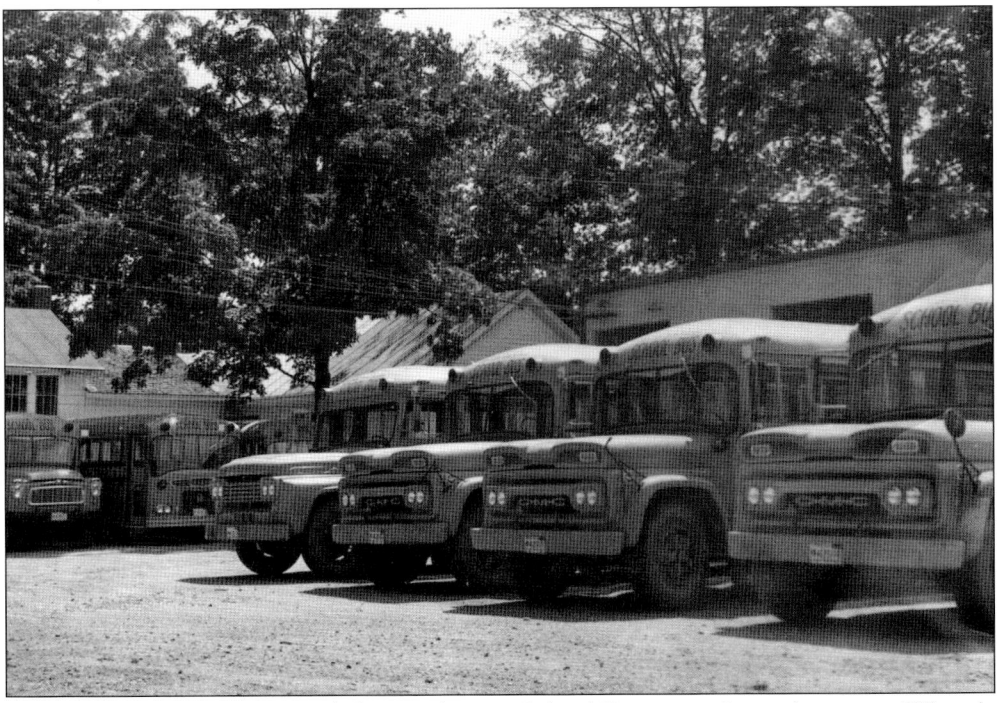

These 1966 school buses served the South Lyon School District and were kept near Whipple Street in South Lyon. (Courtesy Patty Frigon.)

Six

CEMETERIES

Over the years, a number of cemeteries have served the township, including New Hudson Cemetery on Grand River Avenue and Milford Road; the Rose Sherman Family Cemetery, also known as the Bullard Cemetery at Eleven Mile and Martindale Roads; the Kensington Cemetery on Grand River Avenue, west of Kent Lake Road; and the Del Smith Cemetery, also known as the Everett Cemetery on Nine Mile and Chubb Roads.

A pet cemetery, once known as the Happy Hunting Grounds and currently called the War Dog Memorial Cemetery on Milford Road, has interred animals from world-renowned explorers, including Admiral Byrd's pet parrot.

Burials at the New Hudson Cemetery commenced around the same time that New Hudson was formed. The Universalist Church was near the northern boundary of the cemetery. It was later moved to Grand River Avenue and served as an entertainment center. Records show the New Hudson Cemetery has burials dating back to the Revolutionary War, War of 1812, the Civil War, Spanish-American War, World War I, World War II, the Korean Conflict, and Vietnam War. Some of the veterans buried at the cemetery were Jonathan Shores, 1771–1837; Ambrose Orvis, 1758–1844; and William Graham, 1812–1838. Other war veterans interred at the cemetery were Abraham T. Bell, 1842–1869; Albert Foote, 1841–1863; Willard Hufton, 1876–1914; Clarence Scheffer, 1933–1998; Scott Long, 1889–1958; William McKinley, 1915–2006; and Otis Reynolds, 1939–1996.

Today, the New Hudson Cemetery and the War Dog Memorial Cemetery are the only cemeteries still active.

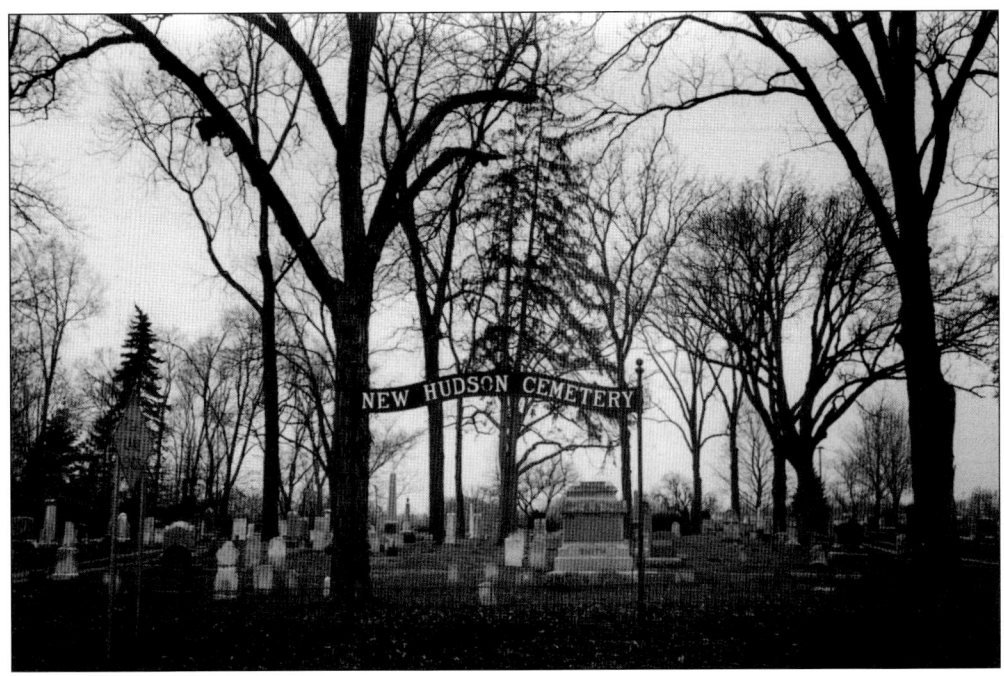

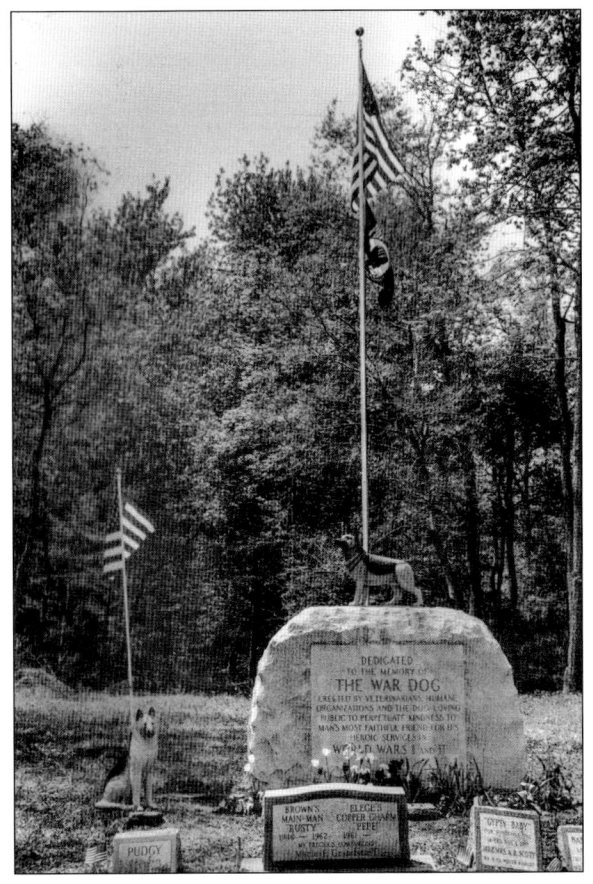

The New Hudson Cemetery is at the six-point road in New Hudson. Originally, the Universalist Church stood on the north side of the property. The church was later jacked up and moved to Grand River Avenue. It became known as Maccabee Hall, a social venue for New Hudson area residents. (Courtesy of Jane and Jack Purslow.)

The Happy Hunting Grounds pet cemetery was established in 1936 by the Elkow family. Located at Milford Road and Eleven Mile Road, it is the final resting place for hundreds of beloved pets. In 2010, military veterans volunteered to refurbish the grounds. The cemetery was renamed the War Dog Memorial Cemetery where interments of US military service dogs continue. (Courtesy of Jane and Jack Purslow.)

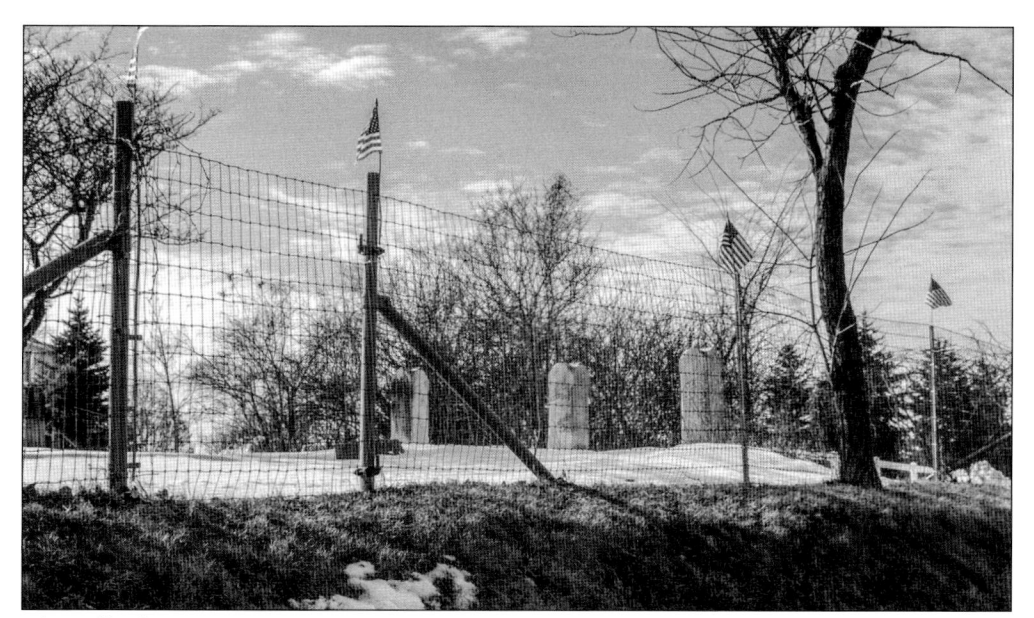

The Bullard Rose Cemetery was a family burial site on Eleven Mile Road between Martindale and Milford Roads. During the 1990s, haunted hayrides took place at the cemetery. Tractors pulled covered farm wagons from the annual Halloween party on Martindale Road, and upon arrival at the cemetery, the tractor driver would typically say he ran out of fuel. Meanwhile, a teenager hid behind a tombstone in the cemetery and jumped out at the kids for the perfect holiday scare. (Courtesy of Jane and Jack Purslow.)

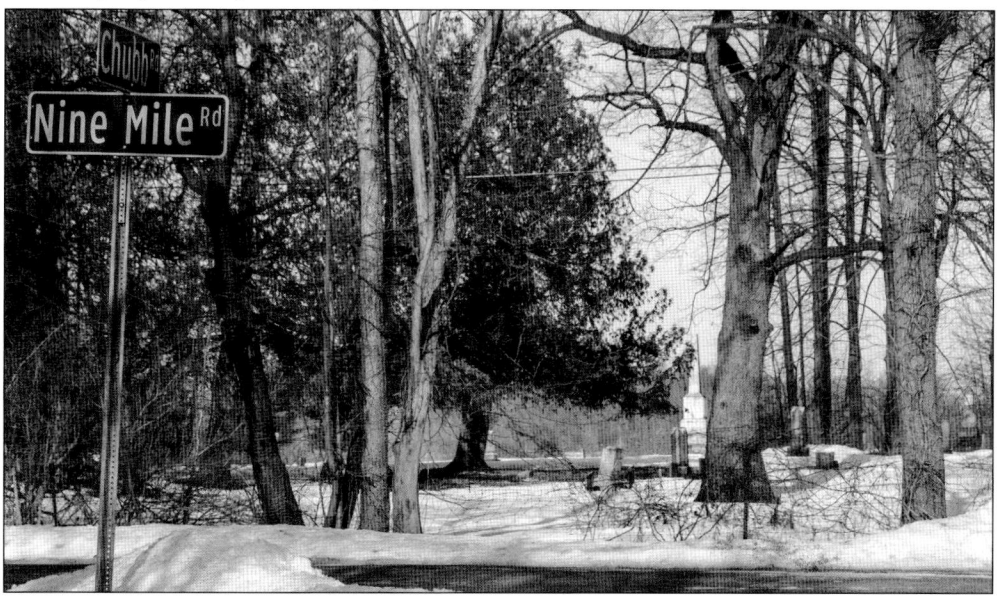

The Everett Cemetery on the northwest corner of Nine Mile Road and Chubb Road is located on the old Delbert Smith Farm. Many of the Whipple family lived on Nine Mile Road and are buried at Everett. A considerable number of roads in the township were named after people like Herman Griswold, who was interred in the cemetery. Some of the monuments that still stand date back to before the turn of the 20th century. The last burial in Everett was in 1943. (Courtesy of Jane and Jack Purslow.)

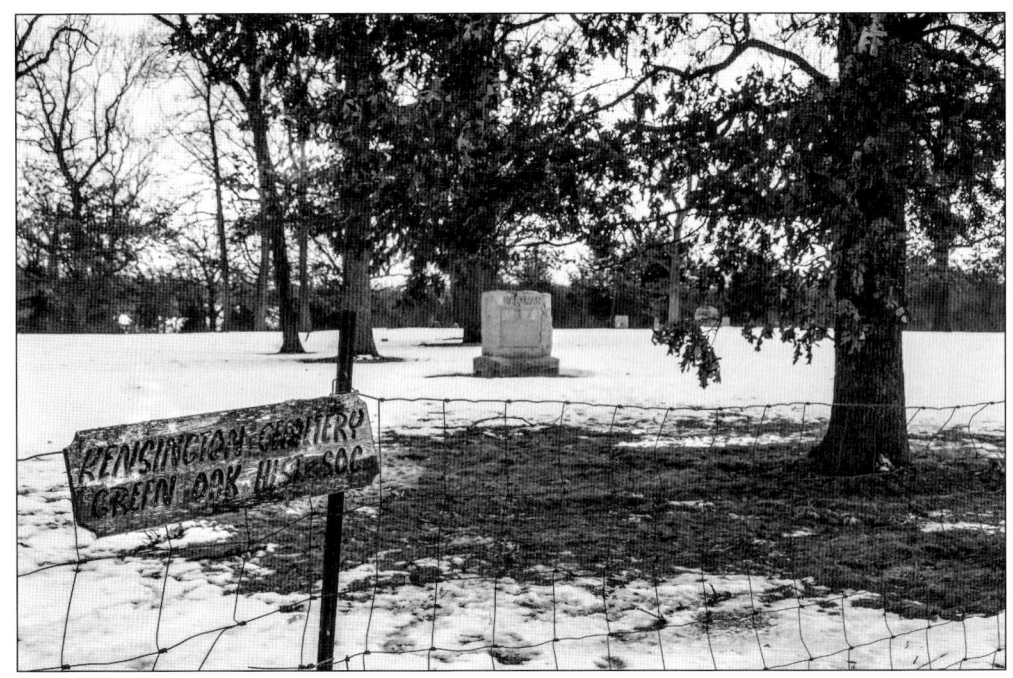

Kensington Cemetery is located on Old Grand River Avenue, west of Kent Lake Road. Ownership of the cemetery was shared between Lyon Township and Green Oak Township. Abram Wood, who died in 1905, was a Civil War veteran and is buried in Kensington. Several members of the Daughters of the American Revolution are also buried at the cemetery. William S. Kingsley, a Civil War veteran who lived from 1828 to 1912, was the last interment. (Courtesy of Jane and Jack Purslow.)

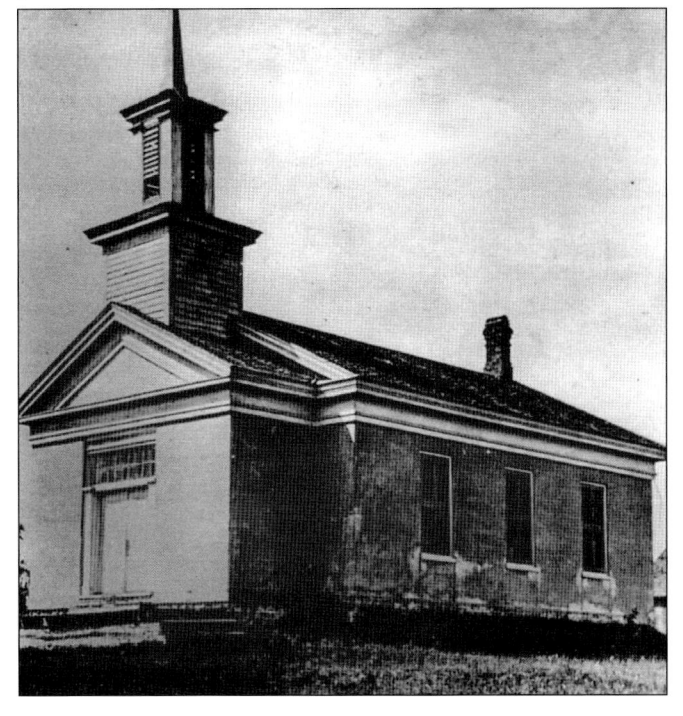

Kensington Church was adjacent to the Kensington Cemetery in the small Kensington community. The church and cemetery closed when the bank's wildcat notes were deemed worthless. (Courtesy of the Lyon Township Library.)

Seven
Interstate 96 Expressway

In the early 1950s, before construction on I-96 began, New Hudson was a thriving community that centered at a six-point intersection—Milford Road, Grand River Avenue, and Pontiac Trail Road. Grand River Avenue was a three lane road and was a vital connection to the main route from Detroit to Lansing, the state capital. The middle lane was used as a passing lane and was considered a dangerous spot where accidents were reported. Many roads were made of sand. If motorists were going from New Hudson to East Lansing, it took all morning to get there.

New Hudson had seven gas stations and six restaurants to serve all the travelers going through town. When the expressway came in, the traffic was routed on the much more efficient highway and away from Lyon Township. As a result, many of the businesses were shuttered. As the popularity of the expressway grew, its effects on commerce went full circle by 2004. I-96 became a harbinger of new businesses because of visibility to motorists and its prime location near the highway.

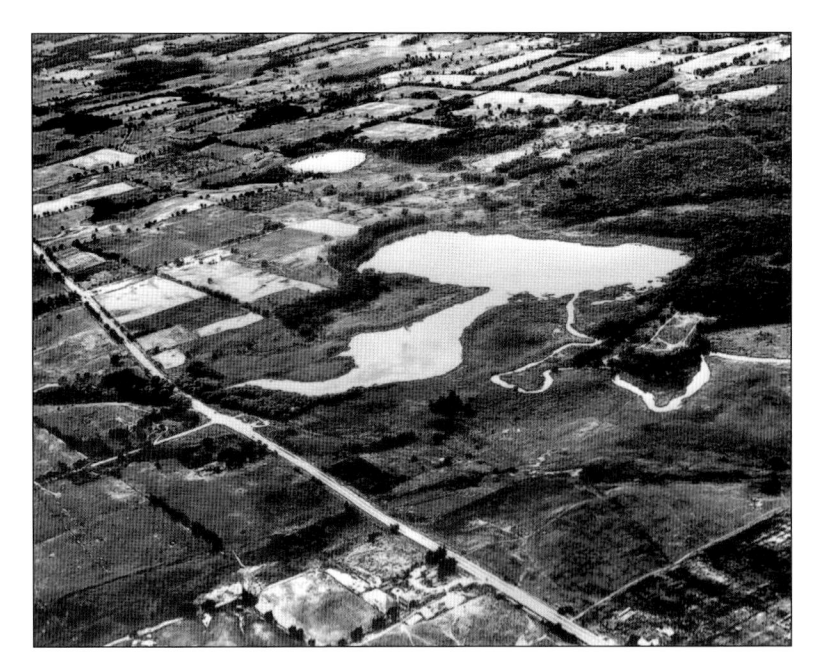

A dam at Grand River, c. 1946, blocked the Huron River to expand the 60-acre Kent Lake to a 1,200-acre lake in the newly formed Kensington Metropark, which opened in 1948. (Courtesy of the Lyon Township Library.)

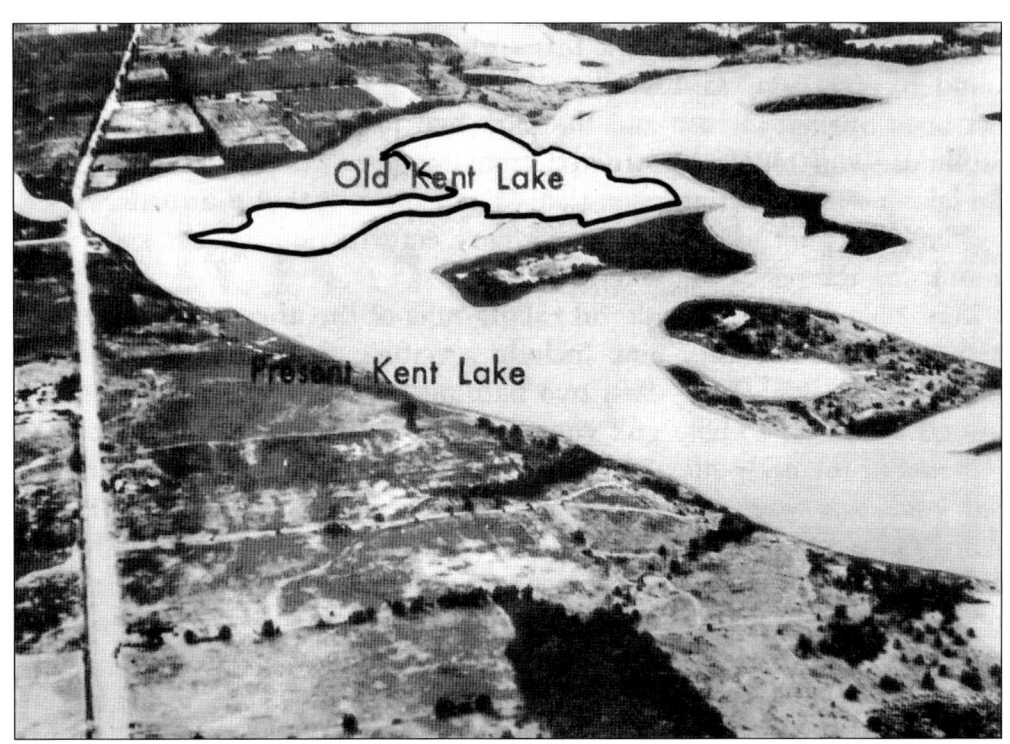

Superimposed over the old Kent Lake is the artist's conception of the new flooded Kent Lake's shoreline. (Courtesy of the Lyon Township Library.)

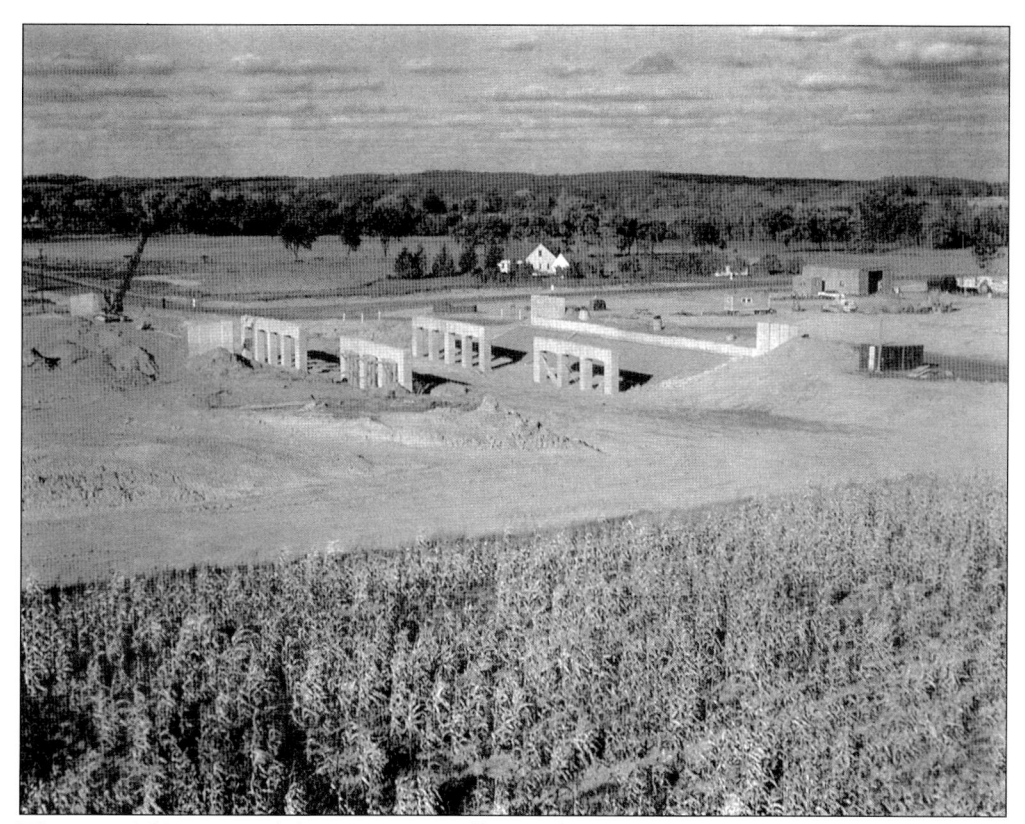

This is a 1956 picture of the supporting pillars under construction for the I-96 bridge on the expressway at Exit 155 at Milford Road. Significant traffic rerouting on Milford Road occurred to accommodate the freeway construction. (Courtesy of Doug Canfield.)

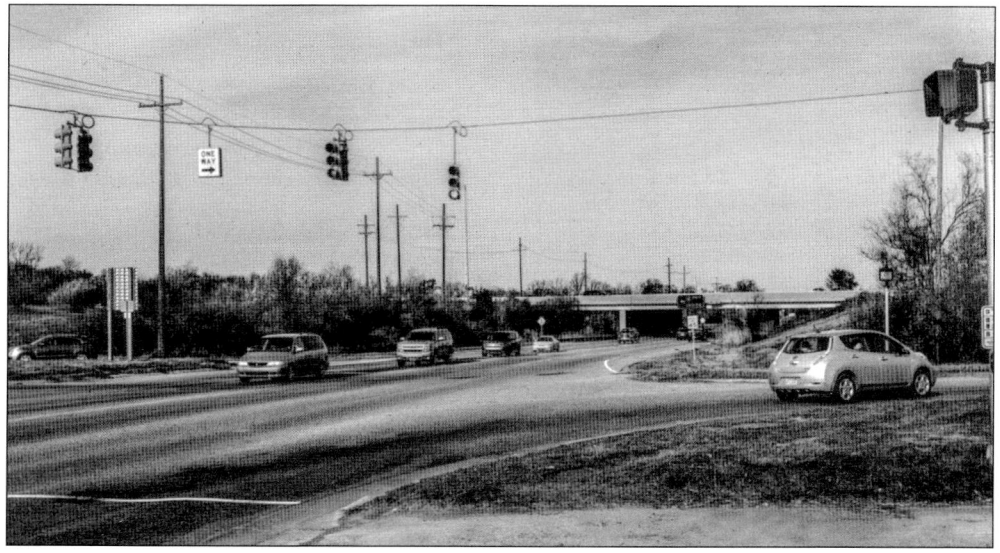

This is a 2014 picture of the bridge on Milford Road at Exit 155. (Courtesy of Jane and Jack Purslow.)

93

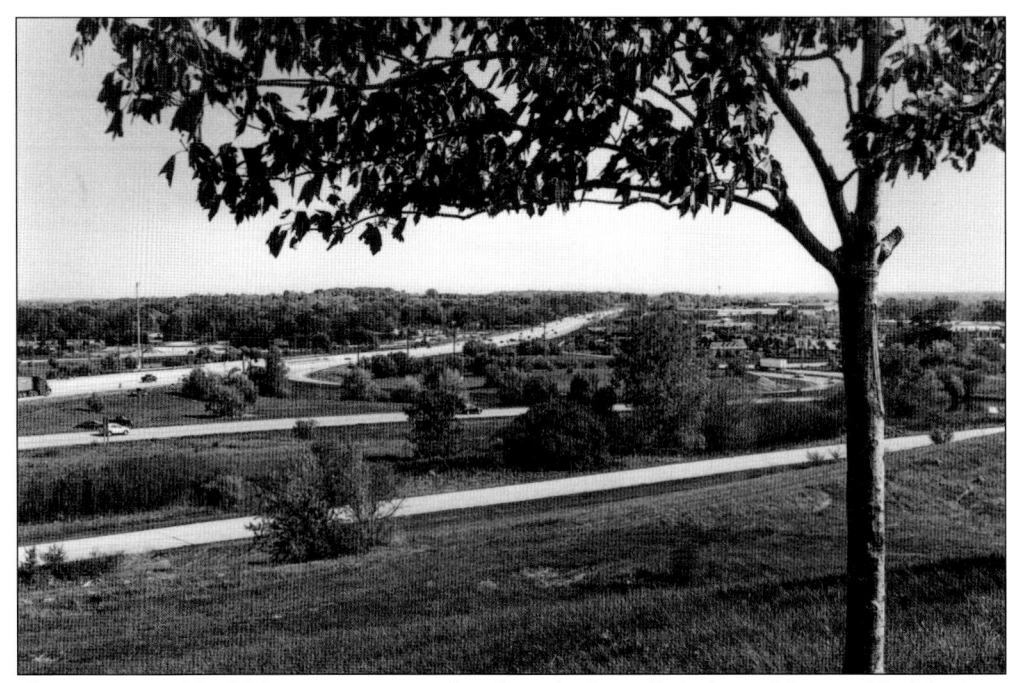

This overview of the I-96 expressway was taken from the James F. Atchison Memorial Park looking east in 2012. (Courtesy of Jane and Jack Purslow.)

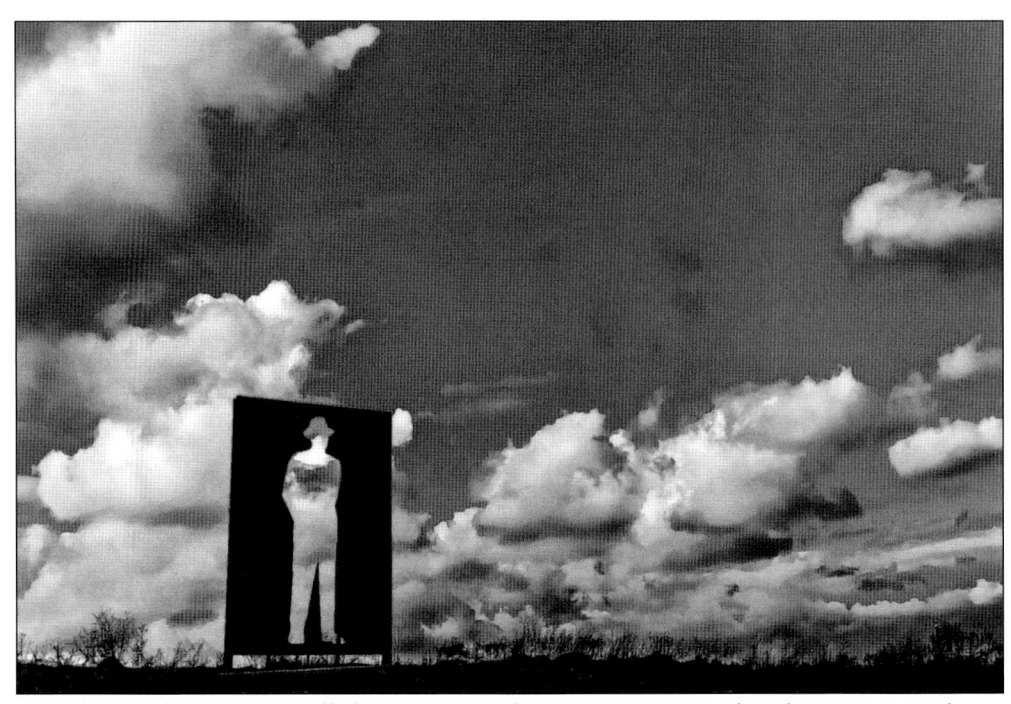

This abstract, by internationally known artist John Sauve, was erected in the James F. Atchison Memorial Park and overlooks the expressway. (Courtesy of Jane and Jack Purslow.)

Eight
TODAY

By 2013, Lyon Township had grown from a sleepy village to the fastest-growing single-family residential development in Oakland County, Michigan. It is also one of the most rapidly growing communities for overall development in the southeast part of the state.

In July 1963, zip codes were introduced by the United States Postal Service. Lyon Township had the dubious honor of having zip codes from five communities—New Hudson, Northville, Milford, South Lyon, and Wixom, which to this day has led to considerable confusion among residents and businesses. Many homes and businesses were physically located in the six square miles of the township, but they have mailing addresses from other communities.

The township boards and committees provide leadership to ensure a quality of life for its residents, protecting their health, welfare, and safety. Today, the Grand River Avenue and I-96 corridors are hallmarks of commercial and industrial growth.

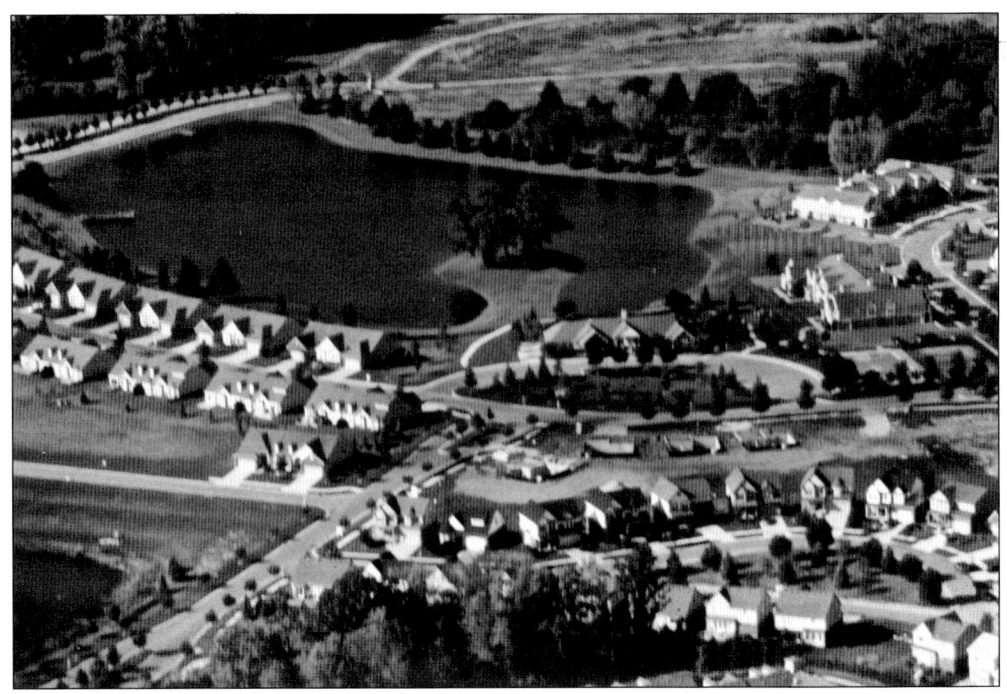

This is a typical subdivision in the township. Varying housing options include single-family homes, condominiums, and owner-occupied apartments. The open space with walking and bike paths provide an ambience of tranquility that is no doubt the envy of city dwellers. (Courtesy of Lyon Township.)

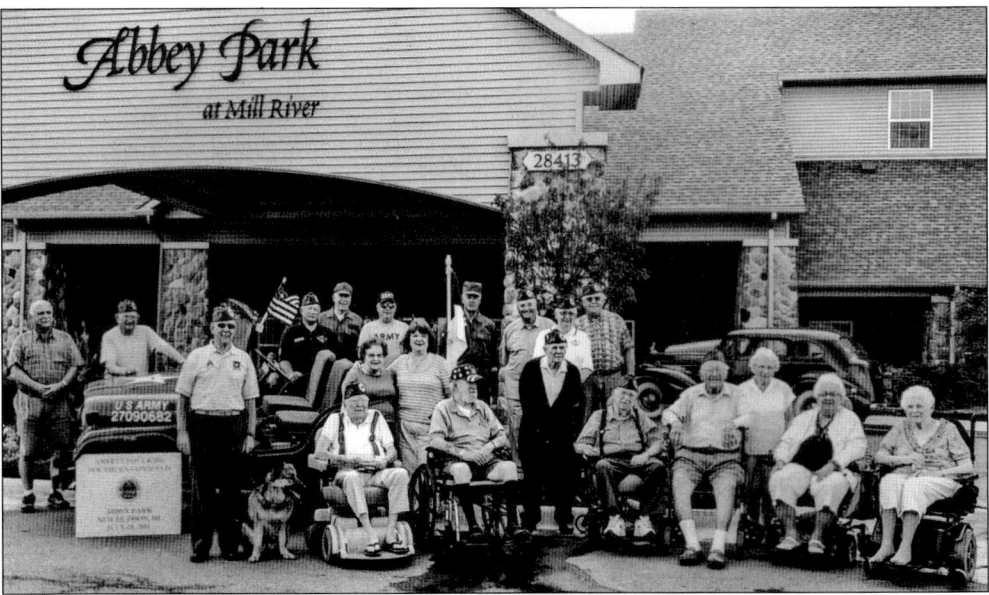

Many of the residents at Abbey Park at Mill River, a senior living facility, are veterans from World War II, the Korean Conflict, and Vietnam. A branch of the American Veterans (AMVETS) Post No. 2006 meets monthly to share memories. Pictured here are veterans, wives, and other Abbey Park residents at the conclusion of a meeting. Note the Army jeep shown. (Courtesy of Jane and Jack Purslow.)

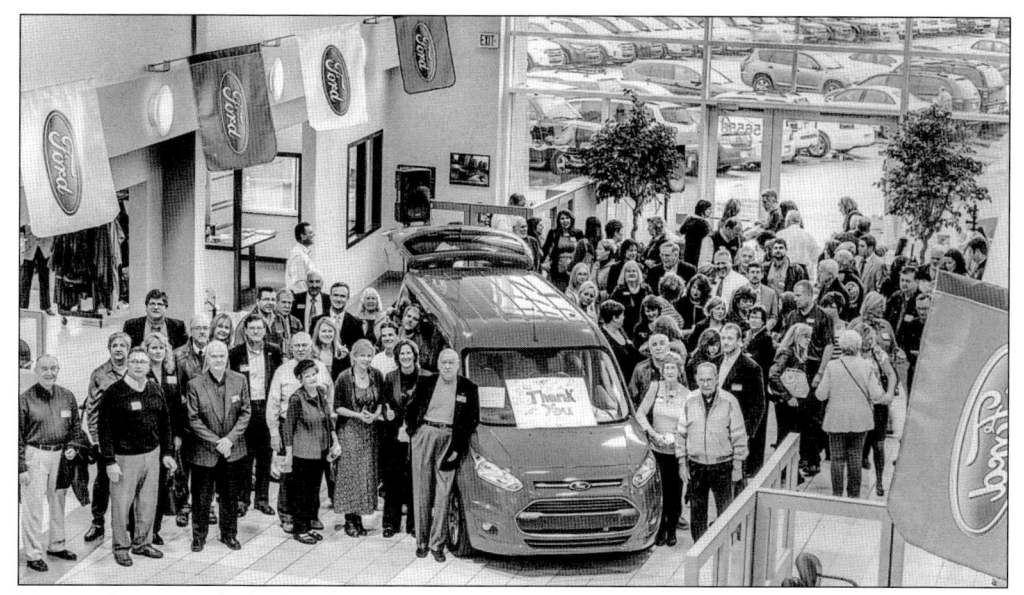

New Hudson once had a board of commerce that catered to agricultural issues. The South Lyon Area Chamber of Commerce replaced that board. The main goal remains the same—to promote business. It has evolved to meet the needs of current businesses and offers training, education, and networking opportunities. The chamber arranges periodic breakfasts hosted by a member business. This 2013 picture shows members of other area chambers, which often come together at events. (Courtesy of Jane and Jack Purslow.)

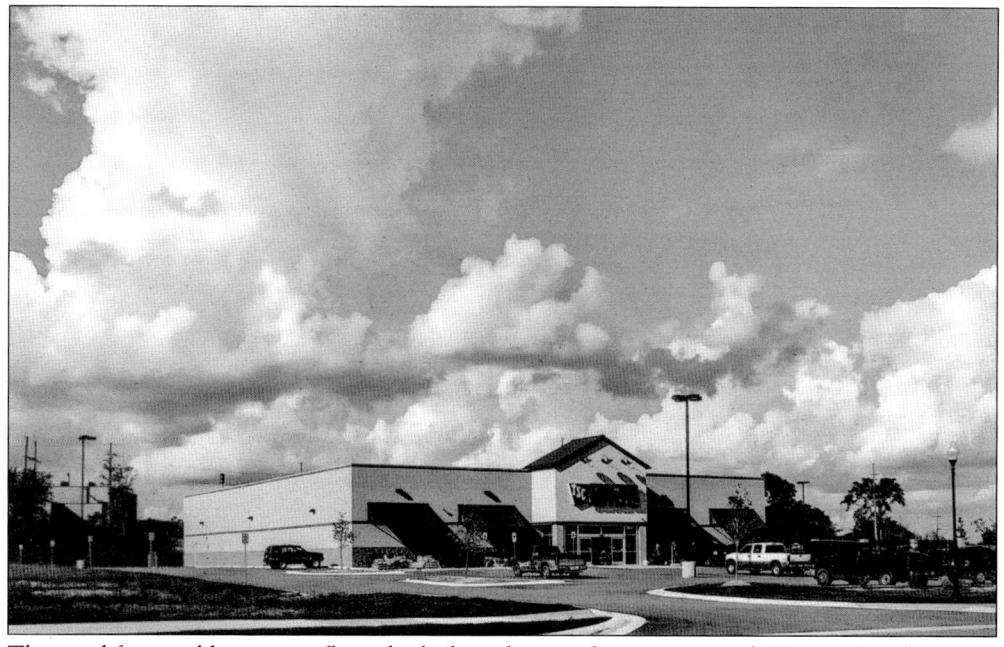

The need for retail businesses flourished when the population increased. Tractor Supply, one of the supporting companies, is located on the ring road and provides materials for full farms, hobby farms, and homes. (Courtesy of Jane and Jack Purslow.)

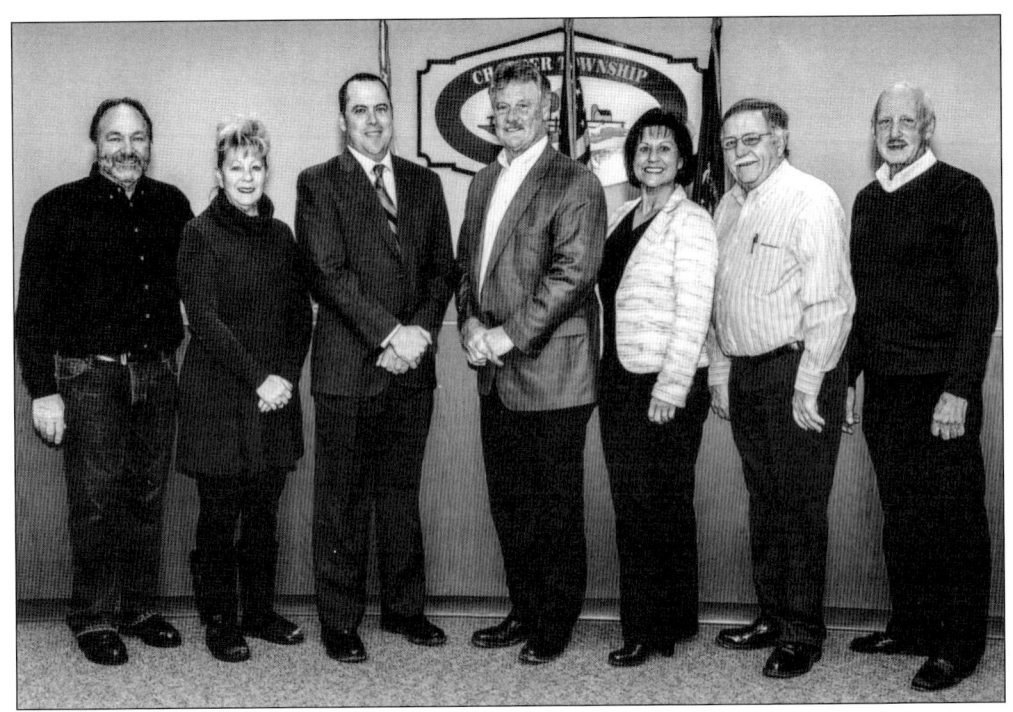

The Lyon Township Board of Trustees includes, from left to right, trustee John Dolan, treasurer Patty Carcone, trustee Sean O'Neil, supervisor Lannie Young, clerk Michele Cash, and trustees John Hicks and Steve Adams. (Courtesy of Jane and Jack Purslow.)

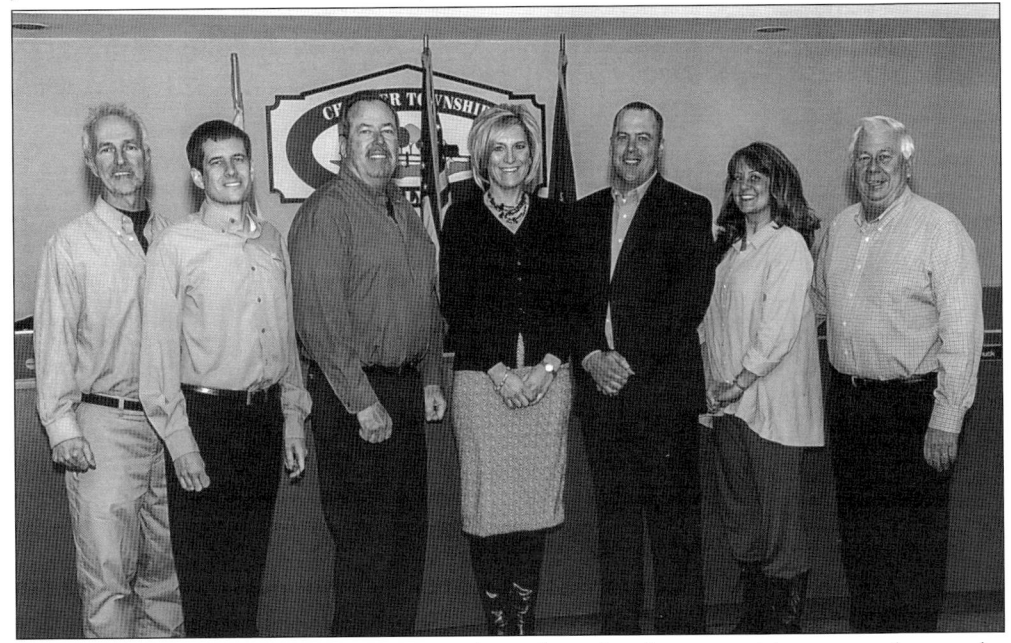

The Lyon Planning Commission recommends residential and commercial property plans to the township board and is instrumental in providing continuity in the community. From left to right are Michael Conflitti, Kris Enlow, Carl Towne, attorney Jennifer Gotti, Sean O'Neil, Deborah Sellis, and Jim Chuck. Ed Campbell is not pictured. (Courtesy of Jane and Jack Purslow.)

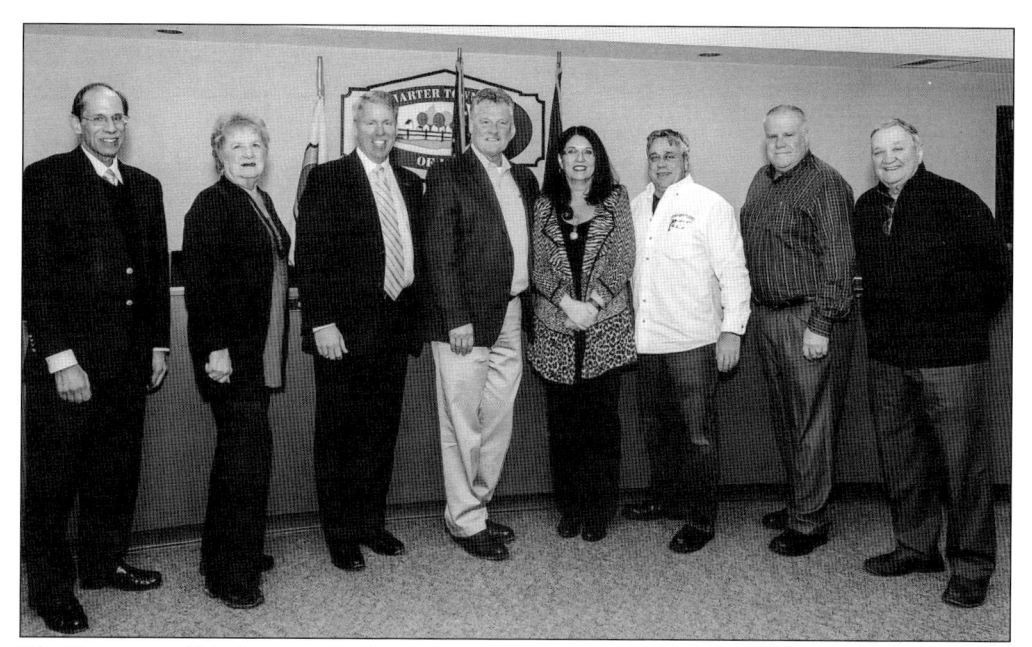

The Downtown Development Authority is commissioned to regenerate and develop the downtown area. Members have been instrumental in providing the infrastructure for the development of the ring roads and roundabouts in New Hudson. From left to right are Chris Doozen, consultant; Rose Case, administrative assistant; Bryan Wallace; Lannie Young; Tamra Ward; Jay Howie, chairman; Robert Heidrich; and John Bell, vice-chairman. Absent from this picture are Vincent DeAngelis and Mark Szerlag. (Courtesy of Jane and Jack Purslow.)

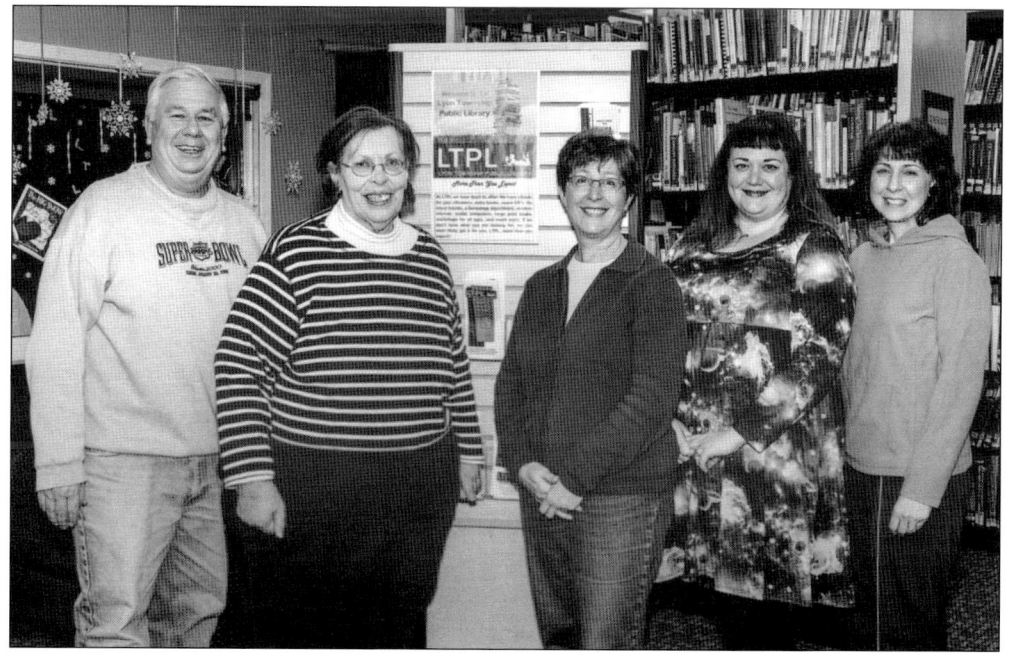

The Lyon Township Library Board includes, from left to right, Jim Chuck, Judy Rae, Alice FitzGerald, library director Holly Teasdle, and Amy Deeds. Missing from the photograph are Mary Pat Fruend and Sue Bell. (Courtesy of Jane and Jack Purslow.)

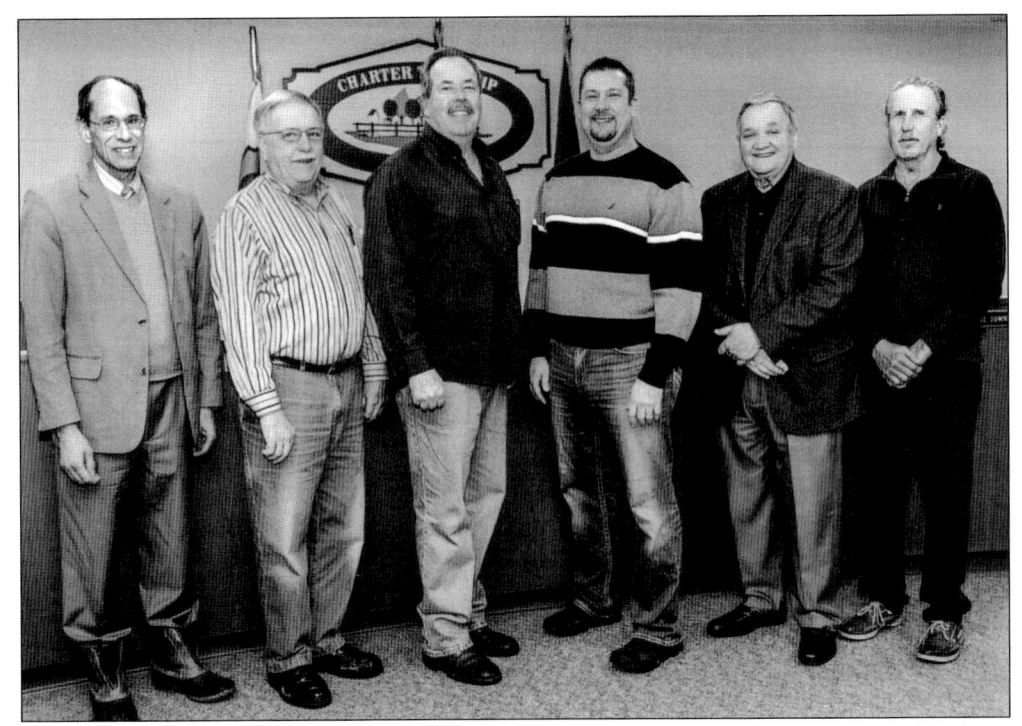

The Lyon Township Park and Recreation Advisory Board reviews proposals for park and facilities use. It makes recommendations to the township board for implementation. Pictured are, from left to right, Chris Doozen, consultant; John Hicks; Carl Towne; Scott Gerlach, chairman; John Bell; and Paul Peters. Missing are Jennie Urtel, Dean Whitcomb, Nancy Kessler, and Jason Bibby. (Courtesy of Jane and Jack Purslow.)

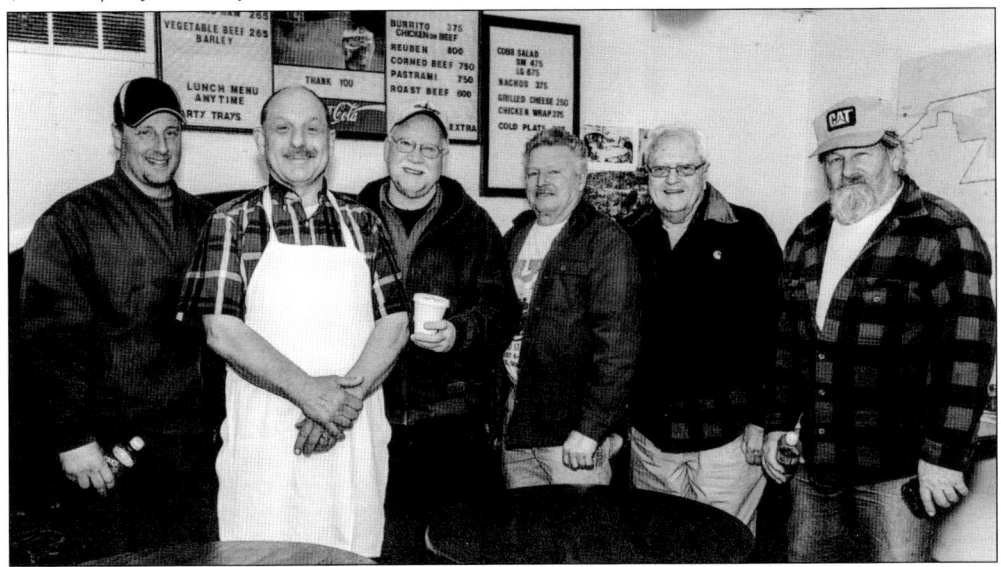

The Table of Knowledge members change daily with whoever shows up for early breakfast to debate and sometimes argue the issues of the day at Bob's Carry Out. From left to right are Phil Jones, Bob Herc, Dana Kittridge, Randy Hall, Bob Langan, and Darrell Fletcher. (Courtesy of Jane and Jack Purslow.)

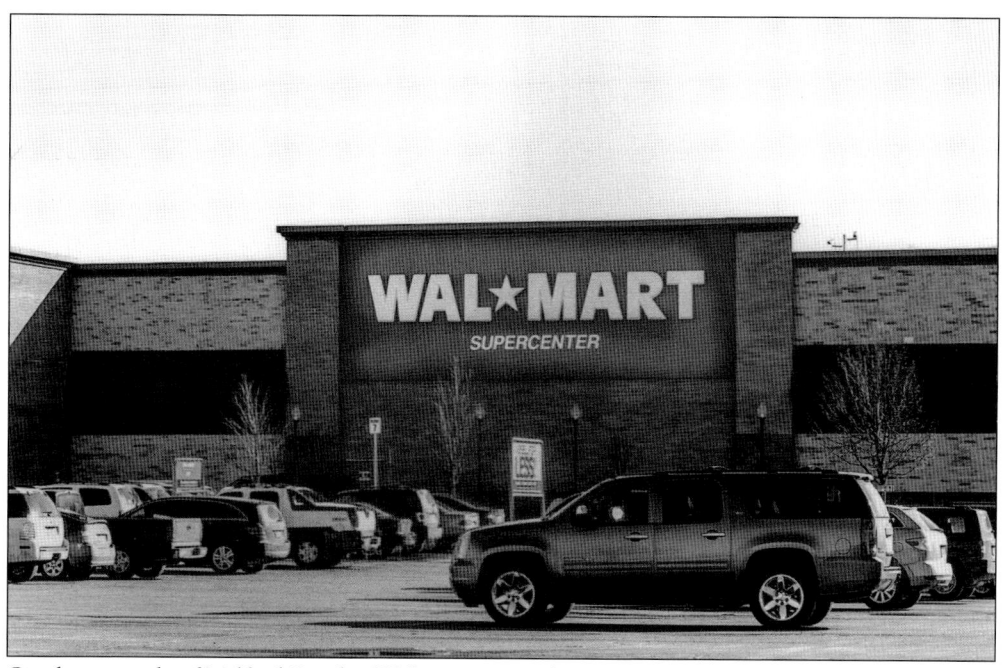

On the east side of Milford Road is Walmart, an anchor at Lyon Center East, the hub of current retail in New Hudson. Other chains represented in that area are Lowe's, Liberty Chevrolet, McDonald's, Applebee's, and several banks. (Courtesy of Jane and Jack Purslow.)

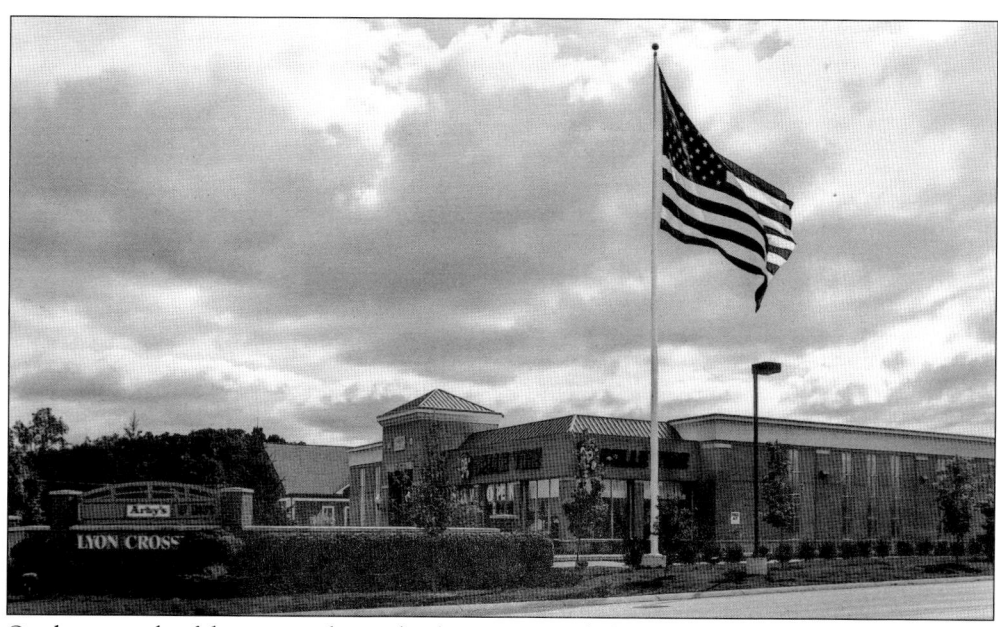

On the west side of the ring road are other businesses, including Belle Tire, Arby's, Tractor Supply, and Flagstar Bank. (Courtesy of Jane and Jack Purslow.)

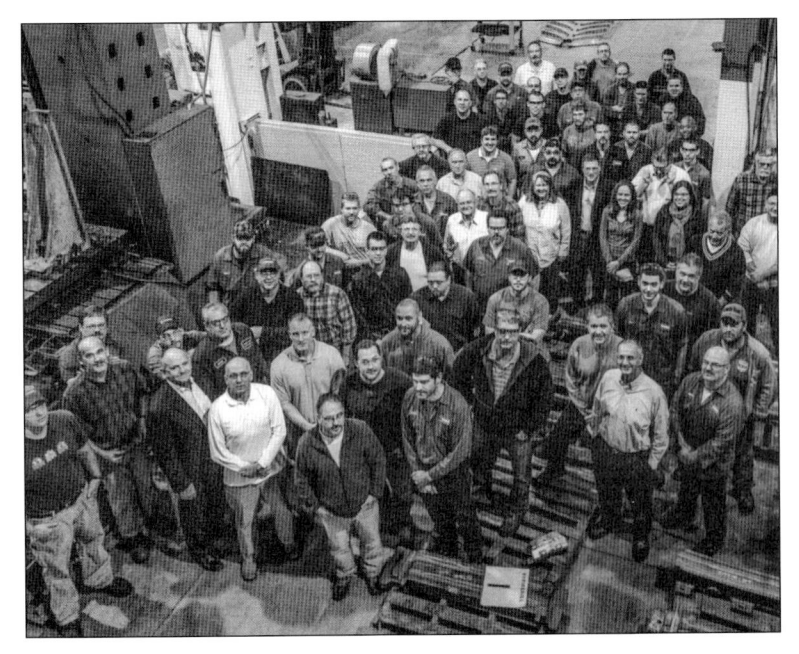

The Richards Tool and Die workforce is shown here during the company's ribbon-cutting ceremony; something the township usually does to welcome new businesses. This new manufacturing business joined the township in 2012. It provides tools for stamping sheet-metal parts for small and large companies. (Courtesy of Jane and Jack Purslow.)

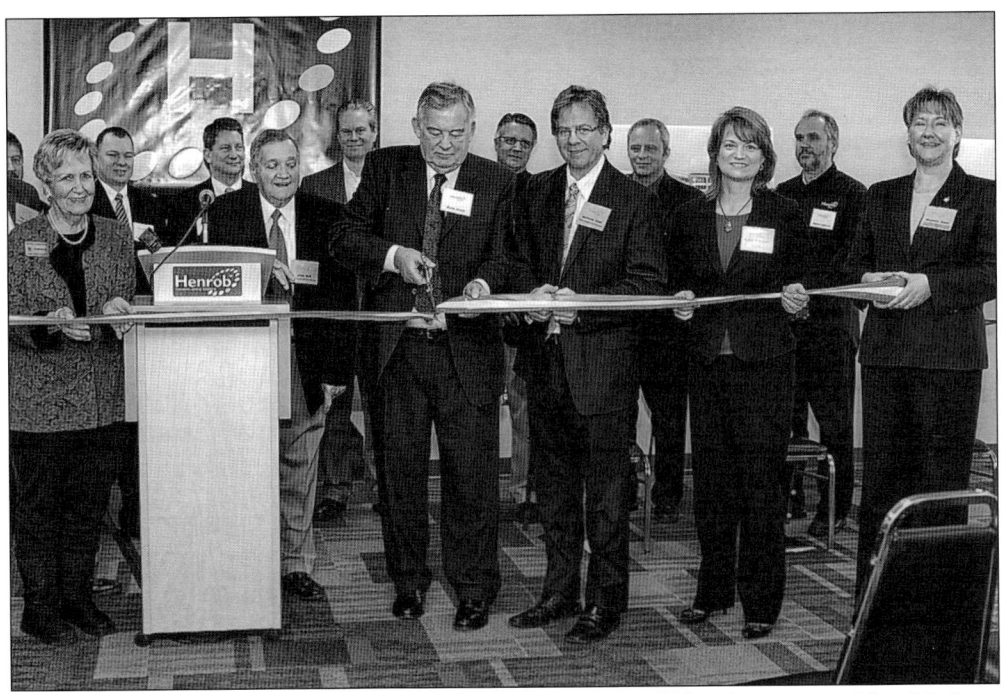

In 2014, Henrob Corporation heralds the opening of their world headquarters in New Hudson. Keith Jones, company president, and Matthew A. Gibb, assistant Oakland County executive, cut the ribbon. Oakland County commissioner Cathy Crawford; John Bell, Downtown Development Authority (DDA) vice-chairperson; and Michelle Aniol, DDA administrator, are among the people shown. Plans are under way to add additional buildings to accommodate the company's growth. (Courtesy of Jane and Jack Purslow.)

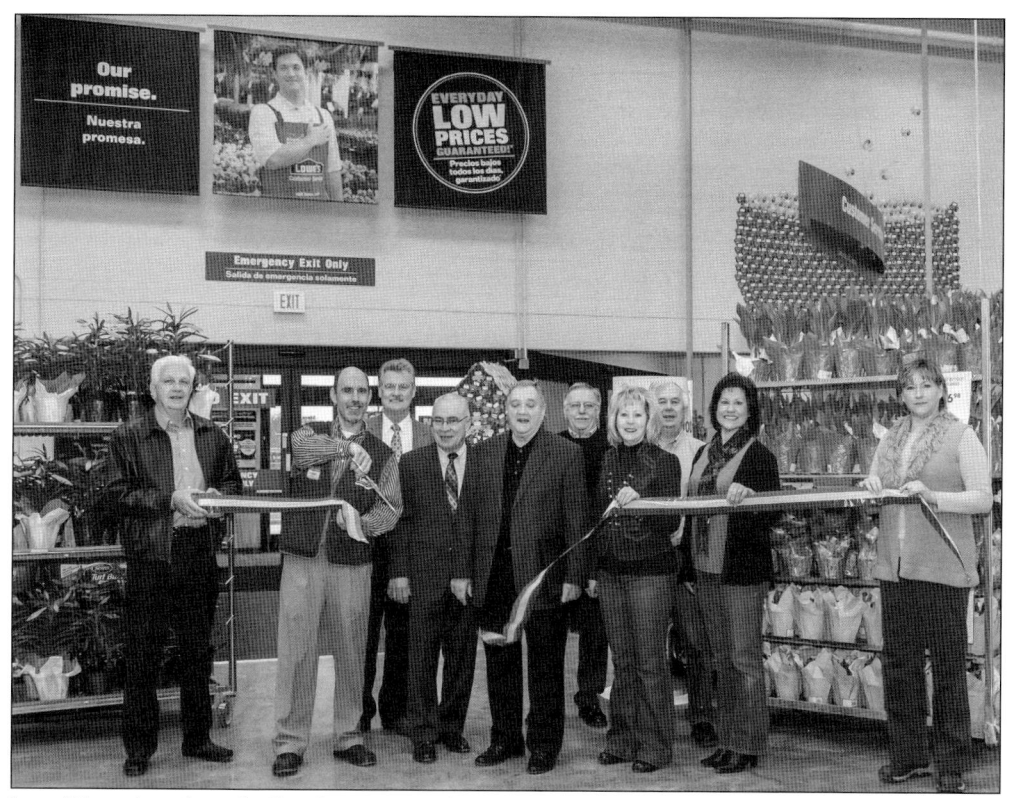

Lyon Township elected officials join in with Lowe's store manager Todd Amprin during a ribbon-cutting ceremony in 2013 as the national chain store launches a new gardening season. (Courtesy of Jane and Jack Purslow.)

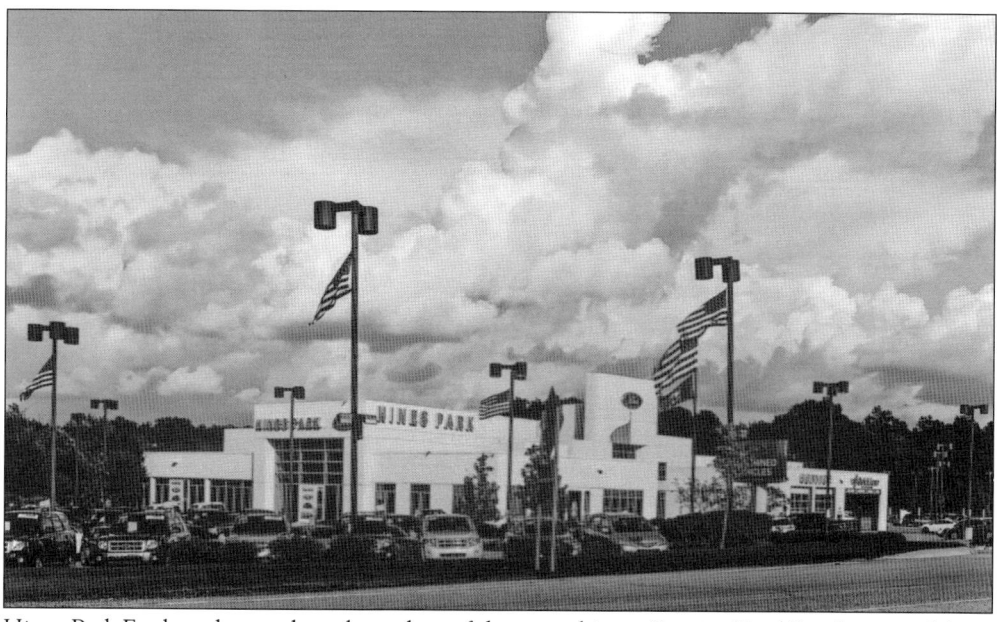

Hines Park Ford on the northern boundary of the township on Pontiac Trail Road is one of three new car and truck dealers in the New Hudson area. (Courtesy of Jane and Jack Purslow.)

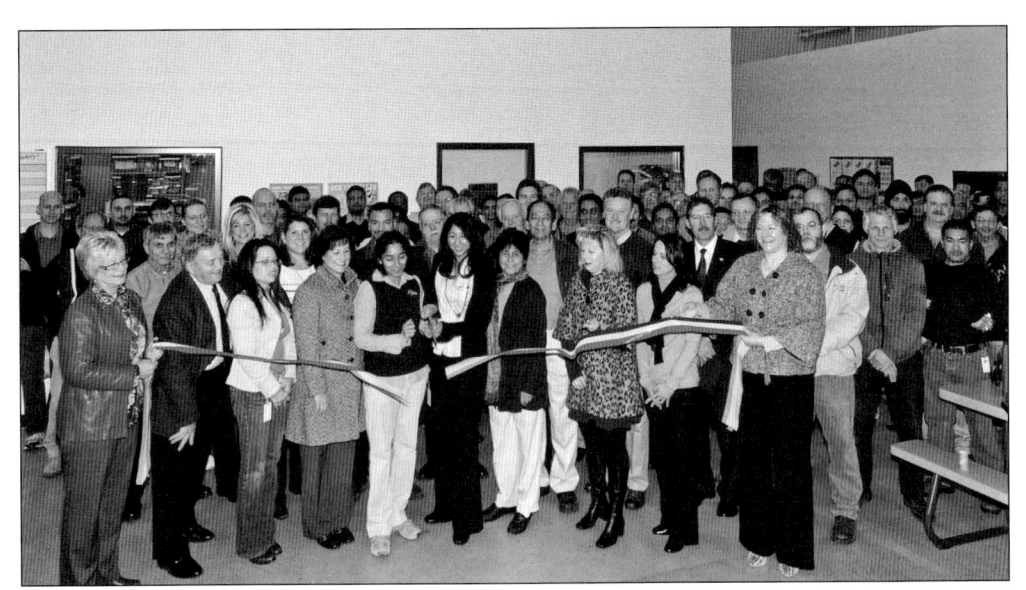

A ribbon cutting at Testek, Inc., welcomes the company that provides intense technology for equipment testing. Testek, Inc., designs and builds custom, complex test systems for aerospace, automotive, and industrial sectors. (Courtesy of Jane and Jack Purslow.)

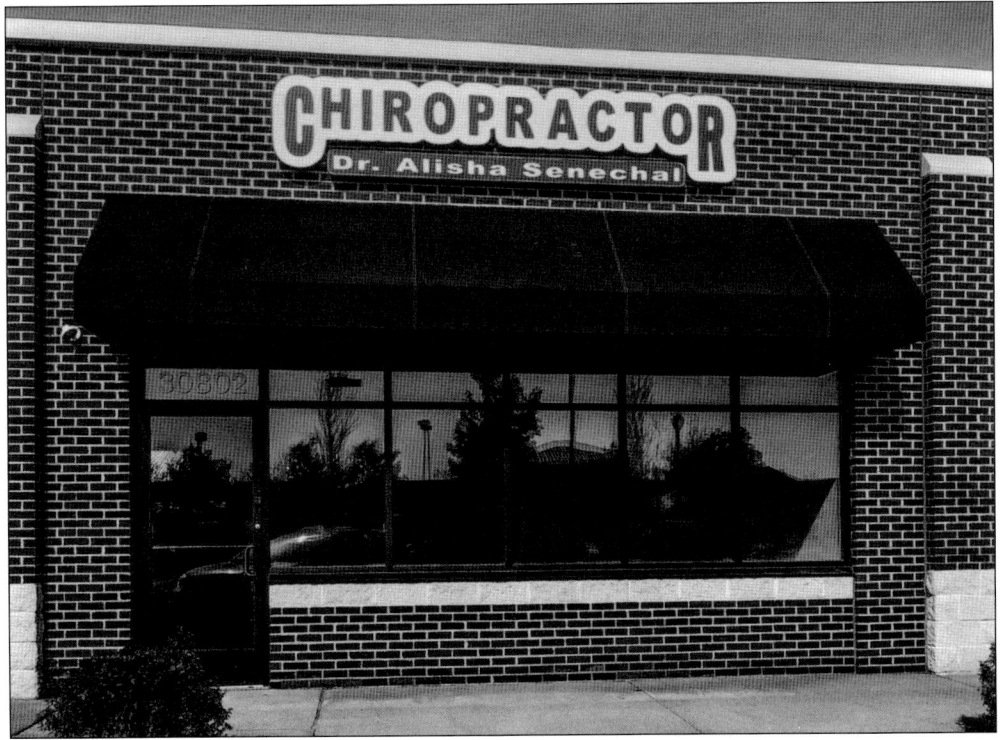

The early settlers from the Eastern states had one medical doctor. There were no dentists at that time. By 2014, medical services have expanded to include four doctors, two dentists, and four drugstores. Following the residential growth in New Hudson, Senechal chiropractic practice moved to Lyon Center Drive East in 2012. The family practice includes another location in Novi. (Courtesy of Jane and Jack Purslow.)

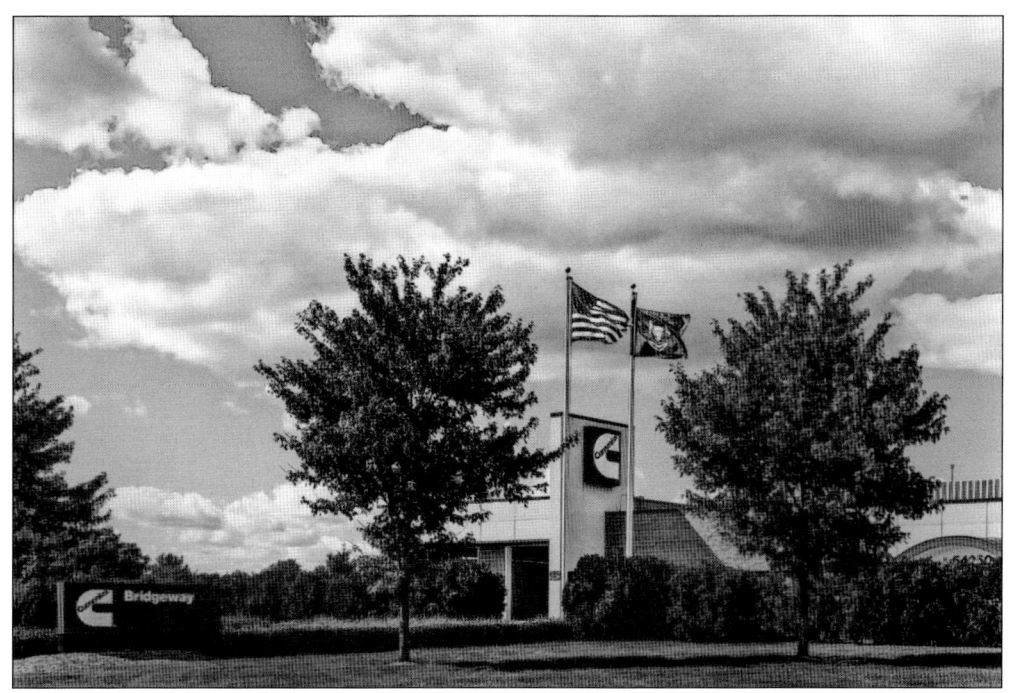

Bridgeway Cummins is located on the Grand River Avenue industrial corridor. The company produces engines and provides services and repairs. Cummins engines are used in buses, commercial trucks, motor homes, and cement mixers. Additionally, the company manufactures generators for use in industrial applications. (Courtesy of Jane and Jack Purslow.)

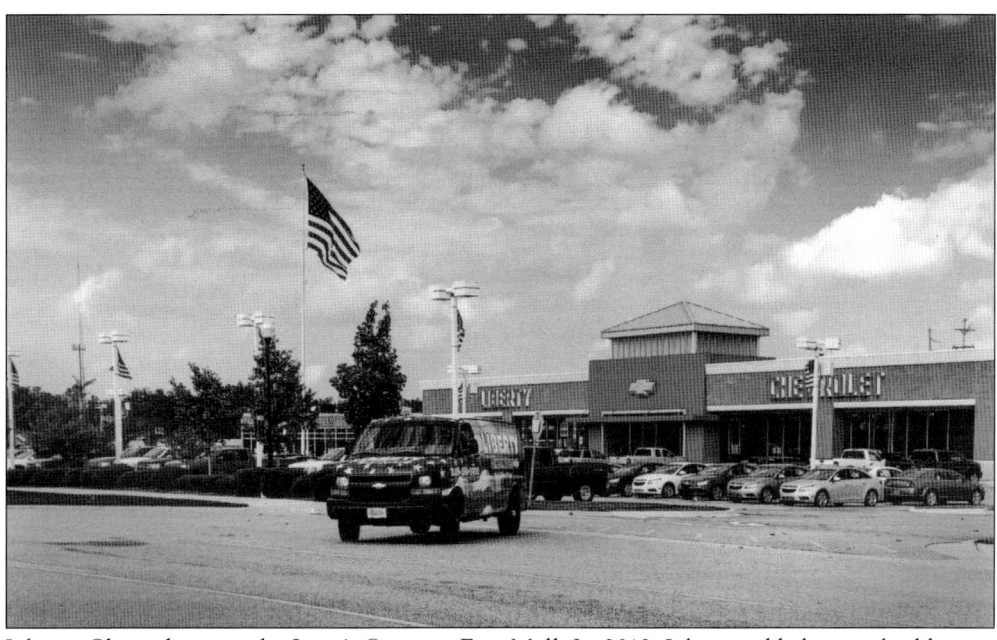

Liberty Chevrolet is in the Lyon's Crossing East Mall. In 2012, Liberty added a new building to house KIA and Hyundai. (Courtesy of Jane and Jack Purslow.)

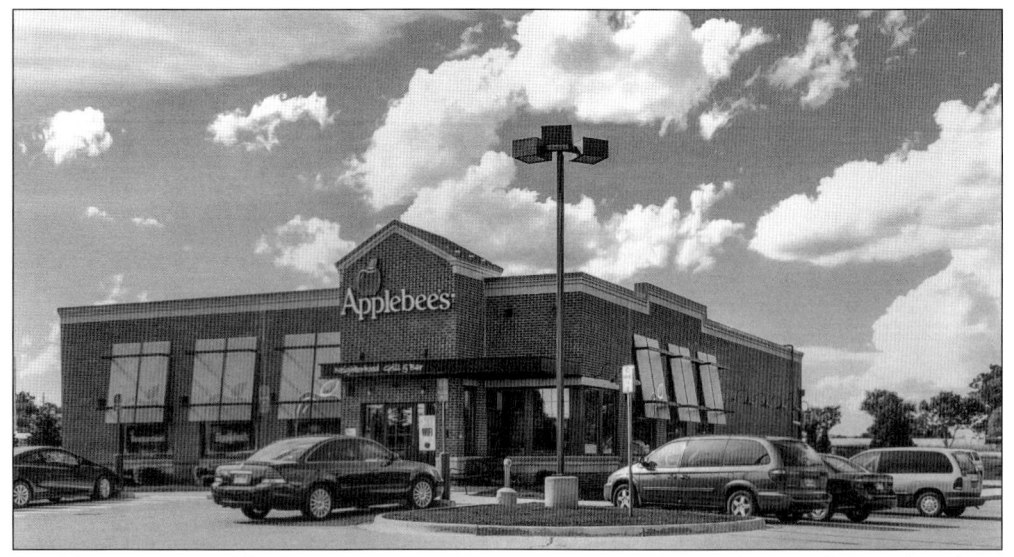

Applebee's was one of the first restaurants in Lyon Center East to provide a stop for travelers along I-96. The restaurant was redecorated in 2011 and includes historical pictures of New Hudson and the surrounding areas. (Courtesy of Jane and Jack Purslow.)

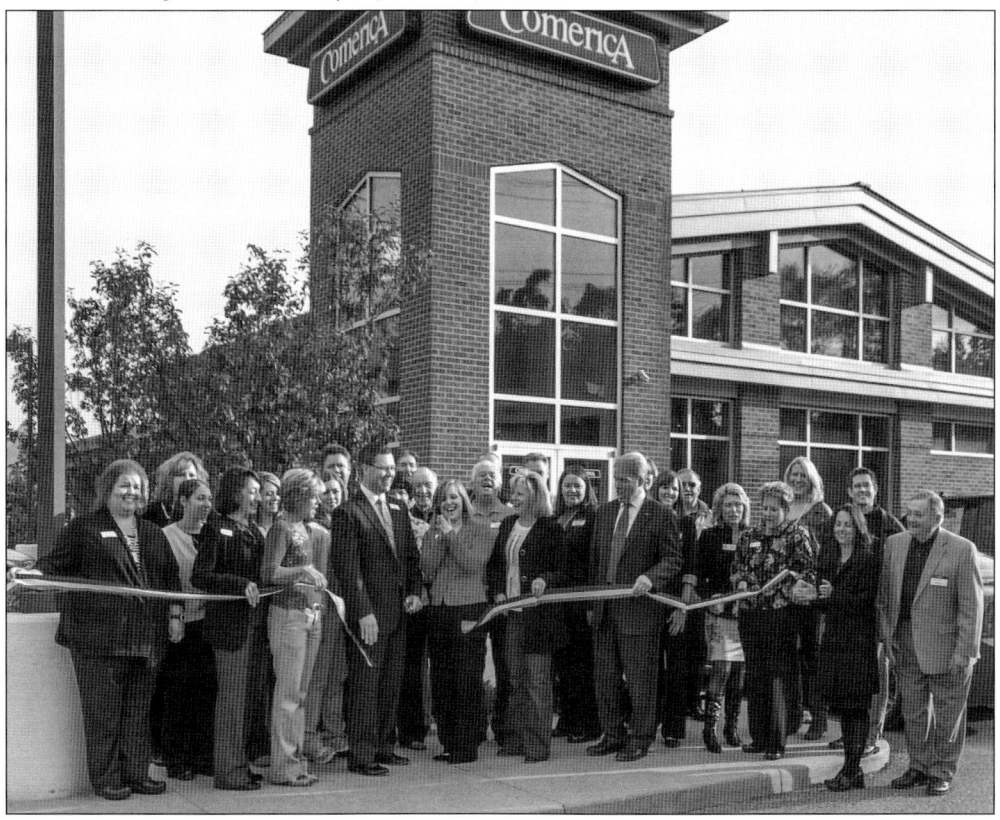

A ribbon-cutting ceremony takes place at the Comerica Bank, located on Grand River Avenue and Pontiac Trail Road, in 2012. The building was originally the location of Dr. Tucker's drugstore and post office in the township's early years. (Courtesy of Jane and Jack Purslow.)

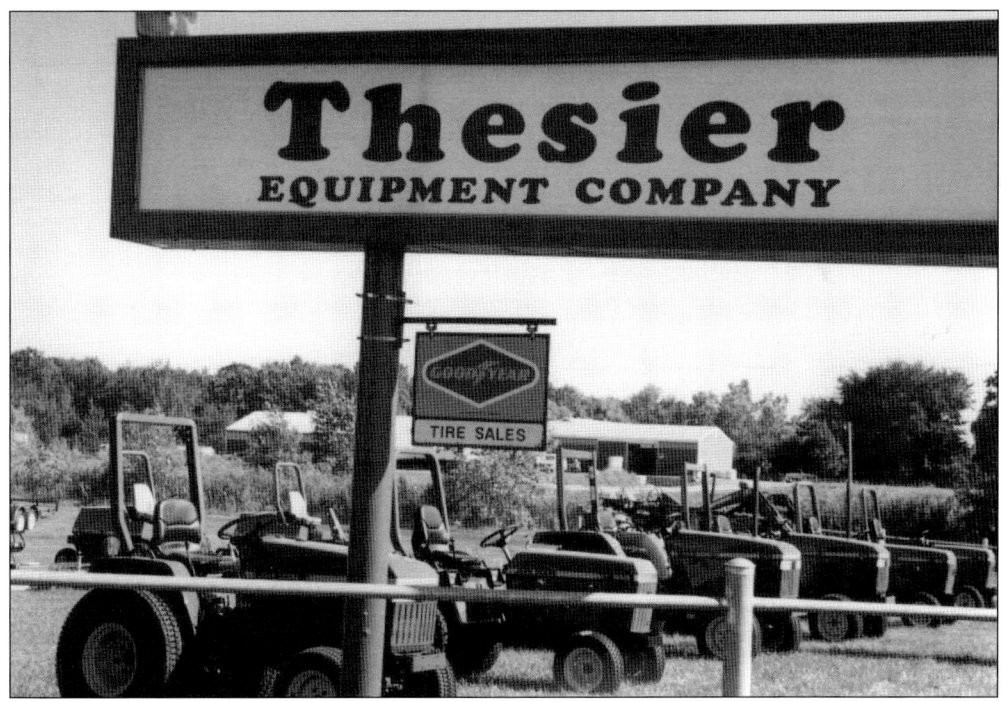

Thesier Equipment Company, currently known as Bader & Son, is centrally located in the township on Pontiac Trail Road and provides tractor and lawn equipment. H.C. Arms, a longtime resident of the area, worked for Thesier for 29 years. The original Thesier Building was a converted dairy barn at a time when farming was prominent in the area, Harms recalled in 2014. (Courtesy of Jane and Jack Purslow.)

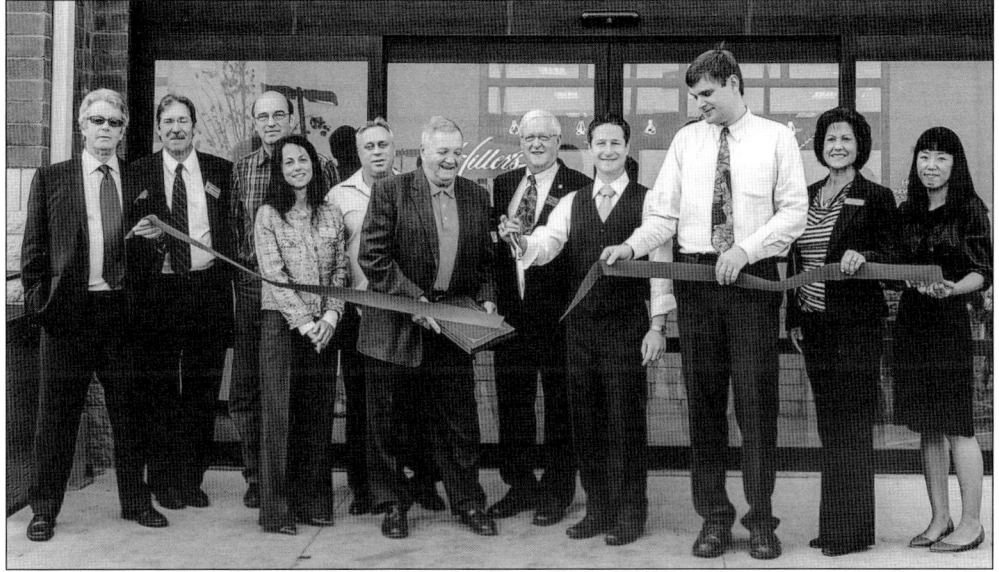

In 2013, Hiller's Market launched one of the newest retail businesses in a growing area of the township on Ten Mile Road and Johns Road. Company owners Jim Hiller and Justin Hiller pride themselves on their efforts to incorporate environmentally friendly options in the building design. They also give shoppers a choice among hard-to-find items. (Courtesy of Jane and Purslow.)

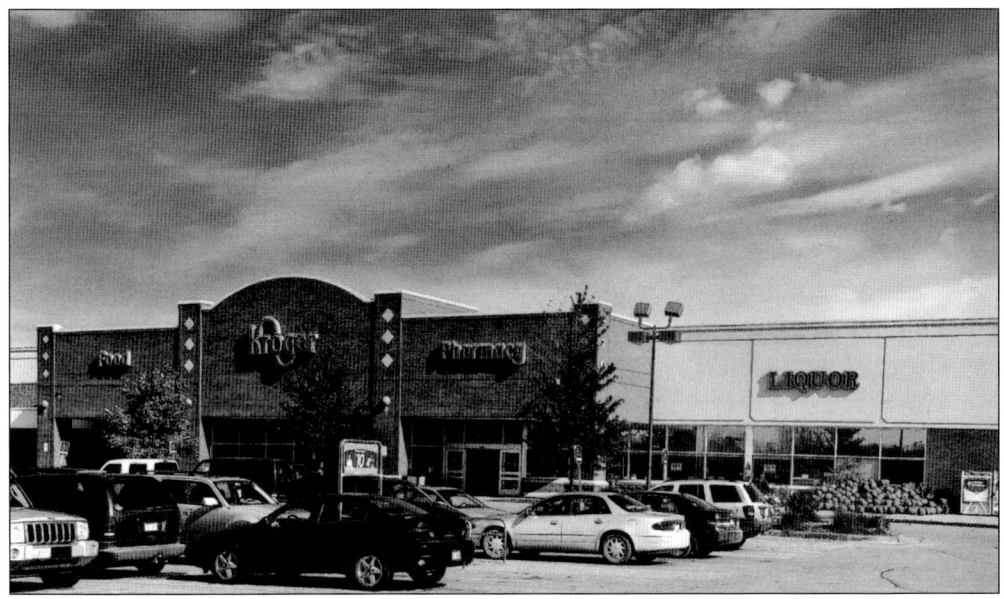

Although a lot of the business development has been on the northern end of the township, the southern end has also seen growth in residential and retail. The businesses in the mall are the center of activity for the area. Kroger supermarket added a gas station in 2013, and it draws a lot of traffic on Pontiac Trail and Eight Mile Roads. (Courtesy of Jane and Jack Purslow.)

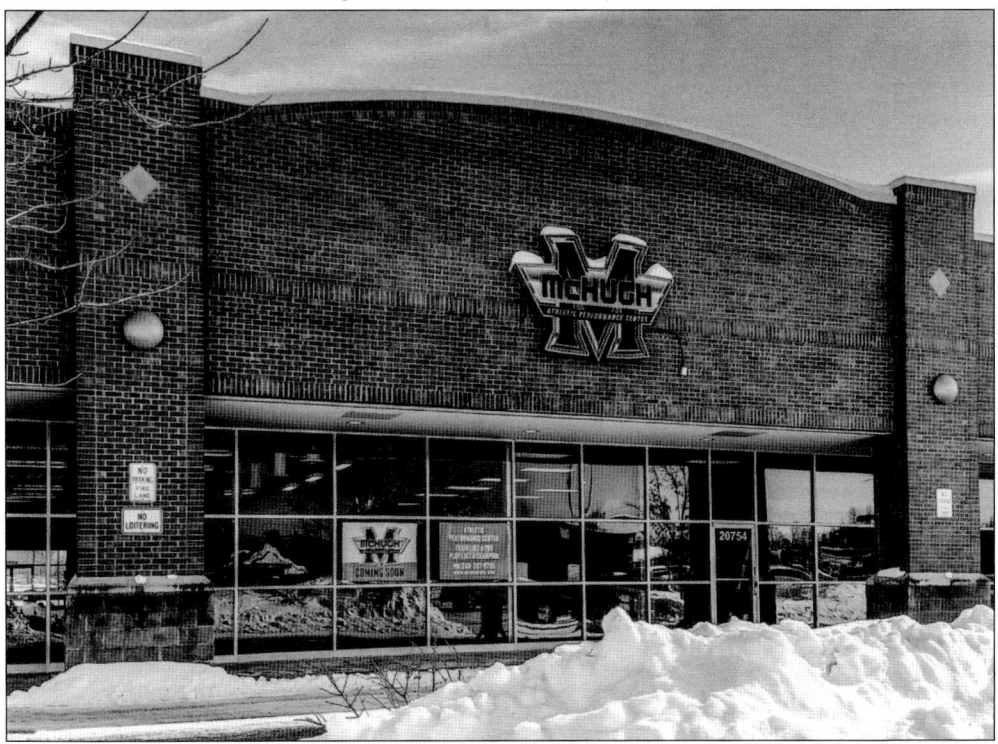

A recent addition to the Kroger shopping center is McHugh Performance Center, which is owned and operated by former National Football League player Sean McHugh. (Courtesy of Jane and Jack Purslow.)

Nine

COMMUNITY SERVICES

A rich history of police, fire, library, and recreational services are the cornerstones of Lyon Township. Police services have been provided by the Oakland County Sheriff's Office with a substation in the Lyon Township municipal center. Some of the services provided are traffic patrol, a crime lab, a special investigative unit, a warrants division, and a fugitive apprehension team.

The formal fire department began with Chief Fred Burt. He was followed by Chief Robert Pollock and then Chief Franklin Knapp, who also owned and operated the gas station at the six-point intersection in New Hudson. Knapp was followed by his son Junior Knapp. Les Cash served the longest as the township's fire chief. He was in the position from 1969 to 2008. Cash was followed by Ron McClain, who was replaced by Kenneth Van Sparrentak in 2013.

The department handles fire suppression, motor vehicle accident rescues, ice rescues, and public fire prevention and education. The department also provides basic life support transport and handled more than 1,100 calls in 2013.

The Lyon Township Public Library was once a branch of the South Lyon Library and was located in a New Hudson school. It moved to the old township hall and finally found a home on Milford Road. There have been two expansions. The library was also used as a community center where families often held reunions. The current director is Holly Teasdle.

The recreational opportunities are boundless at James F. Atchison Memorial Park, which was formerly a landfill that, for a long period of time, provided electricity to the DTE grid. It is now used for many youth sports and festivals.

Special events at the park provide another big draw to the community. The annual Kite Festival brings in thousands of people to see the aerial wonderland as kites, in all sizes, shapes, and value, take flight. The Winter Festival is a cold-weather wonderland with dogsled races and rides, as well as scores of other sports represented. Annual circuses, carnivals, and bike races also take place at the popular meeting ground.

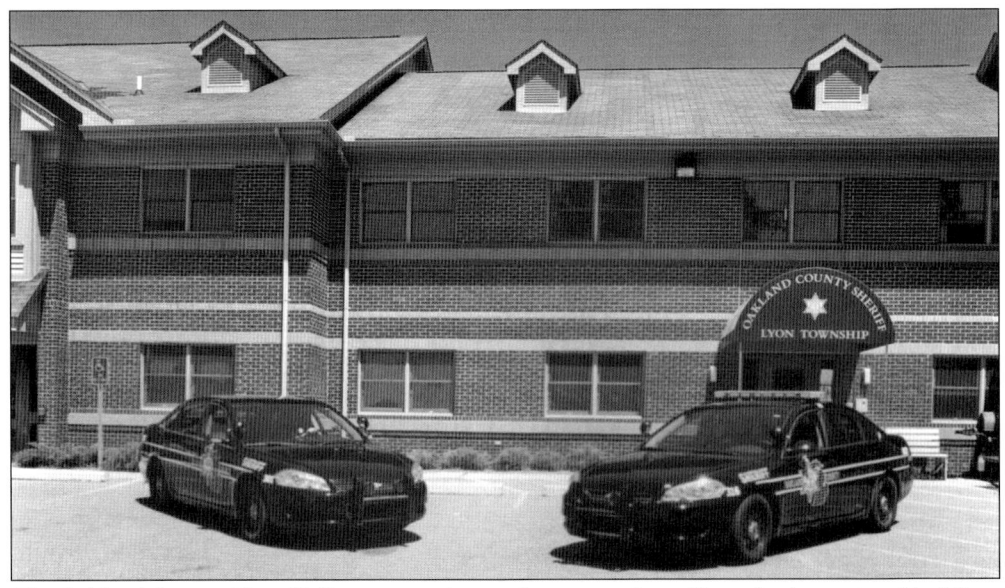

The Oakland County Sheriff's Department has a substation in Lyon Township's municipal building. Past substation commanders included Sergeants Jansson, Wurtz, Sutton, and Crockett. Sgt. Mark Venus is in charge in 2014. The township has seven-day, 24-hour road patrols and detectives on site. This service started in 1982. (Courtesy of Jane and Jack Purslow.)

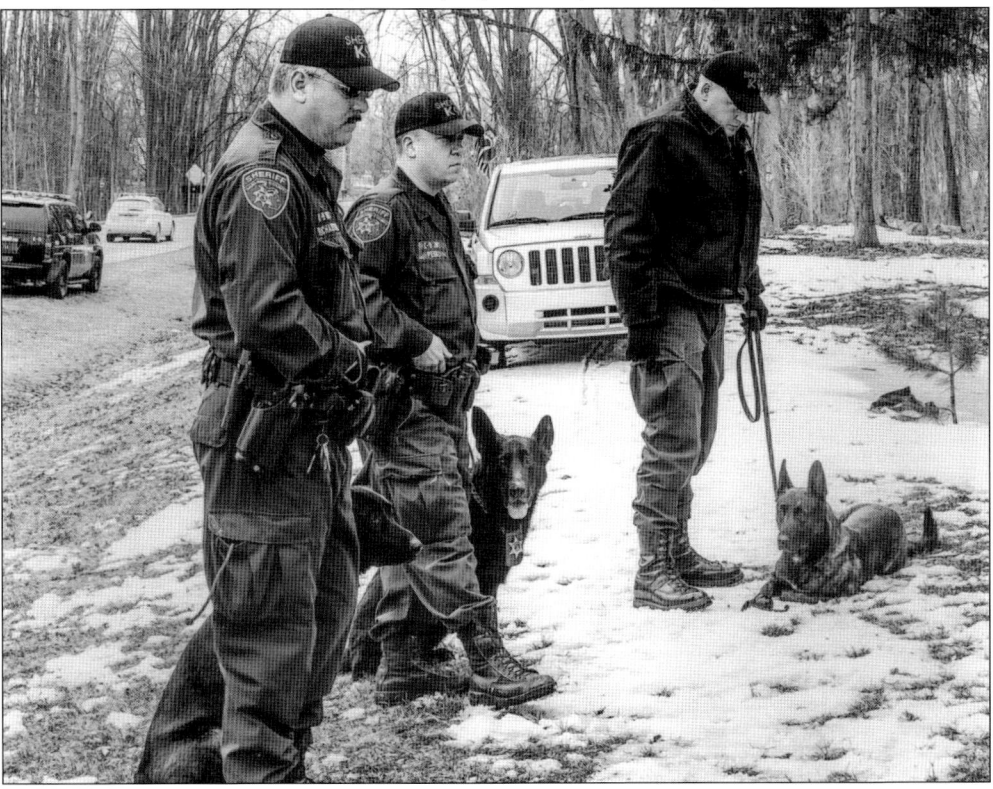

Oakland County Sheriff's Department provides dog tracking, which has been responsible for solving a number of local cases. (Courtesy of Jane and Jack Purslow.)

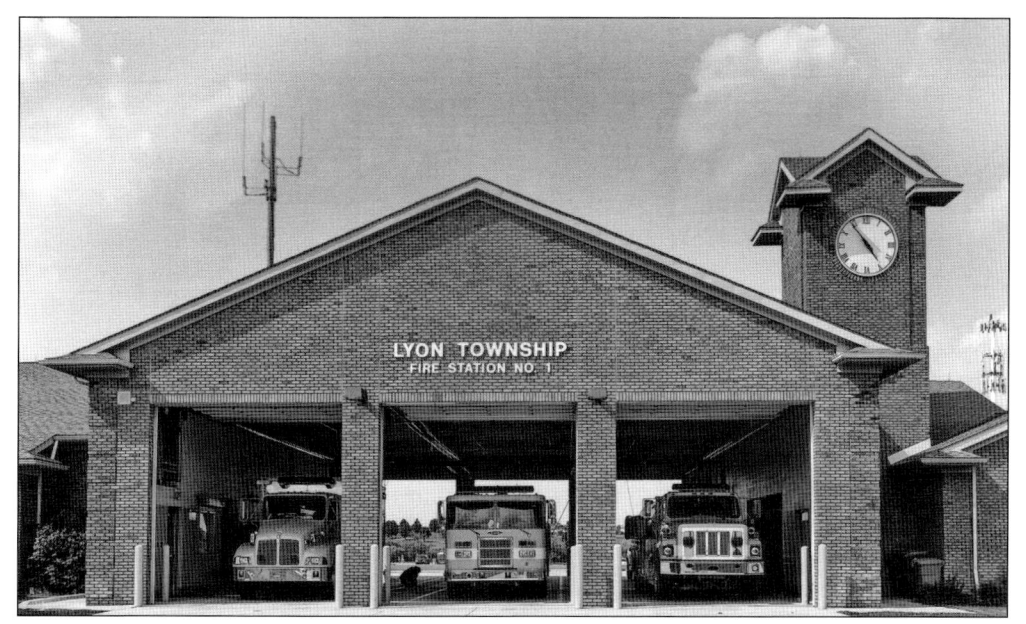

Lyon Township has two fire stations. Station No. 1 is shown here west of the municipal center on Grand River Avenue. Station No. 2 is located on Ten Mile Road east of Milford Road. Fire services and improved response times provided by the fire department has reduced insurance fire ratings, resulting in home insurance savings for residents and businesses. (Courtesy of Jane and Jack Purslow.)

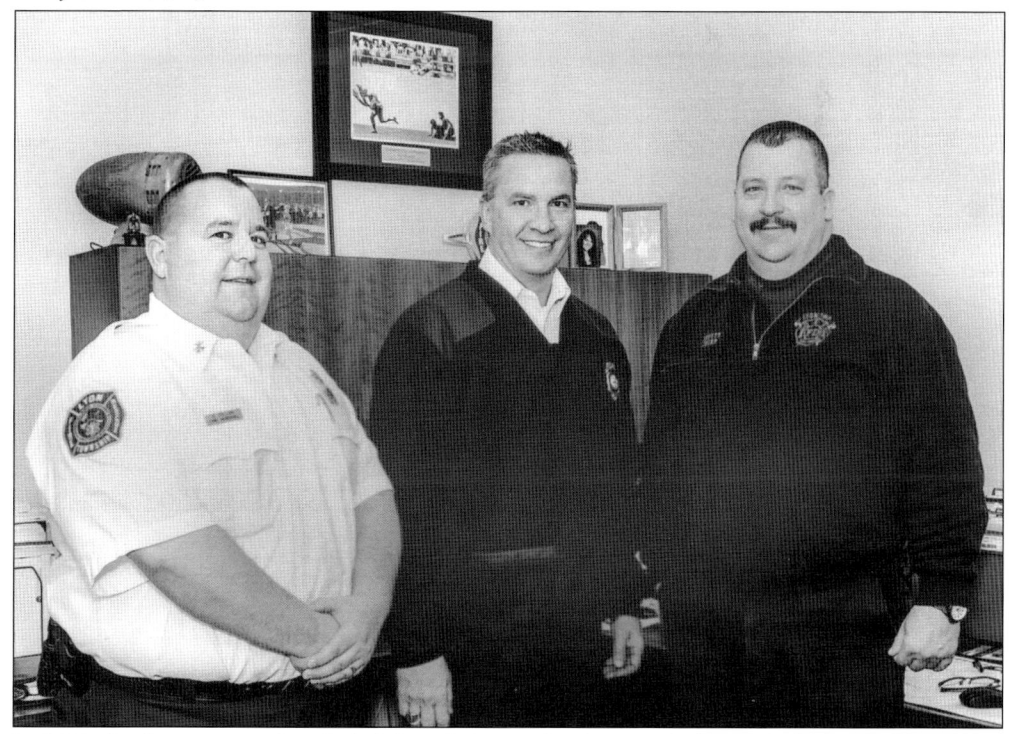

In 2014, the fire command included, from left to right, fire marshal Don Collick, Chief Ken Van Sparrentak, and deputy fire chief Doug Berry. (Courtesy of Jane and Jack Purslow.)

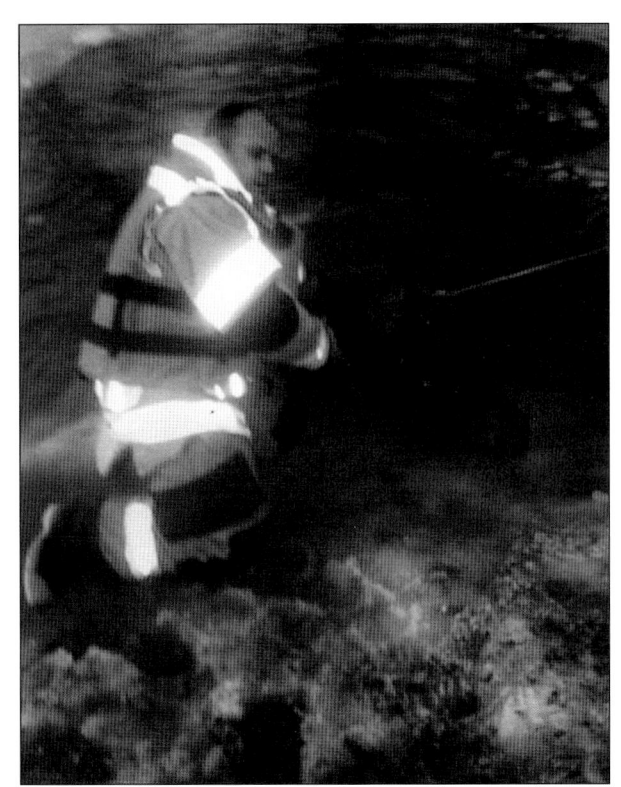

Lyon firefighters came to the rescue of a horse that fell through an icy pond in New Hudson. Fire Marshal Don Collick called Michigan State University Veterinary Department for life support instructions. An animal rescue mask was used to give the horse oxygen. Dandy Acres, a local veterinarian clinic, donated animal masks to the fire department for use on small and big animals. The horse survived the ordeal. (Courtesy of Lyon Township Fire Department.)

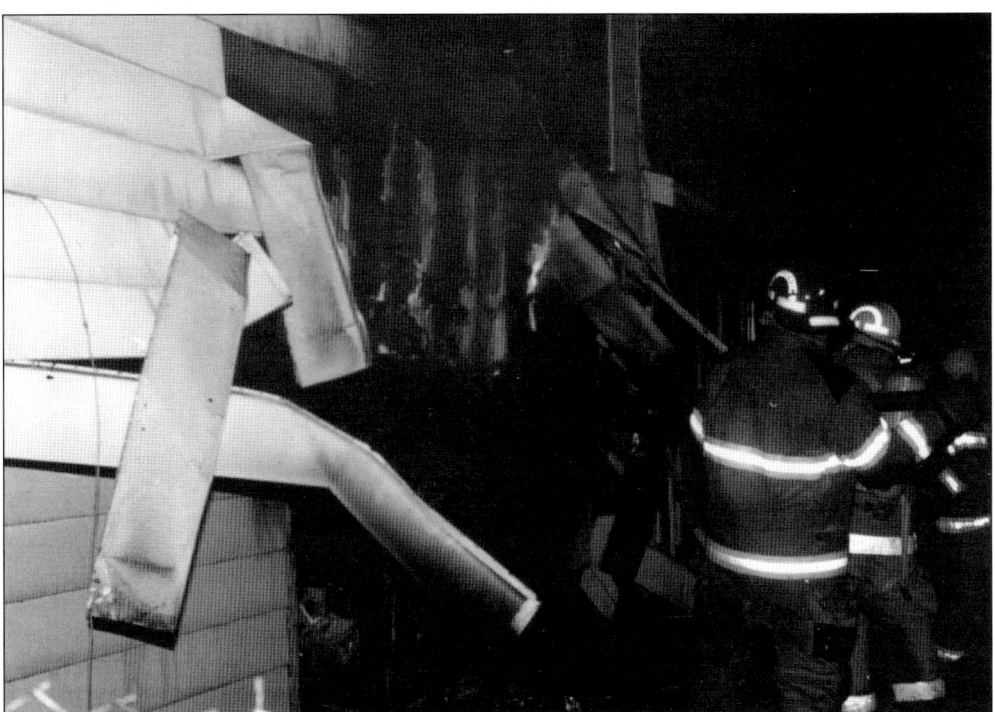

On average, 1,100 calls annually are made to the Lyon Fire Department. This home fire was contained by the quick action of firefighters. (Courtesy of Lyon Township Fire Department.)

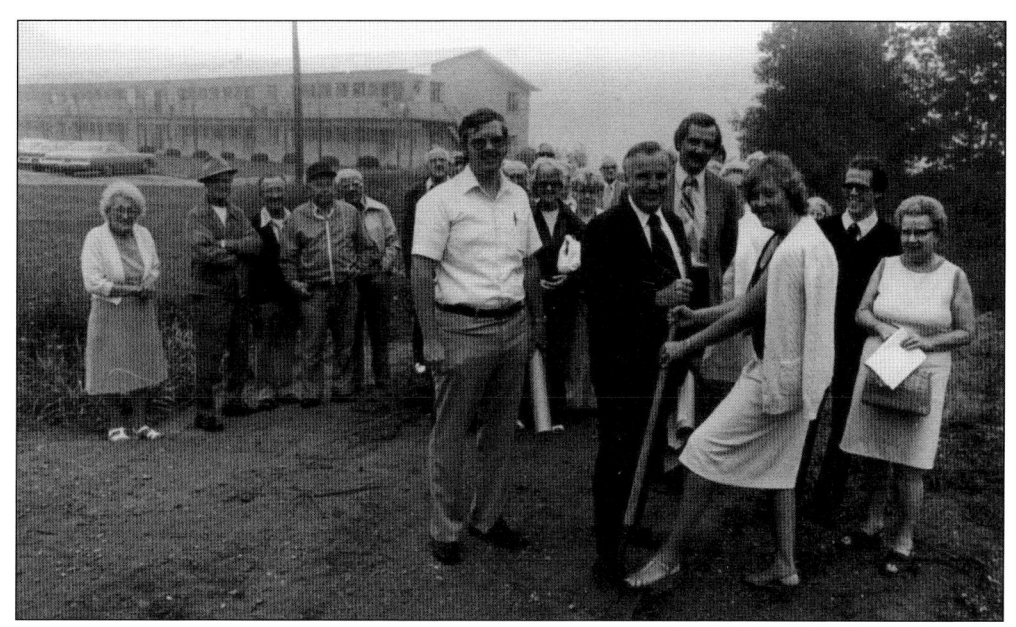

The ground breaking for the new library and community center on Milford Road took place in the spring of 1979. Jim Helfer, who donated the property for the library, and township supervisor Sue Knapp hold the shovel for this ceremony. Also pictured is township clerk Mary Canfield. Residents observe this ceremony in anticipation of the new library, which was formerly at the old township hall. (Courtesy of Lyon Township.)

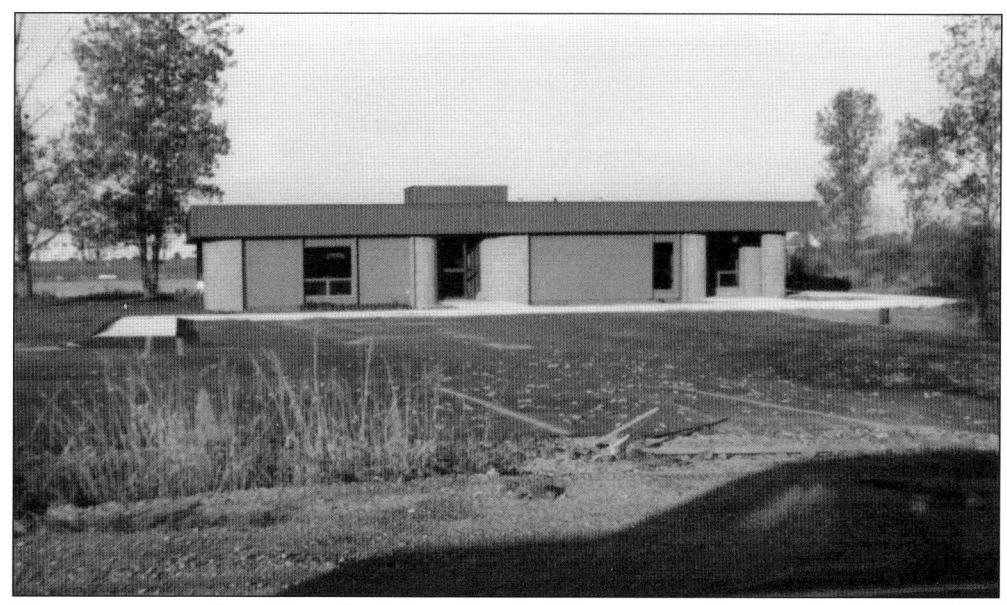

The cost-conscious Lyon Township Library Board of Trustees was able to pay for the new library building on Milford Road with accumulated savings from library operations. (Courtesy of Lyon Township.)

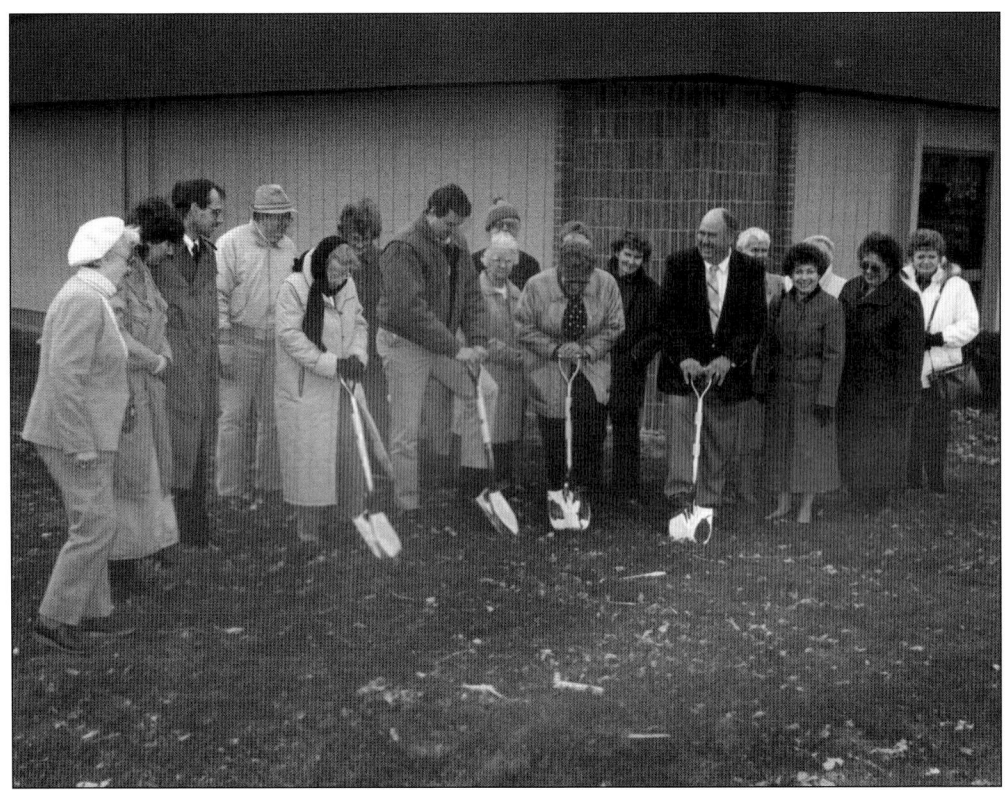

In 1991, a library expansion was needed, and many library supporters came out to the groundbreaking ceremony. Holding the shovels are, from left to right, Mary Canfield, Joe Shigley, Ruby Templeton, and township supervisor Jim Atchison. (Courtesy of the Lyon Township Library.)

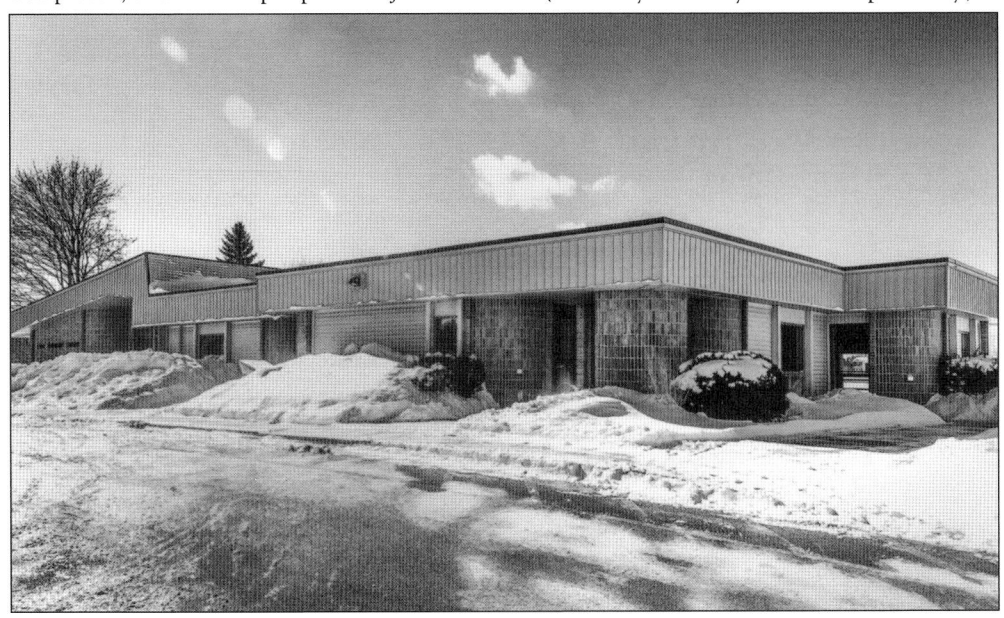

The library building expansion was completed and dedicated on September 15, 1992. (Courtesy of Jane and Jack Purslow.)

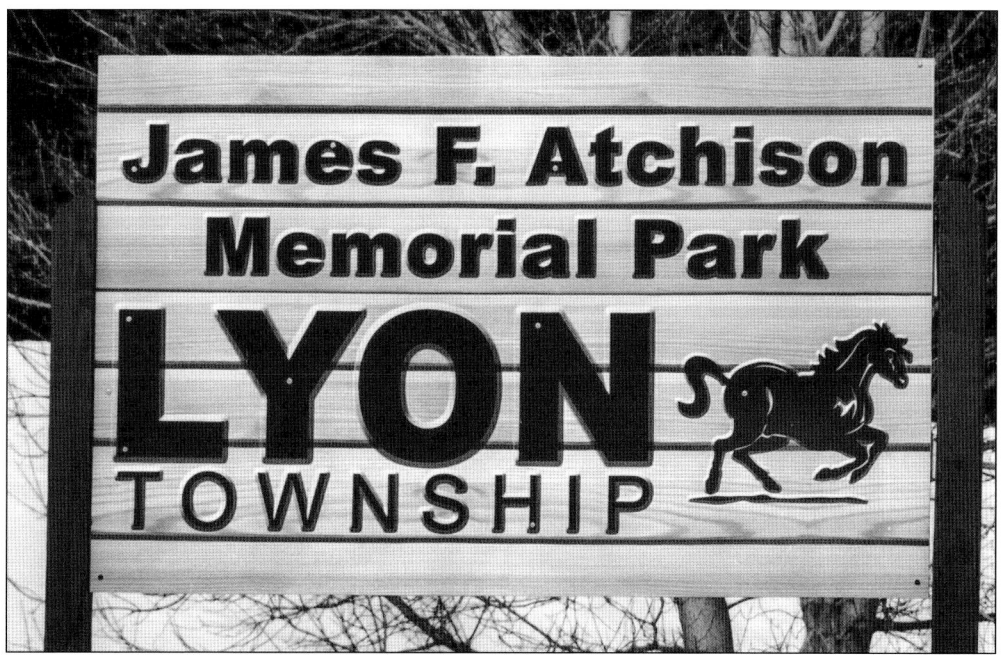

Lyon Township Park was rededicated as the James F. Atchison Memorial Park. James F. Atchison was a former township supervisor. (Courtesy of Jane and Jack Purslow.)

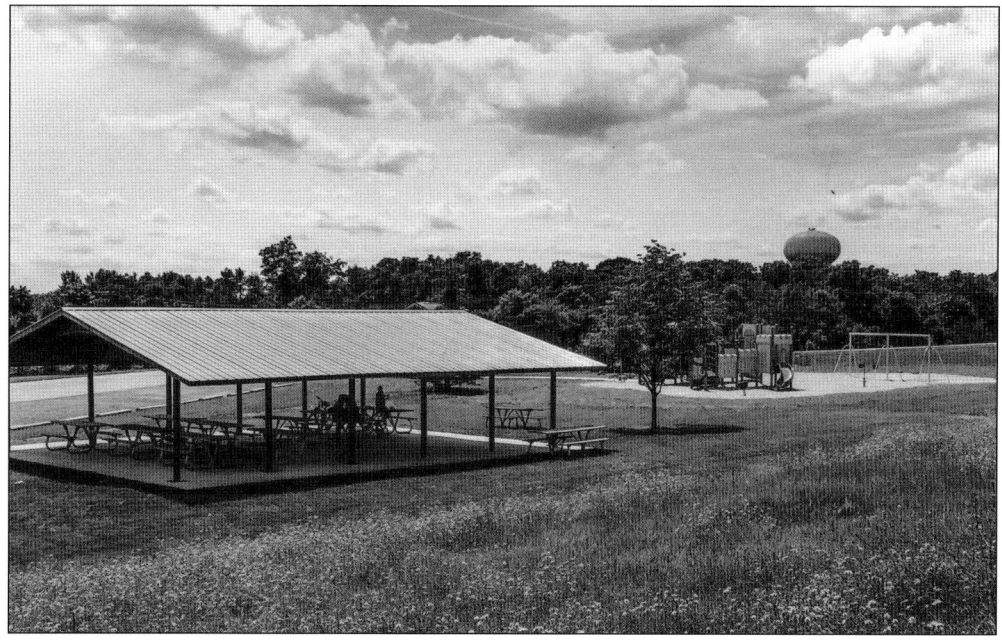

Before it was a park, the area was a landfill. Methane gas developed as a result of the materials in the landfill deteriorating. The gas-fueled engines, coupled to a turbine generator, produced electricity. The township earned royalties for the production of this energy. The park initially had a number of playscapes; however, over time, the ground settled, and they became inoperable. In 2013, a new children's playscape was installed next to the park's new restroom and pavilion. (Courtesy of Jane and Jack Purslow.)

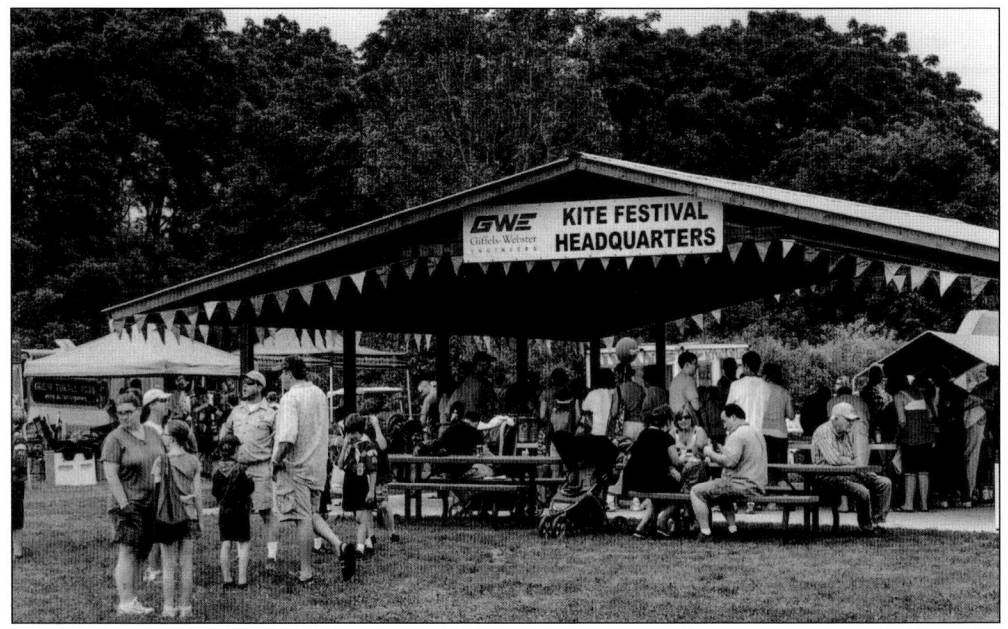

The annual Kite Festival grew from a one-day event at its inception in 2008 to four days by 2014. It included a lot of programs and activities. The headquarters, shown here, was the central hub of operation for the festival. (Courtesy of Jane and Jack Purslow.)

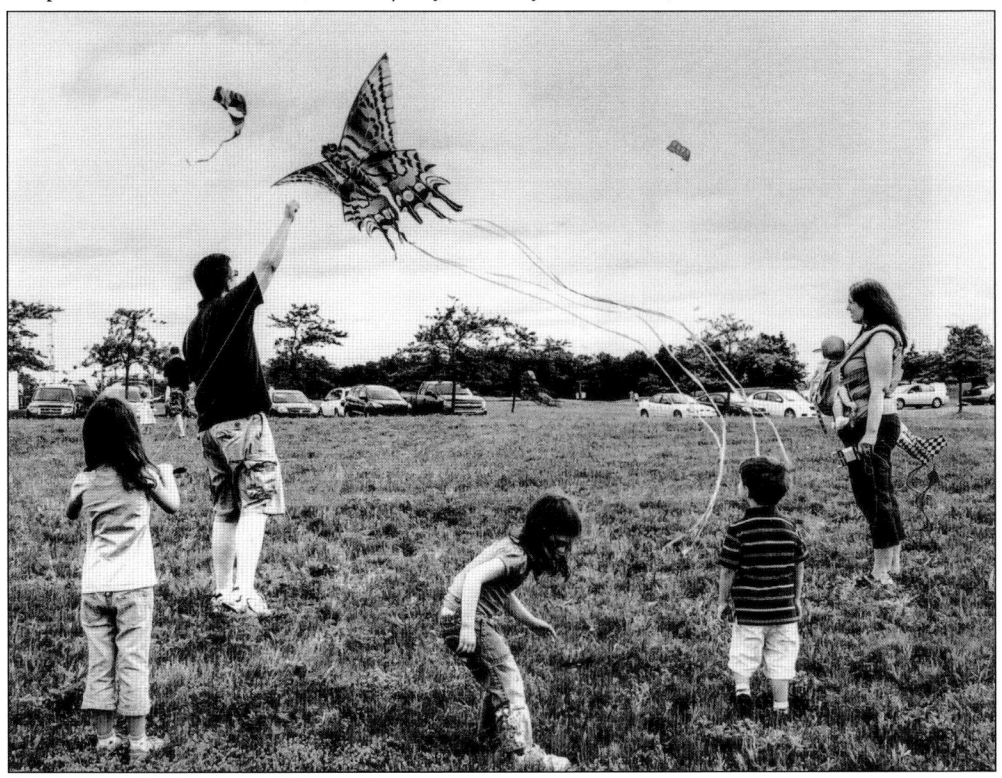

The Kite Festival draws participants and spectators from the Midwest and Canada. (Courtesy of Jane and Jack Purslow.)

Professional kite enthusiasts test their skills at keeping their huge kites in the air. Kites, with tails 125 or longer, dance above the spectators. (Courtesy of Jane and Jack Purslow.)

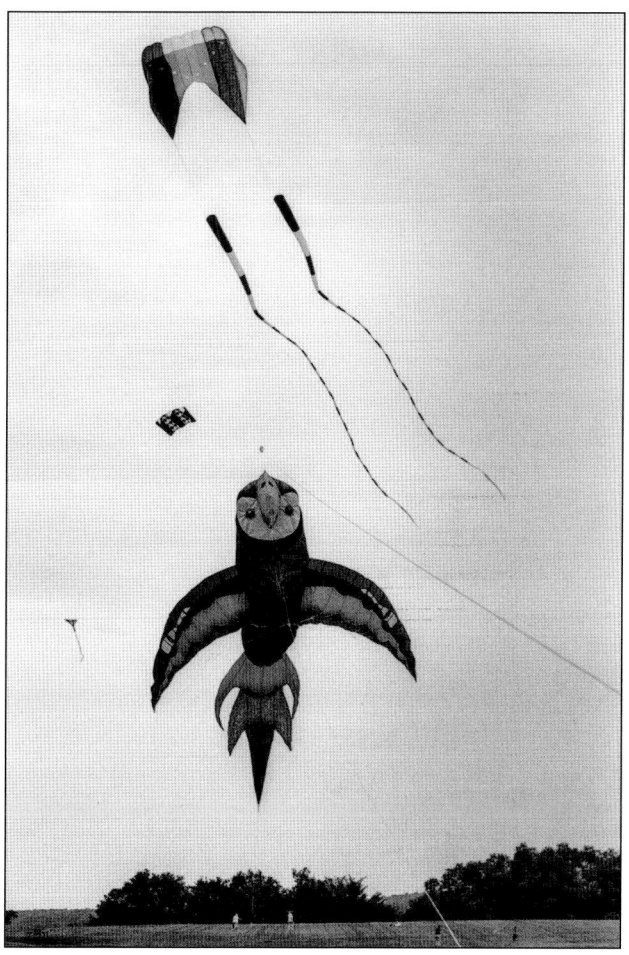

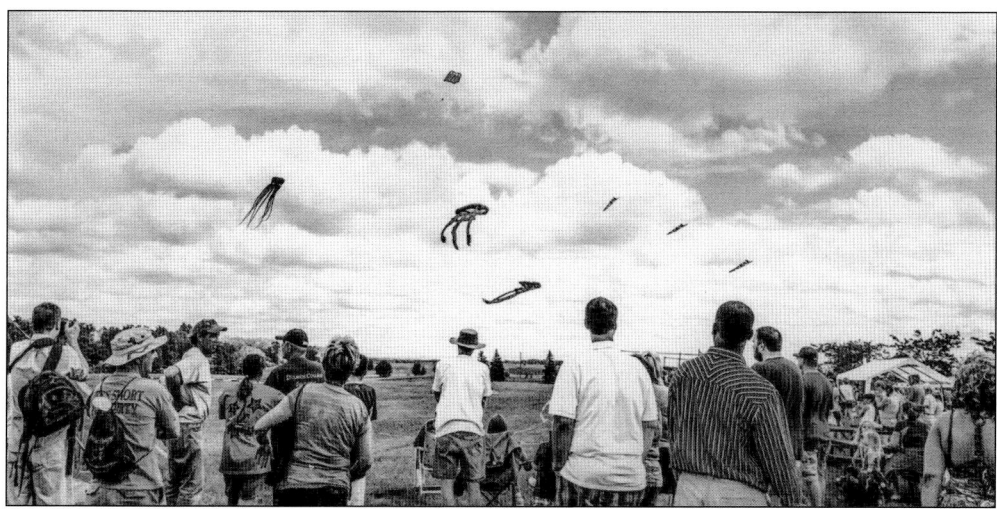

Amateur and professional kiters flock to the park, one of the best locations for kite flying in Oakland County. The ideal conditions result from the park's elevation and thermal air movement coming off the nearby expressway. (Courtesy of Jane and Jack Purslow.)

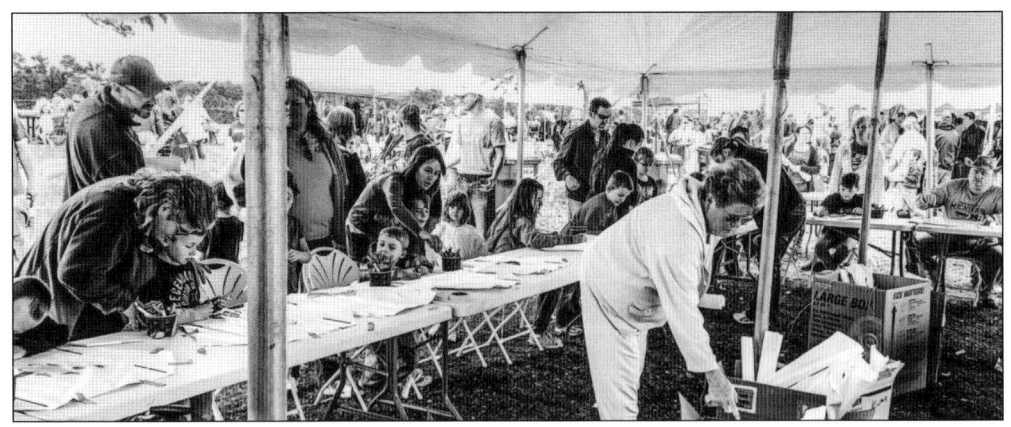

Children decorate their kites given to them free of charge by local businesses that sponsor the Kite Festival. (Courtesy of Jane and Jack Purslow.)

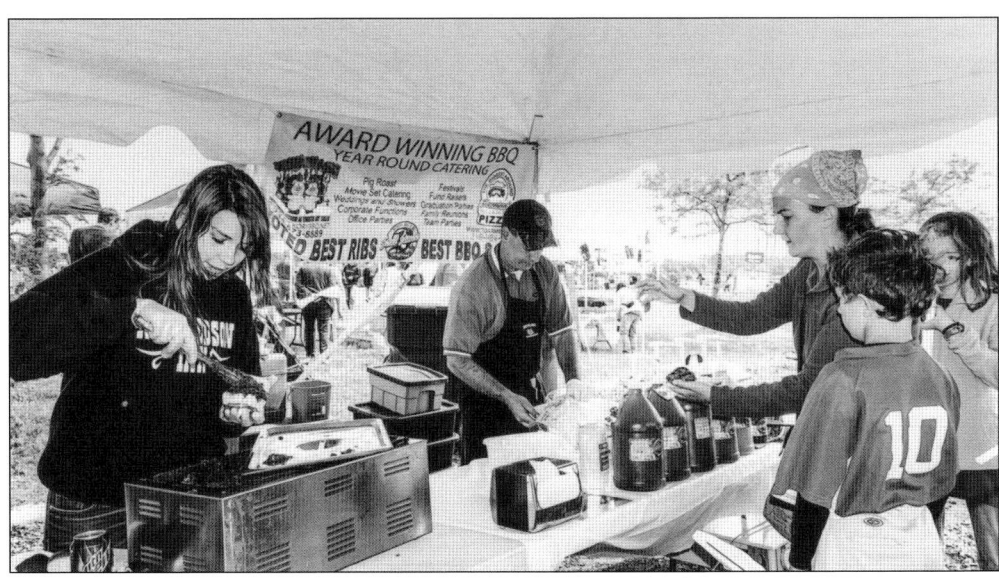

Yearly, area restaurants compete in a best barbecue pulled-pork cook-off during the Kite Festival. Local celebrity judges pick their favorites, and plaques are awarded to the winners. (Courtesy of Jane and Jack Purslow.)

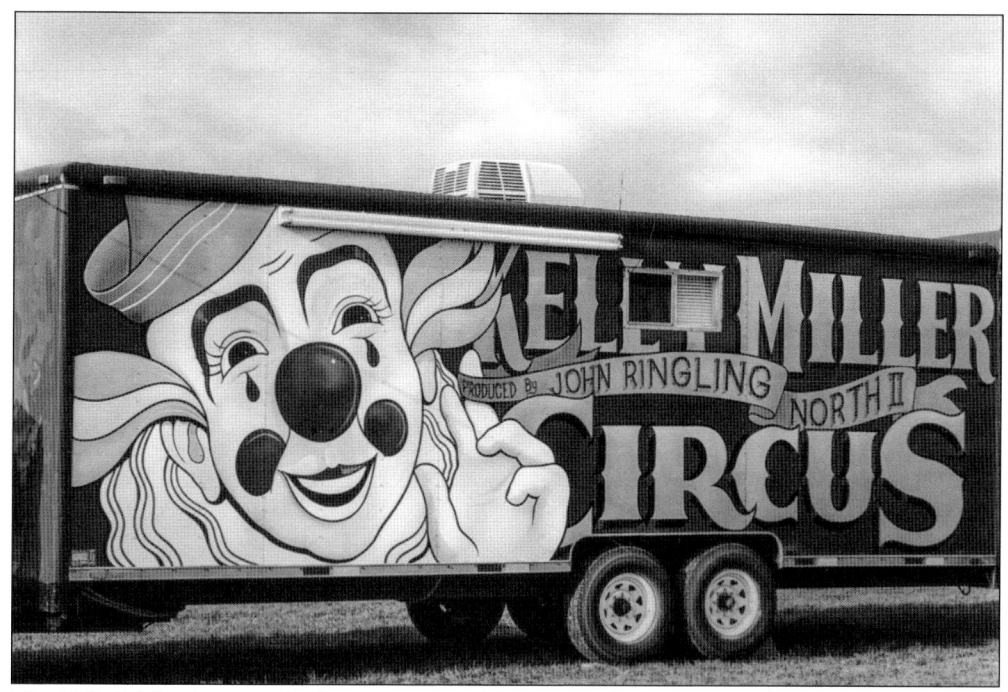

The Kelly Miller Circus, which was sponsored by the South Lyon Area Chamber of Commerce, came to town in 2012. It was a well-attended, one-day event that included a one-ring circus with tigers, elephants, and trapeze performances. (Courtesy of Jane and Jack Purslow.)

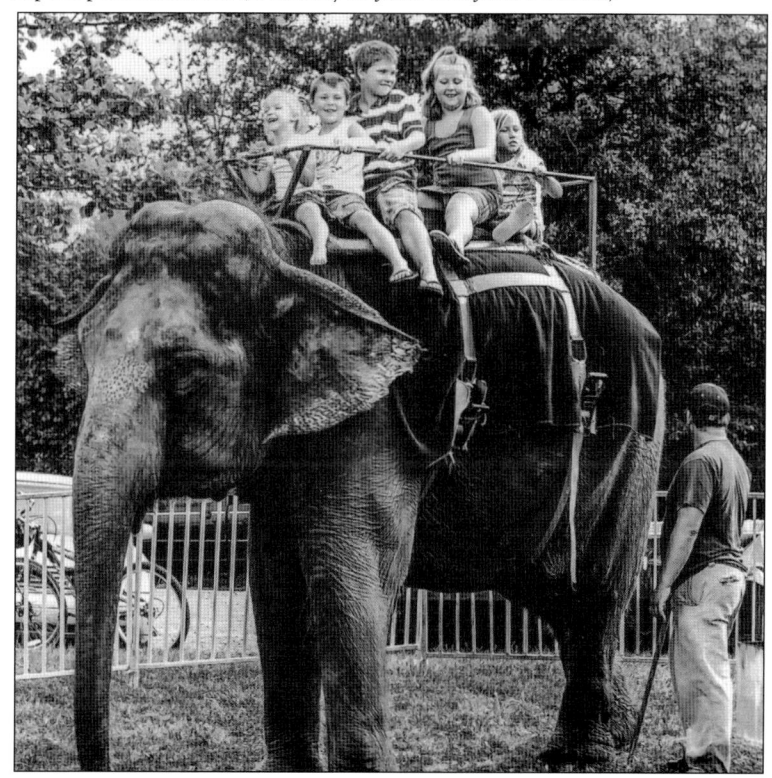

Camel and elephant rides gave kids an extra thrill. People of all ages, including the elderly, took advantage of the unique adventure. (Courtesy of Jane and Jack Purslow.)

119

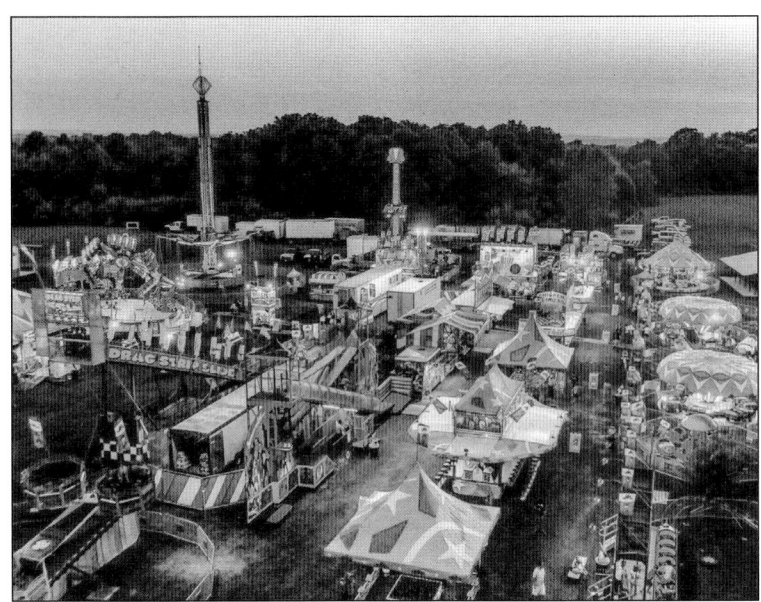

This panoramic view of the township's Summerfest, featuring Wade Carnival in July 2013, was the first such event held in the park. In the early 1940s, a carnival came to the township in an open lot on Grand River Avenue. (Courtesy of Jane and Jack Purslow.)

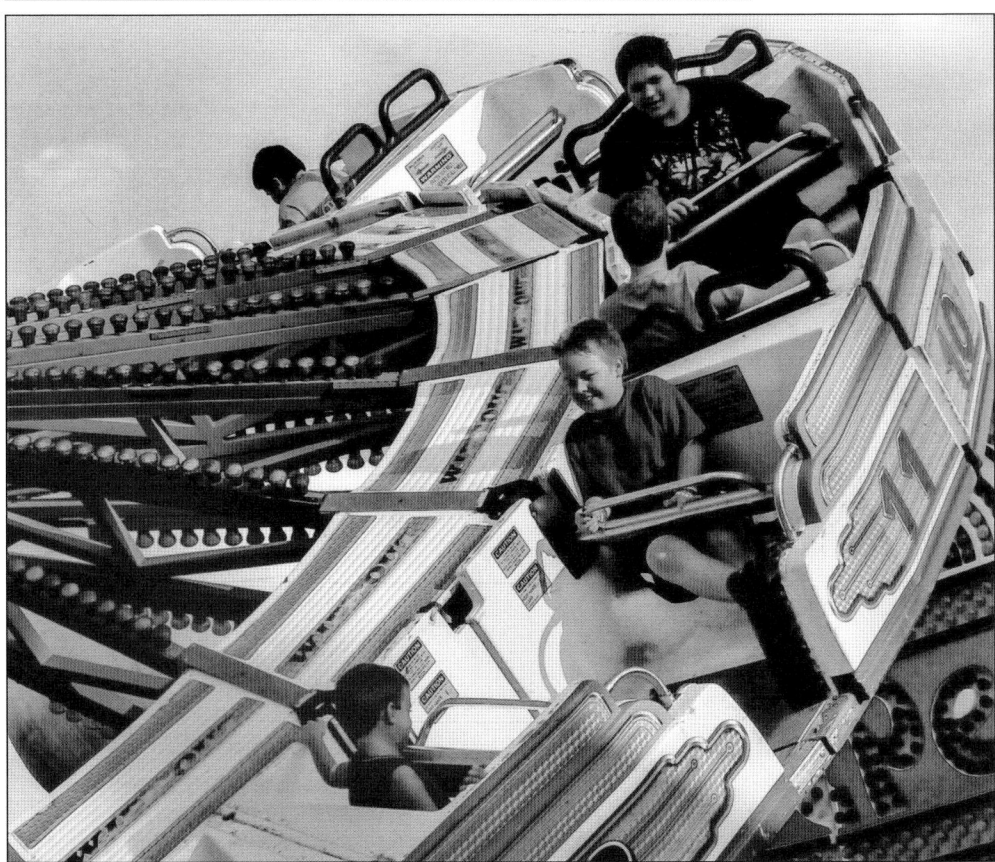

The Summerfest carnival offered a number of thrilling rides, games, and food. Hot-air balloonists unexpectedly chose the festival site to launch their colorfully decorated balloons. It became a wonderful carnival finale. (Courtesy of Jane and Jack Purslow.)

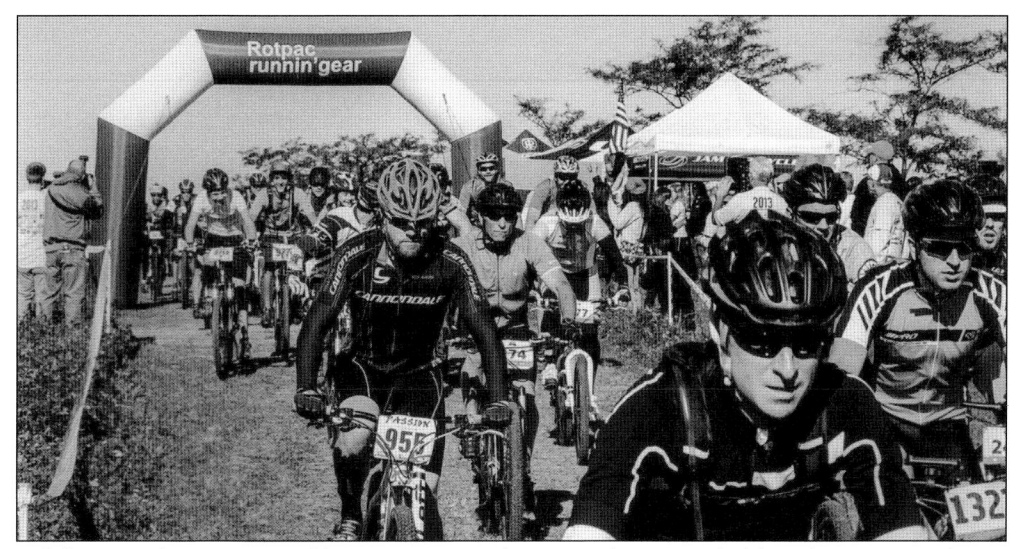

A bike marathon, sponsored by Hometown Bike in Brighton, was held in the summer of 2013 at James F. Atchison Memorial Park. More than 150 cyclists rode the track, and close to 150 spectators observed the events during the course of the day. The grand prize included race-performance bicycles, one of which was won by David Ridley, a Brighton resident. (Courtesy of Jane and Jack Purslow.)

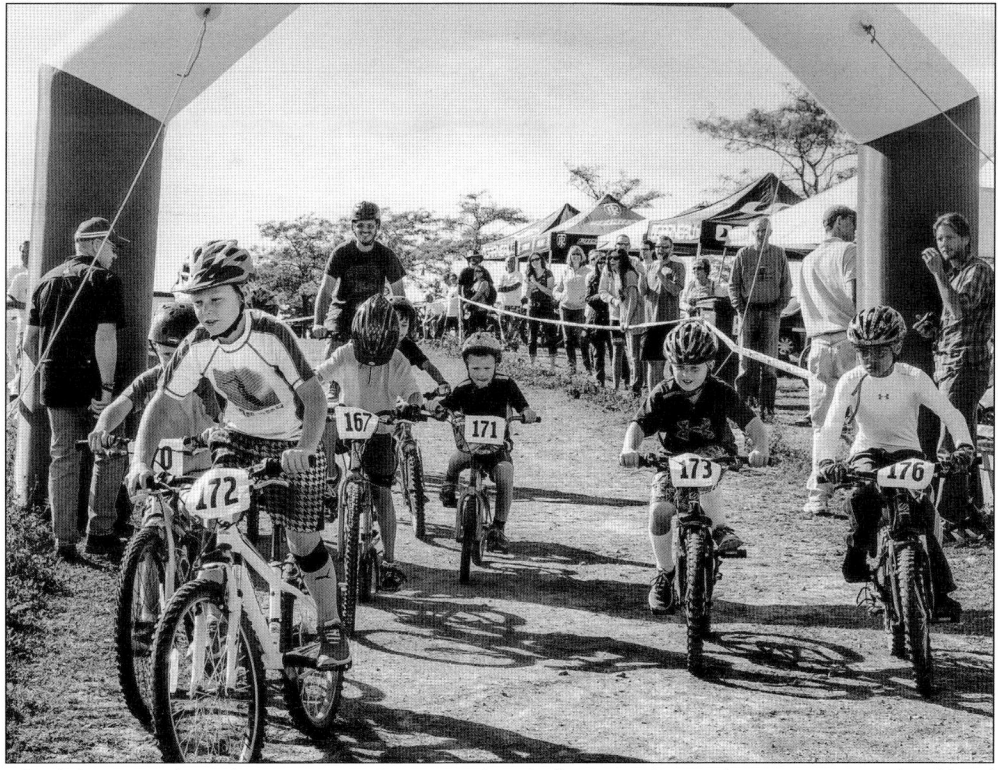

The bike marathon drew interest from people of all ages. The park spectator stands offered 80-percent view of the cyclists at any one time during the field competitions. (Courtesy of Jane and Jack Purslow.)

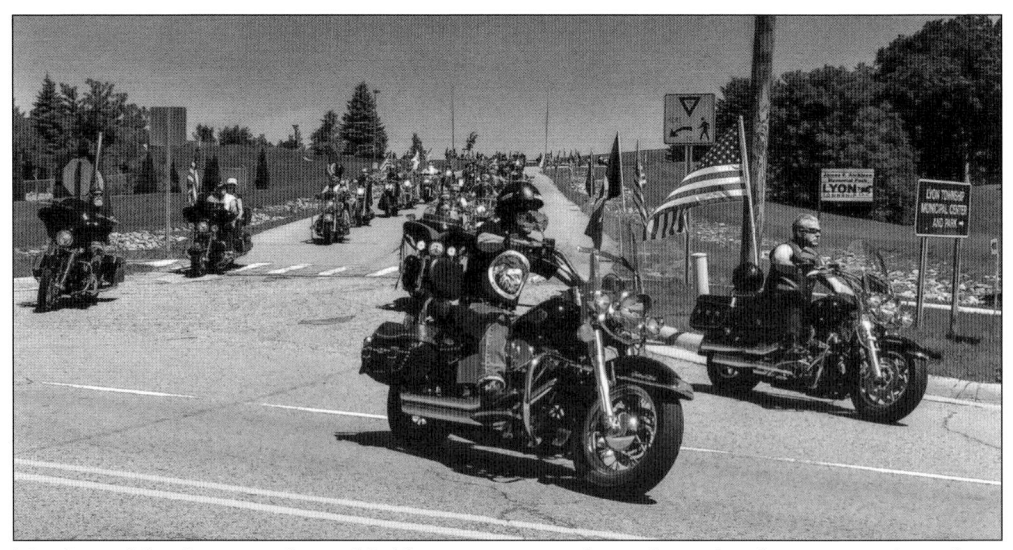

Members of the Operation Injured Soldiers organization leave the park to begin a tour throughout Oakland County to garner attention in support of veterans. This annual event to raise money to provide veterans dream trips, like fishing and hunting. Some of the organizers of the group are Jack Renwick, Dave Harriman, and Alan Hogan, as well as Pam and Andy Bijansky. (Courtesy of Jane and Jack Purslow.)

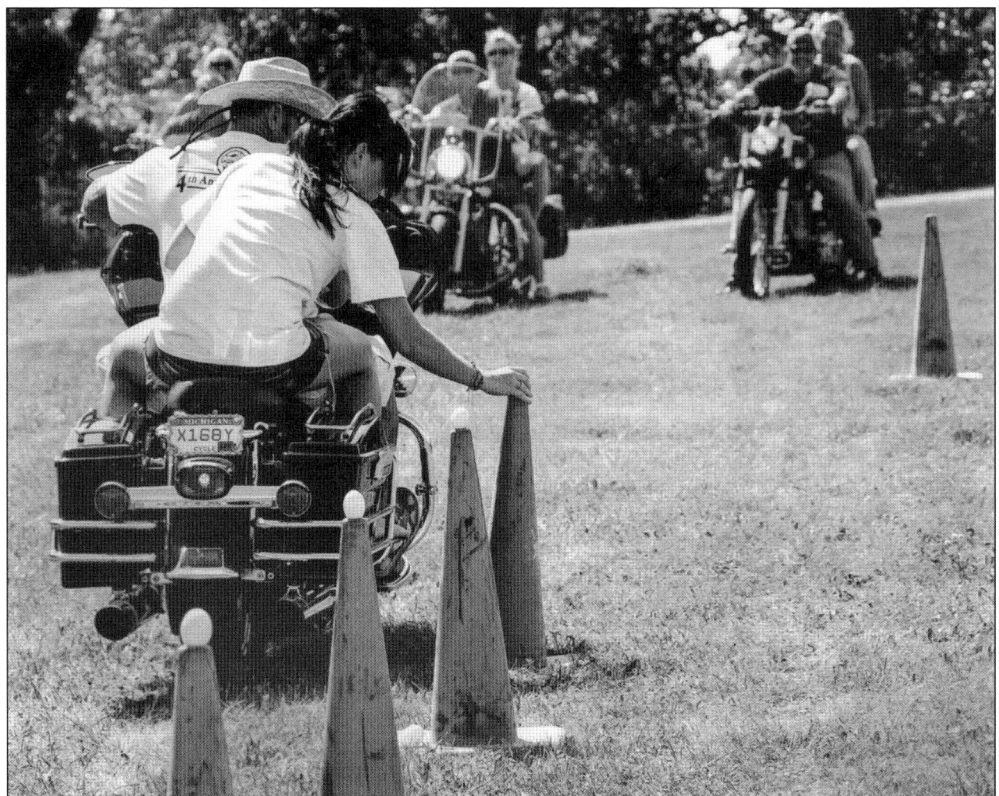

Motorcycle road enthusiasts support Operation Injured Soldiers. A one-day fundraiser in 2013 involved a motorcycle rodeo. Riders competed for trophies. (Courtesy of Jane and Jack Purslow.)

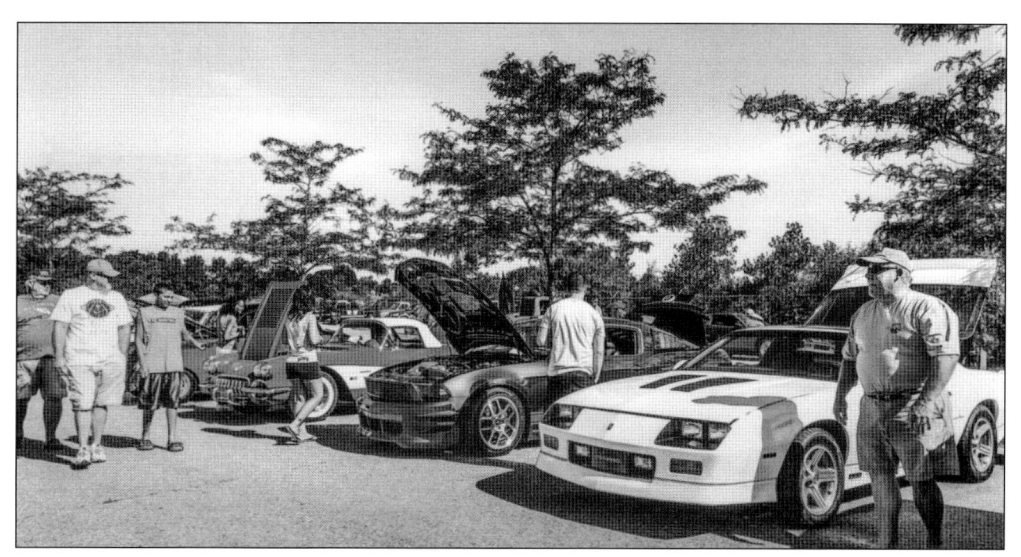

Restored classic cars were on display during the South Lyon Area Spark Plug Club show in the township park in 2013. Area car clubs show off antique, classic, and performance cars. (Courtesy of Jane and Jack Purslow.)

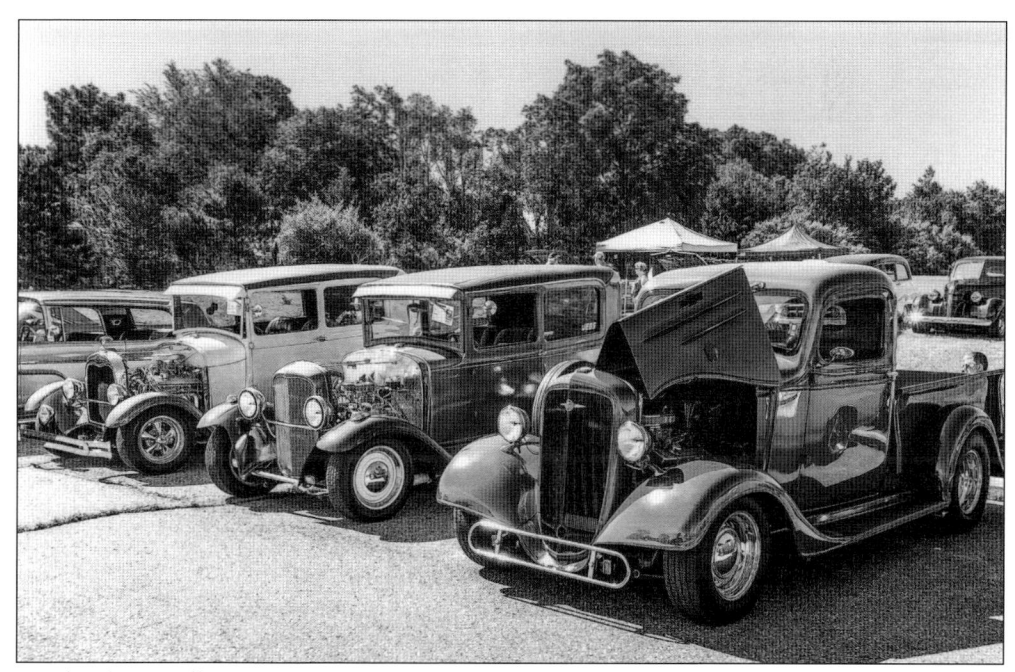

Gearheads from all over Michigan attend the car shows in the township park. They are also drawn to the swap meets to pursue parts and other memorabilia. These events are well attended. Refreshments and live entertainment are part of the venue. (Courtesy of Jane and Jack Purslow.)

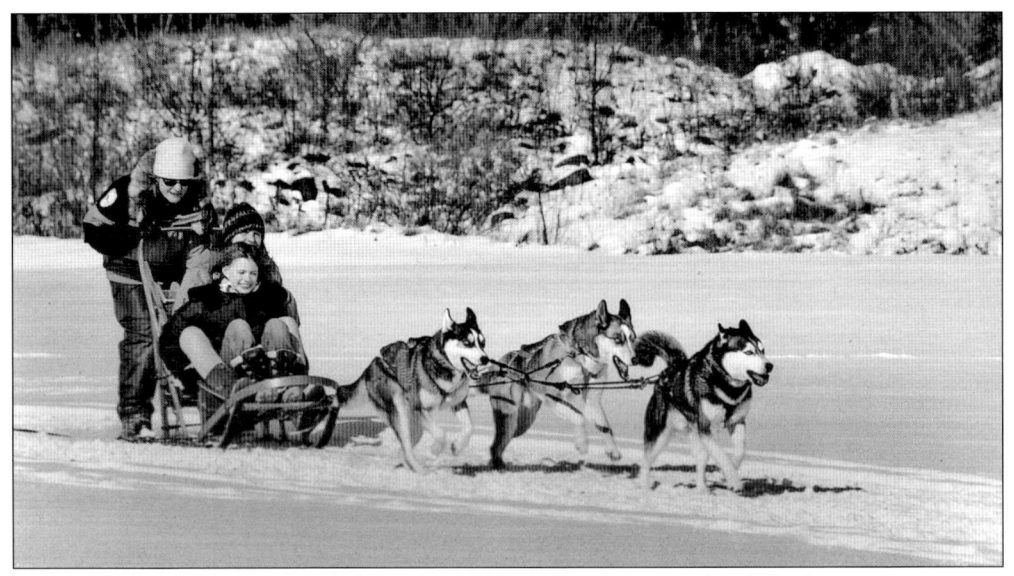

The inaugural Winterfest was held in the park in 2012, featuring dogsled rides, entertainment, and a chilli cook-off to warm up spectators. Local celebrities judged the chilli cook-off. Dogsled teams, from Northern Michigan, were available for rides. (Courtesy of Jane and Jack Purslow.)

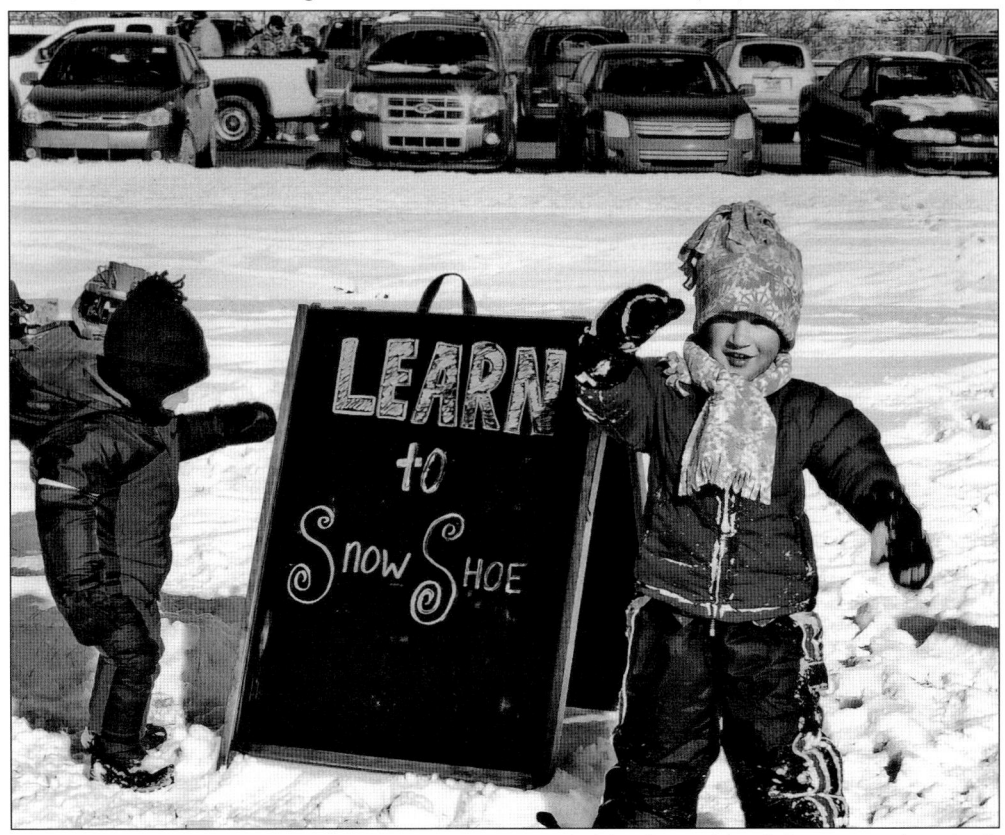

Children learned to snowshoe with instruction provided by the Oakland County Parks, which partnered with the township on this event. (Courtesy of Jane and Jack Purslow.)

Ten

FUTURE

The previous pages describe the agricultural period in Lyon Township's history, when farming dominated the economy and when New Hudson served as a center of community and commercial activity. In the late 1990s, Lyon Township stepped into a new chapter in its history, with large-scale residential development consuming the agricultural land.

It is likely that residential development will continue at an accelerated pace for several reasons. The township is at the leading edge of westward growth in the region. The South Lyon Community School District has become recognized as a top district in the state. Utility extensions throughout the township have made development feasible.

What does the future hold? There will be continued residential development, but neighborhoods will meld together to form a stronger sense of community. The sense of community will be reinforced by public facilities and events, such as the popular bicycle path system and annual Kite Festival.

Commercial agriculture will likely cease, but the rural character of the township will not be completely lost because of the presence of rural-like, large-lot, single-family parcels.

New Hudson will return to its roots as a vibrant mixed-used hamlet. The hamlet may not become the township's key shopping district, but it will be a place for restaurants, small shops, community buildings, and events. The area north of the hamlet, along I-96, will remain the township's main shopping district. Industrial and research uses will be well represented along the Grand River Avenue corridor, east of the New Hudson hamlet.

The extension of utilities will accelerate commercial development on Pontiac Trail Road, south of South Lyon, transforming this corridor into an important shopping district. Residents in the southerly part of the township will also be served by two strategically placed commercial nodes on Ten Mile Road at Milford Road and at Johns Road.

Over time, Lyon Township will become a multifaceted community with a distinct personality, offering a range of facilities and services to meet the diverse needs of longtime residents and newcomers.

—Chris Doozen, McKenna Associates

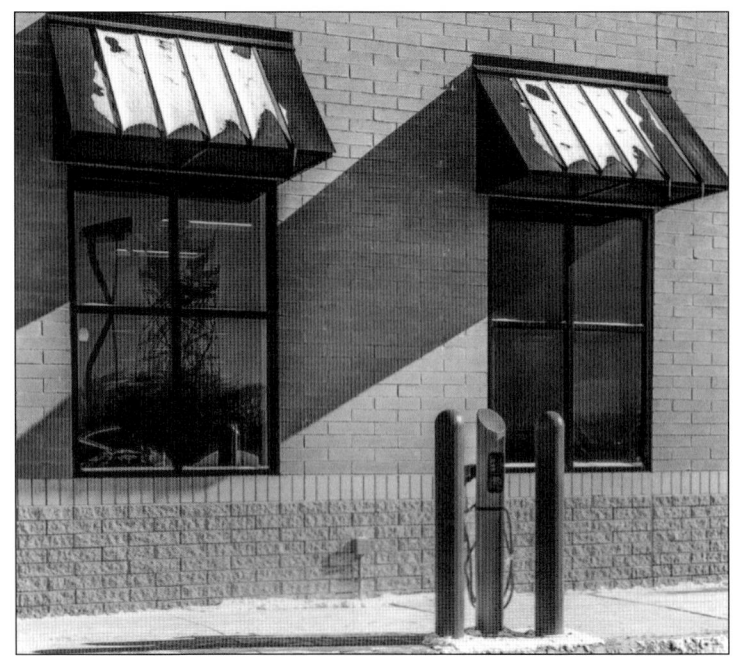

Hiller's Market on Ten Mile Road and Johns Road offers the first free public electric car charging stations in Lyon Township. When they opened in 2013, owners of the market incorporated many environmentally conscious features. (Courtesy of Jane and Jack Purslow.)

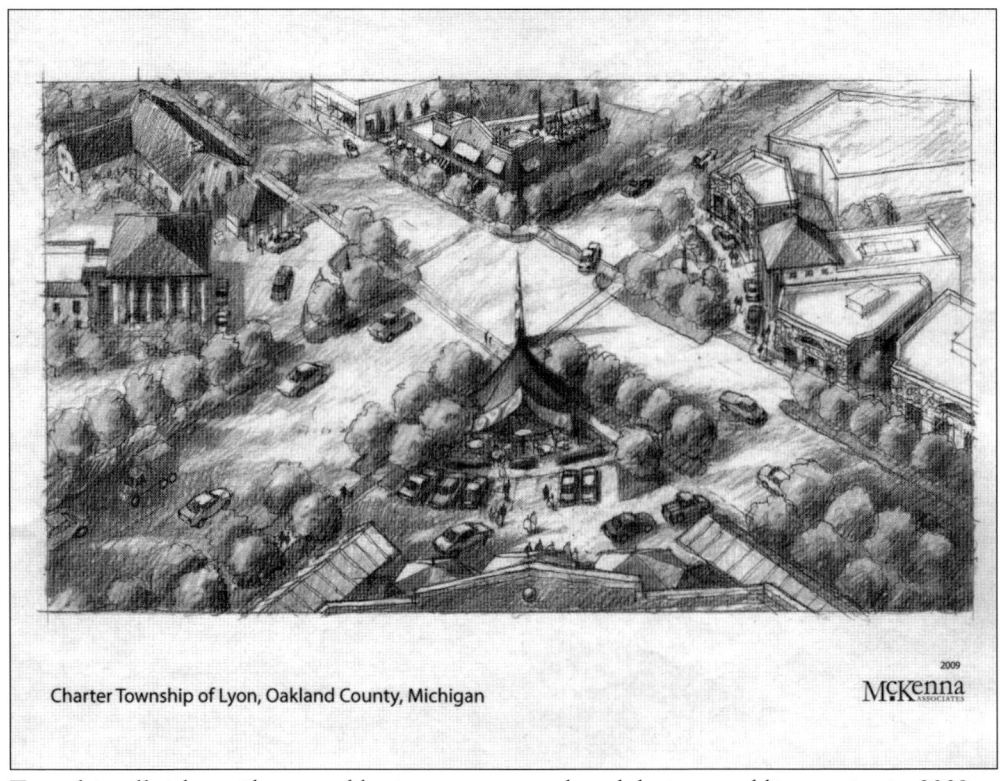

Township officials, residents, and business owners gathered during a public meeting in 2009 to focus on their vision of what New Hudson could look like in the future. Artists were available to hear their comments, and they brought those ideas to life in these conceptual drawings. This is a view of the center intersection of New Hudson. (Courtesy of McKenna Associates.)

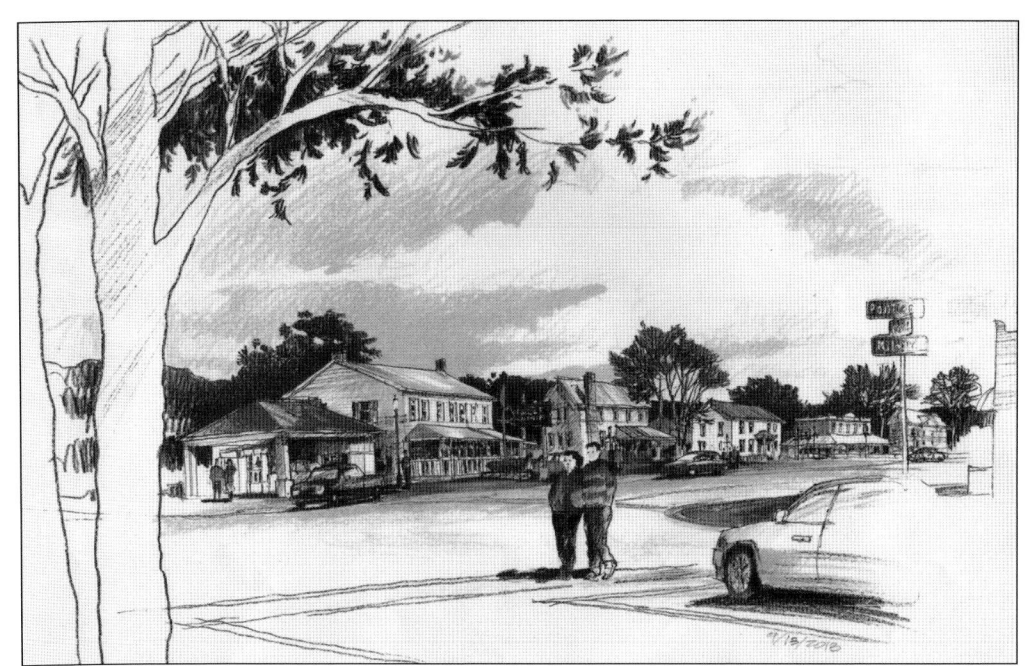

The township has recently adopted new ordinances to reflect a planning technique to support the hamlet development in New Hudson. This rendering shows the north side of Grand River Avenue. Other renderings were made to illustrate the south side. Both included freestanding buildings with varying rooflines that represent a hamlet image. (Courtesy of McKenna Associates.)

New way-finding signs were provided by the Downtown Development Authority in 2013. Travelers are greeted with the township's motto "Honoring yesterday, building tomorrow," and as they exit, drivers see a farewell wish. (Courtesy of Jane and Jack Purslow.)

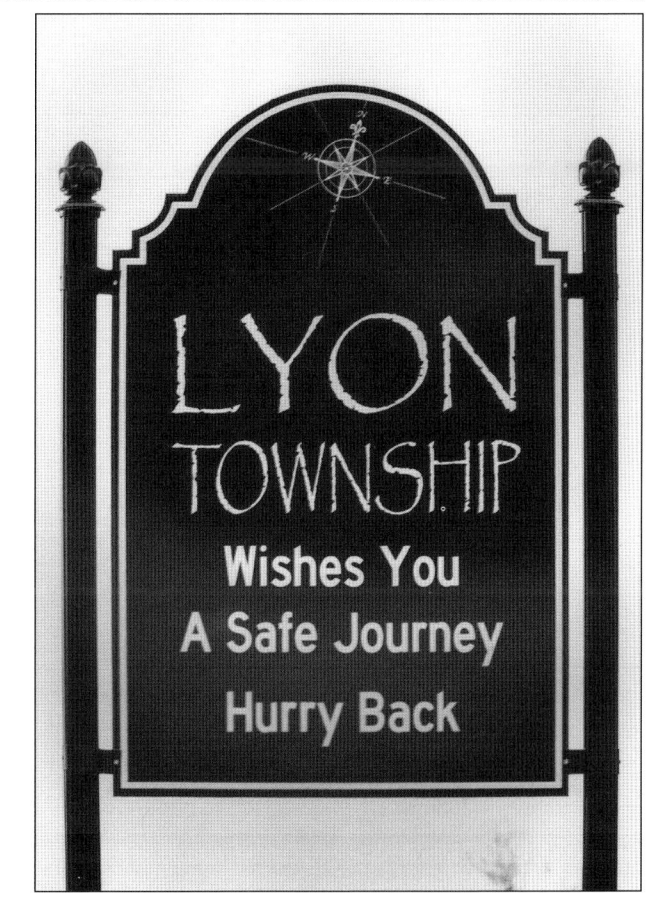

127

Discover Thousands of Local History Books Featuring Millions of Vintage Images

Arcadia Publishing, the leading local history publisher in the United States, is committed to making history accessible and meaningful through publishing books that celebrate and preserve the heritage of America's people and places.

Find more books like this at
www.arcadiapublishing.com

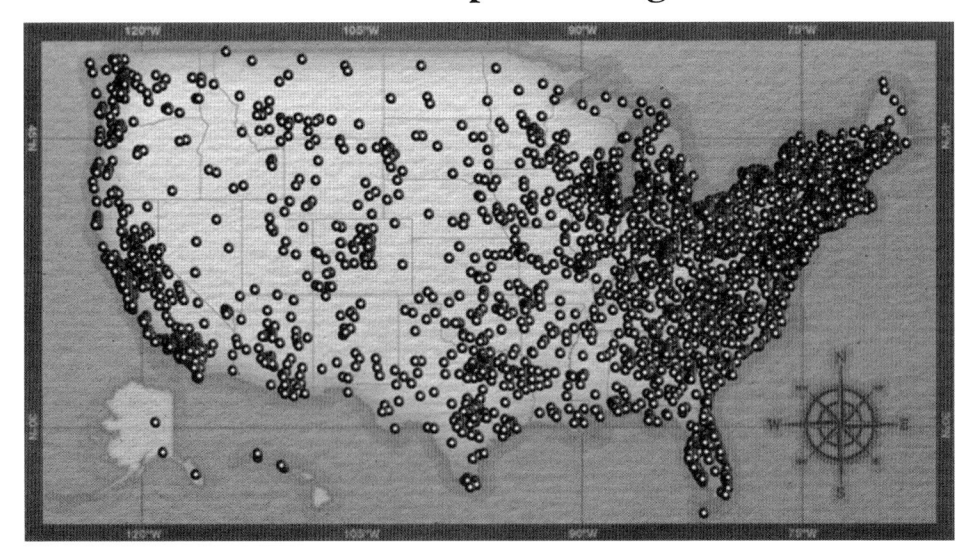

Search for your hometown history, your old stomping grounds, and even your favorite sports team.

Consistent with our mission to preserve history on a local level, this book was printed in South Carolina on American-made paper and manufactured entirely in the United States. Products carrying the accredited Forest Stewardship Council (FSC) label are printed on 100 percent FSC-certified paper.

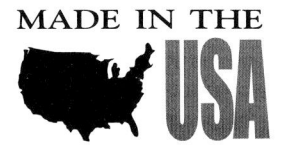

MADE IN THE USA